Autonomous Data Security

Creating a Proactive Enterprise Protection Plan

Priyanka Neelakrishnan

Apress®

Autonomous Data Security: Creating a Proactive Enterprise Protection Plan

Priyanka Neelakrishnan
San Jose, CA, USA

ISBN-13 (pbk): 979-8-8688-0837-1 ISBN-13 (electronic): 979-8-8688-0838-8
https://doi.org/10.1007/979-8-8688-0838-8

Copyright © 2024 by Priyanka Neelakrishnan

This work is subject to copyright. All rights are reserved. whether the whole or part of the material is concerned, specifically the rights of translation, reprinting, reuse of illustrations, recitation, broadcasting, reproduction on microfilms or in any other physical way, and transmission or information storage and retrieval, electronic adaptation, computer software, or by similar or dissimilar methodology now known or hereafter developed.

Trademarked names, logos, and images may appear in this book. Rather than use a trademark symbol with every occurrence of a trademarked name, logo, or image we use the names, logos, and images only in an editorial fashion and to the benefit of the trademark owner, with no intention of infringement of the trademark.

The use in this publication of trade names, trademarks, service marks, and similar terms, even if they are not identified as such, is not to be taken as an expression of opinion as to whether or not they are subject to proprietary rights.

While the advice and information in this book are believed to be true and accurate at the date of publication, neither the authors nor the editors nor the publisher can accept any legal responsibility for any errors or omissions that may be made. The publisher makes no warranty, express or implied, with respect to the material contained herein.

    Managing Director, Apress Media LLC: Welmoed Spahr
    Acquisitions Editor: Susan McDermott
    Development Editor: Laura Berendson
    Editorial Assistant: Jessica Vakili

Cover designed by eStudioCalamar

Distributed to the book trade worldwide by Springer Science+Business Media New York, 1 New York Plaza, Suite 4600, New York, NY 10004-1562, USA. Phone 1-800-SPRINGER, fax (201) 348-4505, e-mail orders-ny@springer-sbm.com, or visit www.springeronline.com. Apress Media, LLC is a California LLC and the sole member (owner) is Springer Science + Business Media Finance Inc (SSBM Finance Inc). SSBM Finance Inc is a **Delaware** corporation.

For information on translations, please e-mail booktranslations@springernature.com; for reprint, paperback, or audio rights, please e-mail bookpermissions@springernature.com.

Apress titles may be purchased in bulk for academic, corporate, or promotional use. eBook versions and licenses are also available for most titles. For more information, reference our Print and eBook Bulk Sales web page at http://www.apress.com/bulk-sales.

Any source code or other supplementary material referenced by the author in this book is available to readers on GitHub. For more detailed information, please visit https://www.apress.com/gp/services/source-code.

If disposing of this product, please recycle the paper.

This book is dedicated to my beloved daughter, Loshni, whose bright spirit illuminates my life. Love you, Losh baby!

And to everyone who prioritizes proactive security, together let's build a secure digital future!

With love and joy, Priyanka

Table of Contents

About the Author xi

About the Technical Reviewer xiii

Acknowledgments xv

Introduction xvii

Chapter 1: Data Security Fundamental Requirements...........................1

What Is Data Security?...3

Understanding Adversaries, Tactics, and Attack Types 5

    Internal Attacks 6

    Internal Attack Types 11

    External Attacks...13

    External Attack Types 14

Building Data Security Requirements 19

    Identifying and Remediation of Confidential Data 20

    Data Security at Coverage Points 25

    Ensuring Business Continuity 29

    Security Solution Configurability 30

    Feedback and Learning 31

    Continuous Monitoring 36

    Scaling...37

Summary..38

TABLE OF CONTENTS

Chapter 2: Traditional Data Security 41

Security Background 42
    User Personas 42
    Common Security Configurations 44
    Data in Motion vs. Data at Rest 58
    Characteristics of DIM vs. DAR 60
    Monitor vs. Prevent 61
Data Security by Channel 64
    Email Security 64
    Network Security 68
    Network Shares 69
    Endpoint Security 70
    BYOD Security 71
    CASB Security 72
Customer Environments 73
    On-Premise 73
    Cloud 74
    Hybrid 75
Limitations of Data Security Solutions 76
    Lack of Comprehensive Coverage 76
    Detection Gaps 77
    Lack of Unified Policies 79
    Poor Matching Technologies 80
    Resiliency, Scalability, Performance 81
    Weak Configuration Options 82
    Poor Usability 82
    Bad Monitoring and Reporting 83
    Poor Upgrade Options 83

TABLE OF CONTENTS

    Inadequate Integrations 84

    Too Expensive for the Value 85

    Poor Customer Support 85

Summary 86

Chapter 3: Thinking Outside Norms 87

Sample Organization and Use Cases 88

    Fictional Use Cases 89

Policy Language 90

    Policy Context Rules 91

    Policy Matching Rules 93

    Exceptions 95

    Creative Policy Language 96

Dependency on Policies 98

    Shortcomings of Security Policies 99

    Learning from Partial Content Matches 103

    Policy Feedback 107

    Test Mode Policies 110

    Match Rule Types 112

Security Violations 116

    Security Violation Remediation 117

    Problems with Existing Violation Structure 119

    Enhancement Options 122

Choosing Target Segment 123

Choosing Deployment Environment and Channels 127

Mode of Usage 130

Utilization Based on Personas 133

TABLE OF CONTENTS

Setup, Deployment, and Maintenance 136
    Installation/Upgrade of Security Software 136
Additional Solutions 140
    Analytics 140
    SaaS Security Posture Management 143
    SPM—Spend Management 144
Summary 145

Chapter 4: Data Security Solution Design 147

Steps to Build a Data Protection Solution 148
    Overarching Goal 149
    Use Cases 150
    Core Components Identification 153
Design of Core Components 161
    Content Detection Engine Internals 161
    Content Detection Engine Components Layout 193
    Policy Engine 199
    Violation Processor 201
    Remediation Execution Engine 205
    Reporting Engine UI 210
    User and Role Processor 214
Summary 216

Chapter 5: Design Towards Autonomy 219

Reasoning Module 220
    Policies Across Channels 223
    Violation Remediations 234
    Storing Partial Matches 238

TABLE OF CONTENTS

Analytics Engine 241
    User Behavior Analysis 241
    Data Trail 253
    Violation Monitoring 256
    Cloud Applications Security Posture Management 260

Statistics Engine 261
    Data Pre-processing Module 262
    Data Visualization Module 263

Feedback Processor 265

Summary 267

Chapter 6: Pro-Active Intelligent Data Security 269

Policy Recommendation System (PRS) 271
    Autonomous Policy Creator 272
    Test Mode Policies Efficacy Tester 273
    Production Policy Deployer 274
    Heuristics 275
    Design 304

Remediation Recommendation System (RRS) 305
    Heuristics 306
    Design 314

Settings Recommendation System (SRS) 315
    Coverage Points Settings 315

Summary 326

Chapter 7: Future Ready Data Security 329

Data Management 330
    Tracking Data 332
    Security Product Enhancements 334

ix

TABLE OF CONTENTS

Data Privacy 335
Intent-Based Security 337
    Configurations 338
    Policies 341
    Violation Remediations 342
AI-Based Detection 344
    Understanding LLM-Based Detection 345
    Incorporating LLM-Based Detection 347
Defend Against AI Threats 351
    Data Privacy and Security 352
    Understanding Trained Models 352
    LLMs: A Threat in Themselves 352
    Safeguarding LLMs from Bad Actors 353
Summary 354

Index 355

About the Author

Priyanka Neelakrishnan is a distinguished data security expert with over a decade of experience in building world-class data protection solutions. Her illustrious career includes pivotal roles at renowned cybersecurity firms such as Palo Alto Networks and Symantec, where she has consistently driven innovation and excellence.

As the Product Line Manager at Palo Alto Networks, Priyanka has been instrumental in conceptualizing, designing, and launching transformative cybersecurity products. Her efforts have led to the widespread adoption of advanced information protection solutions, significantly enhancing enterprise security. During her tenure at Symantec (now Broadcom), Priyanka spearheaded initiatives in on-prem, cloud, and hybrid data protection, notably developing the industry's first cloud data protection solution tailored for large enterprise customers. This groundbreaking solution encompassed all major cloud channels, including email, web, and applications, and featured patented content detection technologies.

Recognized as a go-to authority in the field of data protection, Priyanka is highly regarded for her mentoring capabilities and expertise across a wide range of data security topics. She is also a renowned speaker and independent researcher, contributing extensively to the advancement of the cybersecurity field. Her innovative products and strategic insights have earned her leadership and excellence awards, underscoring her significant contributions to the cybersecurity landscape.

About the Technical Reviewer

Prabhu Narayanasamy is a seasoned data security architect with nearly 20 years of hands-on experience designing and building scalable software solutions for large enterprises. He is currently the Technical Director for the Data Loss Prevention product at Symantec Enterprise Security (now part of Broadcom), where he spearheads the development of large-scale projects spanning both on-premise and cloud product portfolios. He is renowned for his expertise in solving unique data security challenges with innovative product ideas, designing maintainable, high-performance distributed architecture solutions, and ensuring these solutions work effectively for businesses of all sizes. Prabhu holds a master's in Computer Science from North Carolina State University, specializing in algorithms and artificial intelligence.

Acknowledgments

I am deeply grateful to my family—my parents, Neelakrishnan and Umarani; my grandparents, Perumalswamy and Vijayalakshmi; and my brother, Pranesh—for their encouragement and belief in my writing journey. Your love and support have been my foundation.

My daughter, Loshni, has been a constant pillar of strength. Her quick thinking skills and invaluable suggestions have guided me in improving every aspect of my life. Her strong belief in security is an added bonus for me.

I thank every individual whom I have met in my life for enriching my perspectives.

Introduction

Is this just another book on data security? Truly not. This book has been written with great foresight to guide you in building a data security product from scratch. Why do we need such a book? Excellent question! Most books and literature teach you bits and pieces of data security. This results in product silos and does not cater to the businesses out there that are expecting a comprehensive solution that would cover their entire infrastructure, both on-premise and in the cloud.

Very few businesses in this world are well-funded to maintain data security products; however, everyone wants to safeguard their data. They are concerned about the potential consequences they might face if a data breach occurs. The harsh reality is that most businesses are vulnerable, and it often takes only a determined effort to breach any security infrastructure. Many businesses are compelled to maintain data security products due to compliance requirements and data regulations. However, they often do the bare minimum to meet these regulations and show little interest in configuring the products to their fullest potential. Despite this, they are eager to reap the benefits of the solution with minimal effort.

Data security product maintenance shouldn't be taken lightly, even if the security vendor maintains the product and it is hosted in the cloud. It requires regular upkeep from the business perspective, starting from configuring the product to covering their traffic flows and storage repositories, ensuring the right security policies exist that could detect sensitive data from leaking, fight against external threats, and remediate security violations to protect and ensure compliance at all times.

New threats and new ways of how your business can be attacked are discovered every day. Security software needs to be ahead of the attacks to prevent them from happening in the first place. This is what the industry

INTRODUCTION

terms proactive security. Ensuring proactive security in a security product requires a well-thought-out design. A robust foundation is essential for building security modules capable of thwarting threats that range from simple employee negligence to sophisticated AI-powered attacks. To achieve this, security vendors must engage in extensive research and development. This effort ensures the creation of exceptional products that address a wide array of customer use cases, providing comprehensive protection against an evolving landscape of security threats.

This book is written primarily with security vendors, cybersecurity enthusiasts, and organizations in mind. There is a lot of content for each of you, and I have discussed many concepts that could expand your thinking. I should mention this book does not spoon-feed and detail out step-by-step instructions. Instead, it encourages you to think beyond security and focus on the true customer requirements. What do customers need? Why do they need it, and what do you have to do? How should you design a model that can withstand the test of time?

Let's assume that you are a CISO of an organization. Do you have to gain knowledge of how security products work to provide comprehensive coverage? Absolutely! As a CISO, you might be responsible for choosing the security strategy for your whole company. You need to evaluate and decide on the security products. Security vendors are skillful enough to show you what works better and completely leave out what their products don't cover. You, as a CISO, need to know what questions to ask. How to evaluate a product? Does it make sense to invest in a security product given your use cases and limited security budget? There would be hundreds of questions like this in your mind. I've tried to balance it out in this book, arguing from both sides—specifically as a security vendor, what can you deliver, and as an organization, what you should expect.

Many organizations procure security products, then within a year or two decide that these products don't solve their use cases and go and buy more products to supplement the existing product or change security vendors and try out something new. It takes months, if not years, to configure a product with all the security policies and integrate their business tools for a smooth organizational flow. I have come to the understanding that it is not realistic to expect organizations to configure the security products to address all their use cases. They may start with the basics, but it is the job of the security product to take it further. In most cases, administrators from the organizations don't know what they need, and they like to monitor everything to the point that it overwhelms them, causing them to miss critical issues.

In this book, I take you, my dear readers, on a ride through the security rollercoaster, covering core requirements and use cases, addressing your fears, and most importantly, making sure you understand what limitations exist today and how to think holistically to build a comprehensive security product. This book covers the design of core components necessary for a product to run without loss of detection coverage in great detail. Component interactions are critical to building a scalable product that can address customers of any size. I lay out a solution building up step-by-step to a product that can learn itself and build upon the security policies that the customer has started with, helping them in automating violation remediation to the point that the security product can run autonomously with minimal manual intervention. Be it the cloud, on-premise, or a hybrid of environments starting from Cloud Access Security Broker (CASB) to Bring Your Own Device (BYOD), this book covers it all.

I firmly believe in technological developments and expect technologies to be used constructively for a safe digital world. No one should be avoiding technologies fearing the security aspect of them, specifically businesses. We have progressed through thousands of years of growth and should guarantee a safe future for our future generations.

I'm confident that you will find the concepts discussed in this book enjoyable and valuable. Whether you're a teacher, a security architect, or a CEO, this book is designed to serve as a lasting guide on data security design and the creation of a proactive enterprise security plan. Enjoy!

CHAPTER 1

Data Security Fundamental Requirements

When I started my career in cybersecurity, specifically focusing on data security, I quickly understood the common pursuit among security vendors. It was evident that each vendor was striving to build a solution offering comprehensive coverage across myriad access points, thwart external threats and attacks, and staunch the flow of data leaks. In essence, they were searching for a mythical creature—an all-encompassing unicorn—to alleviate all security concerns in one fell swoop.

The solution seemed glaringly obvious to me—keep the data shielded from the outside world. Lock down all entry points, store the data securely, and access it only through verified channels. How hard could it possibly be? I found myself grappling with a similar question when confronted with the topic of cancer. Why couldn't the brilliant minds in the medical field devise a medication that could halt the progression of cancerous cells within our bodies? Why wait until a diagnosis? Why not take a proactive stance? All *why's*! The sheer magnitude of the effort dedicated to finding a cure for cancer left me stunned. Over 250 years of research! Two and a half centuries! It's staggering, isn't it?

CHAPTER 1   DATA SECURITY FUNDAMENTAL REQUIREMENTS

Little did I know, then, that my initial assumptions couldn't have been further from the truth. In a peculiar twist of fate, the intricacies of cybersecurity defense bore a striking resemblance to the battle against cancer. While many may promise their ability to ensure security, the unequivocal guarantee of protection remains an elusive challenge. Much like a delicate house of cards, our security measures' efficacy stands firm until a skilled hacker discovers a way to breach our defenses. Throughout the pages of this book, we will discuss attackers and how they persistently try to break the system, and what security vendors and enterprises can do to thwart such persistent attempts. But beware, for it's only a matter of time until one of these predators, primarily motivated by financial gain, pounces on our vulnerabilities. We should have a system that is one step ahead to defeat the attackers, and as the technologies evolve, attackers become powerful day by day.

I set out to approach security from a different perspective, far away from conventional boundaries, and understand the true essence of our goal. What is the fundamental objective and what would be a solution that would stand the test of time? It is critical in cybersecurity to understand the fact that many of us believe. Given any security product, time, and computing power, a hacker could crack the product. By brute force, an attacker could test all permutations and combinations while looking for all the vulnerabilities. Don't we know this fact? Our systems should be intelligent enough to understand the behavior of an attacker and proactively take measures to protect. Isn't it? Of course, this isn't as straightforward as I put it out here. Often, attackers operate using legitimate credentials, making it challenging for us to distinguish between genuine users and potential threats.

CHAPTER 1 DATA SECURITY FUNDAMENTAL REQUIREMENTS

What Is Data Security?

Data security refers to safeguarding sensitive data without compromising its integrity and availability. In this chapter, I will discuss the requirements for a world-class data protection solution, starting from the ground up, while emphasizing the need for data protection.

In its simplest form, every organization deals with data, which can be broadly categorized into two main types: internal and external. Internal data encompasses an array of organizational information, including trade documents, tax statements, employee records, sales data, intellectual property, and more. Essentially, this data originates from and belongs to the organization itself.

On the other hand, external data pertains to information owned by the customers or clients that the organization serves. For instance, in a banking context, external data may include a customer's personally identifiable information and transaction history. Unlike internal data, the source of external data lies outside the organization, with customers or clients being the primary owners.

Consider Figure 1-1, which portrays different kinds of data under various departments in a banking organization. See if you can distinguish external data from internal data.

CHAPTER 1   DATA SECURITY FUNDAMENTAL REQUIREMENTS

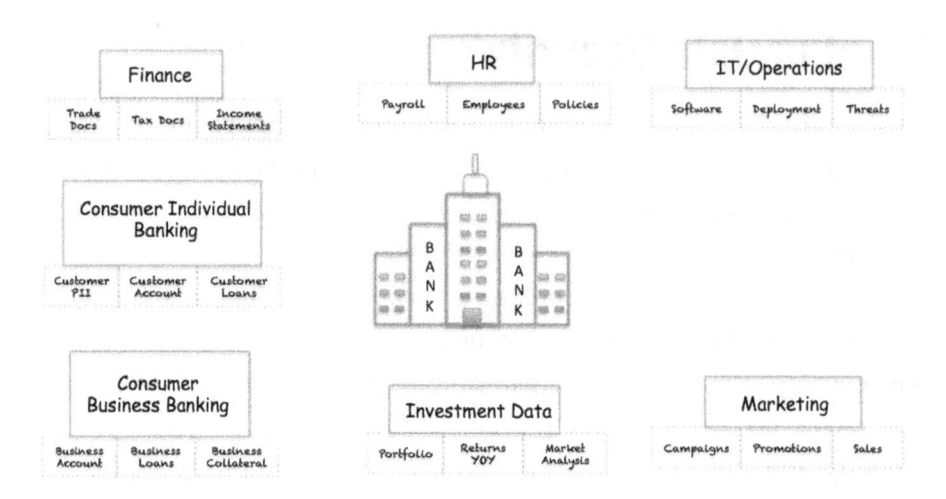

Figure 1-1. External and Internal Data in a Banking Organization

Protecting internal and external data is a top priority for every organization. It's not just common sense; it's essential for maintaining a competitive edge, building trust with clients, safeguarding the brand, and complying with audit regulations. Internal and external data are equally important, as protecting them is critical to an organization's success. From Figure 1-1, it's evident just how vital it is for the banking organization to safeguard the depicted data. Considering the potential ramifications, one can easily envision the significant harm it could inflict on the banking entity.

From the perspective of security vendors, the objective is clear: deliver data security solutions that ensure a company's confidential data never falls out of its control. To do this effectively, it's crucial to define two key terms: confidential data and data control. Confidential data encompasses any sensitive, private, or proprietary information within an organization, while data control refers to the practice of restricting access to authorized users only.

In my years of experience, I've observed that security products often swing between two extremes: being too lenient, allowing suspicious data to slip through, or too strict, blocking legitimate activities. Striking the right balance is paramount. As a fundamental requirement, security products

CHAPTER 1   DATA SECURITY FUNDAMENTAL REQUIREMENTS

should never disrupt genuine business operations. For instance, consider a sales team needing to share past sales reports via a shared folder or an employee reaching out to a customer via external email. Security measures should monitor operations without hindering them unless there's a genuine threat of data leakage.

Thus far, three critical aspects that a data security solution should prioritize are: differentiating and protecting confidential data, never disrupting legitimate business practices, and always ensuring and guaranteeing that confidential, sensitive data never leaves an organization's control.

At the heart of data security lies the challenge of safeguarding information with utmost efficiency and effectiveness. Should our approach be reactive or proactive? Before we dive deeper into this question, it's crucial to grasp the nature of our adversaries. Understanding them better will help us refine our strategies and requirements.

Understanding Adversaries, Tactics, and Attack Types

The adversaries I am referring to are the attackers who attempt to break in and gain control. Attackers ex-filtrate confidential data out of the organization's control. Similar to how we broadly classified the data as internal and external, attackers can also be classified as internal and external. Internal attackers work for the organization we are trying to protect. External attackers do not work and have no authorized access to the business systems and the organization's internal infrastructure.

Figure 1-2, on the left side, illustrates how external attackers attempt to breach the organization's firewall since they lack access to the internal network. They employ various methods, such as bots, to cause harm to the organization. On the right side of Figure 1-2, you can observe an internal malicious user attempting to attack the internal infrastructure.

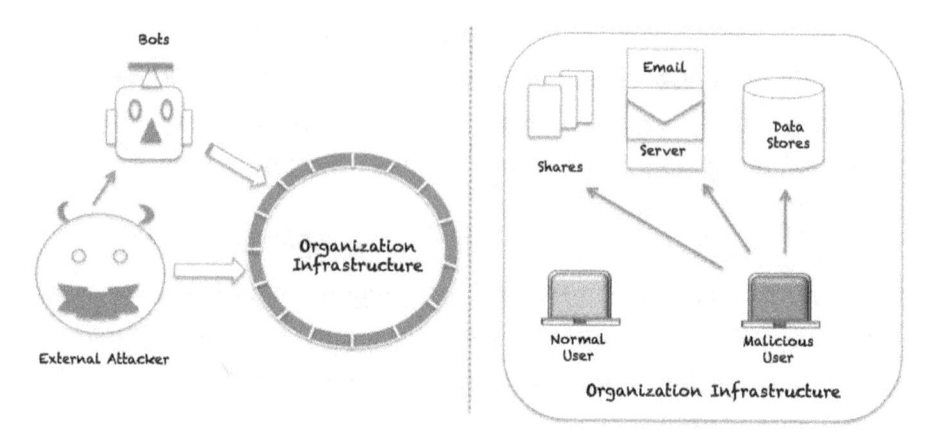

CHAPTER 1   DATA SECURITY FUNDAMENTAL REQUIREMENTS

Figure 1-2. *External and Internal Attackers Attacking an Organization Infrastructure*

Next, it is critical to understand the measures carried out by internal and external users to gain control in designing effective solutions. While extensively discussing various types of attacks is beyond the scope of this book, let us examine the major types.

Internal Attacks

Malicious insiders primarily perpetrated internal attacks. However, external users can also carry out internal attacks by gaining access and masquerading as legitimate system users. As they effectively impersonate internal users, I have classified these instances as internal attacks for the clarity of this book's readers. Internal attackers are responsible for "insider threats," and not all threats stem from employees with malicious intent. Often, employees inadvertently engage in such actions without considering the ramifications. Some may remain unaware, even after repeating the behavior multiple times. To date, most security measures within organizations focus on preventing external attacks rather than internal ones. **Guarding against internal attacks proves to be exceptionally challenging.**

CHAPTER 1   DATA SECURITY FUNDAMENTAL REQUIREMENTS

Now let's dive deep into the topic of malicious insiders to understand them better.

Malicious Insider

An adversary from within an organization, commonly referred to as a malicious insider, is an individual with nefarious intentions seeking to compromise the security of the business by illicitly acquiring sensitive data. Essentially, these are individuals who exploit their authorized access privileges to clandestinely transfer proprietary and confidential information from the organization. This threat can emanate from any member within the organization, or even from an individual who retains unrevoked access privileges post-employment. Frequently, such individuals are found to be disgruntled or motivated by personal gain, posing a significant risk to the organization upon departure.

Cost of Insider Threats

As per the 2023 IBM security report[1], the average cost incurred by an organization due to a single data breach amounts to $4.45 million. Additionally, a separate statistical report highlights that, in the year 2023, the United States witnessed 3205 reported cases of data breaches. These figures underscore a cause for concern, emphasizing the financial implications and the growing prevalence of such security violations.

---

[1] https://www.ibm.com/reports/data-breach?utm_content=SRCWW&p1=Search&p4=43700077724064033&p5=p&acs_info=ZmluYWxfdXJsOiAiaHR0cHM6Ly93d3cu aWJtLmNvbS9yZXBvcnRzL2RhdGEtYnJlYWNoIgo&gclid=CjwKCAiA5L2tBhBTEiwAd SxJX895yGLShkQpeDPTtR-PJo_k5sospH27maXmJ98FmXAZWgN2gEft8BoCPNQQAvD_ BwE&gclsrc=aw.ds

CHAPTER 1   DATA SECURITY FUNDAMENTAL REQUIREMENTS

Insiders were responsible for more than 50% of data breaches, and according to a report from cybersecurity-insiders[2] 74% of organizations today are susceptible to insider threats. Certain effects of a data breach are irreversible, like damage to a company's brand image—once lost it can't be restored. It is natural for all organizations worldwide to increase their investment to protect against such insider data breaches.

Over 50% of data breaches can be attributed to insiders, with a cybersecurity-insiders report indicating that 74% of organizations currently face vulnerability to insider threats. The repercussions of a data breach, such as irreversible harm to a company's brand image, underscore the critical nature of this issue, as reputational damage is often irreparable. Hence, organizations on a global scale find themselves compelled to enhance their investments in bolstering defenses against data breaches instigated by insiders.

Are All Insider Threats Malignant?

Yes! Every data breach, regardless of its scale, inflicts irreparable harm on an organization. Nevertheless, it's essential to recognize that not all data breaches result from employees with malicious intent. According to a survey, negligent employees inadvertently cause a significant 80% of such security violations. Contrary to some apprehensions, the world is not as perilous as certain individuals might perceive. Let's delve into the categorization of insider threats.

Negligent Users—Accidental Data Exposure

Within this category, insider threats involve individuals who unintentionally expose data without any malicious intent. Often, to streamline tasks and save time, they opt for the path of least resistance,

---

[2]https://www.cybersecurity-insiders.com/portfolio/2023-insider-threat-report-gurucul/

CHAPTER 1 DATA SECURITY FUNDAMENTAL REQUIREMENTS

colloquially known as "shortcuts," leading to inadvertent exposure of confidential information. Illustrative instances include an employee aiming to impress their supervisor by emailing confidential data to their personal account for remote work, another unintentionally sending proprietary data to the wrong recipient, or an employee inadvertently falling victim to a phishing attack.

Figure 1-3 shows a negligent user accidentally cc'ing all employees in his organization on an email that contains confidential data.

Figure 1-3. *Negligent User—Accidental Data Exposure*

Negligent Users—Losing Credentials

Figure 1-4 shows a negligent user who lost his laptop where he had all his laptop login credentials on a sticky note.

CHAPTER 1   DATA SECURITY FUNDAMENTAL REQUIREMENTS

Figure 1-4. *Negligent User—Losing Credentials*

As depicted in Figure 1-4, this category comprises individuals who inadvertently leaked or lost their credentials, often without realizing the potential harm inflicted on the organization. Malicious actors may exploit these compromised credentials to cause harm. Examples include an employee losing a laptop, another misplacing a diary containing usernames and passwords for critical company accounts, or an employee with access to confidential data leaving their laptop unlocked.

Malicious Intent Users

This category represents a minimal 10% of threats, primarily driven by financial motives. Individuals with malicious intent, often fueled by frustration with their employer, actively seek opportunities to extract confidential data from the organization through any available means. Examples include a disgruntled employee deliberately leaking sensitive information to a competitor, an employee intending to establish their own business resorting to data theft, or an individual seeking revenge on their supervisor by disclosing confidential data.

CHAPTER 1 DATA SECURITY FUNDAMENTAL REQUIREMENTS

Figure 1-5 shows a malicious user (disgruntled employee) who attempts to break the server to cause physical damage to the organization.

Figure 1-5. Malicious User—Causing Physical Damage to Organization

Internal Attack Types

As you'll discover in the later chapters of the book, I'm going to unveil a few strategies to root out these behaviors associated with ill intent and proactively prevent such occurrences. For now, let's see how these threats manifest in the real world. Are you ready?

Data Theft/Exfiltration Attacks

Since insiders have access to all internal systems, they can easily carry out operations that aren't possible for external users, such as copying data between corporate folders, emailing sensitive information outside the organization, downloading data from corporate to personal drives, and abusing access privileges to view and download confidential proprietary data.

Destruction Attacks

Malicious insiders may intentionally delete confidential and important files, bring down servers and networks by executing malicious software, expose sensitive files to the world by granting access to external users, give away their credentials to hackers, or impede critical operations and business functions to cause damage to the organization.

Cyber-Espionage Attacks

Insiders may engage in espionage, providing competitors with access to highly valuable intellectual property. Competitors may recruit individuals to undertake espionage on their behalf to gain a competitive advantage. In some cases, these stolen pieces of information may be used by these malicious individuals to kick-start their enterprise. Disgruntled employees typically exhibit this type of behavior.

Financial Attacks

Disgruntled or financially motivated employees with bad intent embezzle funds by creating fictitious transactions. Malicious insiders may perform insider trading by using privileged undisclosed proprietary information to make stock trades for financial gains. Such illegal activities can result in financial losses for investors and cause irreparable damage to the organization's reputation.

Figure 1-6 depicts the main motivations behind internal attacks. Financial gain is not the sole driving factor. While money-motivated attacks may be mitigated, those perpetrated by internal employees seeking a challenge or to satisfy their ego pose a greater challenge to contain. Internal employees can be convinced to commit crimes too.

CHAPTER 1 DATA SECURITY FUNDAMENTAL REQUIREMENTS

Figure 1-6. *Motivations for Internal Attacks by Internal Users*

External Attacks

Once more, external attacks may stem from similar motivations as internal ones: financial gain, revenge, espionage, cyber warfare, or simply the thrill of the challenge. They can orchestrate each type of attack discussed below through diverse means. In many cases, it would be a combination of attacks meticulously planned and precisely executed to inflict maximum damage. Figure 1-7 depicts different types of external attacks that exist.

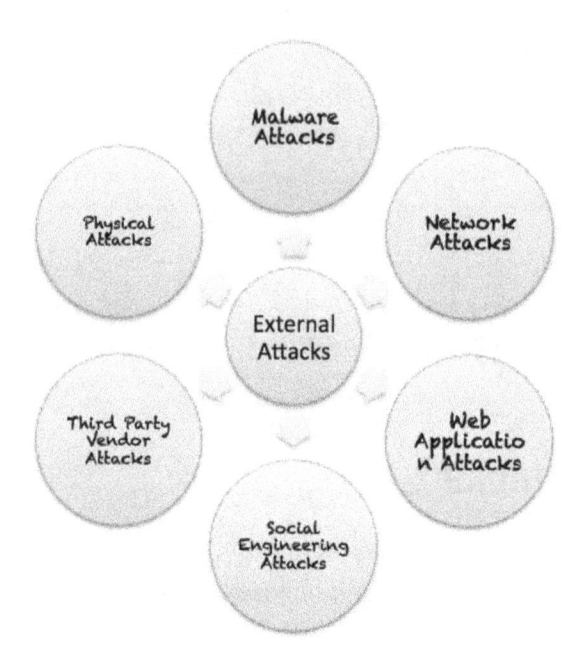

CHAPTER 1   DATA SECURITY FUNDAMENTAL REQUIREMENTS

Figure 1-7. *Types of External Attacks*

External Attack Types

Malware Attacks

Malware is a malicious program intentionally created to attack a computer, a server, or any infrastructure to gain unauthorized access without the knowledge of the end user. Malware can manifest in different forms, such as the following:

- **Ransomware**: Encrypt files for a ransom
- **Adware**: Malicious ads to extract information
- **Viruses**: Programs to destroy or ex-filtrate data
- **Worms**: Replicating viruses to exhaust resources

CHAPTER 1   DATA SECURITY FUNDAMENTAL REQUIREMENTS

- **Bots**: Infect a system to launch other attacks
- **Spyware and keyloggers**: Spies on activities
- **POS**: Point of Sale attack to extract transaction data
- **Trojans**: Attack in the background to gain data access
- **Phishing**: Fraudulent emails/messages to trick end-users

These are the most common types of attacks, as it is easy to execute with fewer resources and money. Statistics state that there are usually billions of malware attacks in any single year and 10% of organizations worldwide get attacked every year.

Network Attacks

Network attacks, as the name implies, are carried out on an organizational network infrastructure to gain access to assets. Sometimes, the motive of the attack is not to gain access but to destroy the infrastructure and cause damage. Other subsequent attacks can be carried on top of the initial network attack once the attacker gains access to the network. Most commonly, attackers start with targeting network perimeters.

> *"The network perimeter is the boundary between an organization's internal network and the internet. Attackers focus on the perimeter, looking for vulnerabilities."*

Network attacks can include the following:

- **Denial of Service (DOS)**: Sending large amounts of invalid data to a network/server
- **Distributed Denial of Service (DDOS)**: Using a fleet of devices to attack a network/server

- **Man in the Middle (MITM)**: Intercepting traffic to steal secure data

- **Packet Sniffing**: Eavesdropping to inspect the packets looking for sensitive data

- **DNS Spoofing**: Poisoning the DNS entries to redirect traffic to a fraudulent server

Web Application Attacks

Application attacks occur as a result of attackers gaining control by exploiting the vulnerabilities in applications used by users in an organization. These attacks are hard to guard against as they often need to be exposed through either port 80 or 443.

Common application attacks can include the following:

- **SQL Injection**: Introducing malicious SQL code into application input fields

- **Cross-site Scripting**: Inserting Javascript into web pages

- **Cross-site request Forgery**: Tricking authenticated users to perform malicious actions

- **Application Redirects/Forwards**: Forwarding users to malicious sites

- **Fuzzing**: Sending random input data to web applications

- **Path Traversal**: Manipulate file paths in web applications

CHAPTER 1   DATA SECURITY FUNDAMENTAL REQUIREMENTS

Social Engineering Attacks

Exploiting users psychologically through devious schemes to induce mistakes or make them give their sensitive data away. 98% of cyberattacks today throughout the world are of this type, by far the largest, and 85% of organizations are vulnerable to this. These attack schemes typically manipulate human minds by invoking feelings of empathy, urgency, scarcity, or fear. Hence, they are difficult to tackle and control.

Common social engineering attacks can include the following:

- **Phishing/Smishing**: Sending fraudulent emails or SMS to trick users

- **Whaling**: Targeted on a single individual by leveraging continuous personal communication

- **Baiting/Luring**: Providing falsified information to trick users

- **Diversion**: Persuading users to pick up or drop off packages

- **Pre-texting**: Composing plausible scenarios to trick users by seeking empathy

- **Quid pro quo**: Tricking users to give away information for a service offering

Third-Party Vendor Attacks

This is also termed a supply chain attack, where attackers exploit the vulnerabilities of third-party components, typically libraries, used in an application. This can lead to severe trust issues between the targeted organization and the application software vendor. Government offices and financial organizations take this seriously and mandate periodic audits and high compliance requirements for all the software they use internally.

CHAPTER 1   DATA SECURITY FUNDAMENTAL REQUIREMENTS

These types of attacks are typically orchestrated by attackers using one of the following schemes:

- **Vendor Software Compromise**: Breaching the third-party application systems or software

- **Vendor Account Takeover**: Take over admin accounts to orchestrate attacks

- **Credential Theft**: Stealing legitimate user credentials stored in the application for attacks

- **Misconfiguration**: Exploiting misconfiguration of the third-party software

Physical Attacks

Attackers employ malicious tactics to breach an organization's physical infrastructure, targeting hardware components and users. To counter such threats, organizations deploy robust physical security measures to safeguard critical infrastructure effectively.

Physical Attacks include the following:

- **Physical Stealing/Destruction**: Physically stealing or destroying hardware components

- **Tailgating**: Gain access by tailgating employees into the organization

- **Dumpster Diving**: Looking for information in trash cans and dumpsters

- **Tampering**: Tampering with hardware components delivered to the organization

CHAPTER 1 DATA SECURITY FUNDAMENTAL REQUIREMENTS

Building Data Security Requirements

After analyzing both internal and external attacks, a common theme emerges, the extraction of sensitive information from the organization. This may occur through actions by internal employees, attacks impersonating legitimate users, or targeting the organization's resources. Therefore, safeguarding the organization's most valuable data remains the primary use case. I encourage all readers to consider closely, the customer requirements, including business use cases, deployment environments, and constraints, when developing effective security solutions. With that in mind, let's establish security requirements in their most basic form. Subsequently, in the following chapters, we will refine and expand upon these requirements.

Fundamentally, the requirements can be broken down into functional and non-functional requirements. For example, performance is a non-functional requirement, and encrypting sensitive data may be one of the functional requirements. However, I would like to consider all of them together, as we often tend to ignore or delay addressing non-functional requirements, making it challenging to incorporate them into the products we develop.

Since we all know that data exists in organizations, Figure 1-8 represents the summary of actions to be done to protect data. This has been folded into requirements in the subsequent sections.

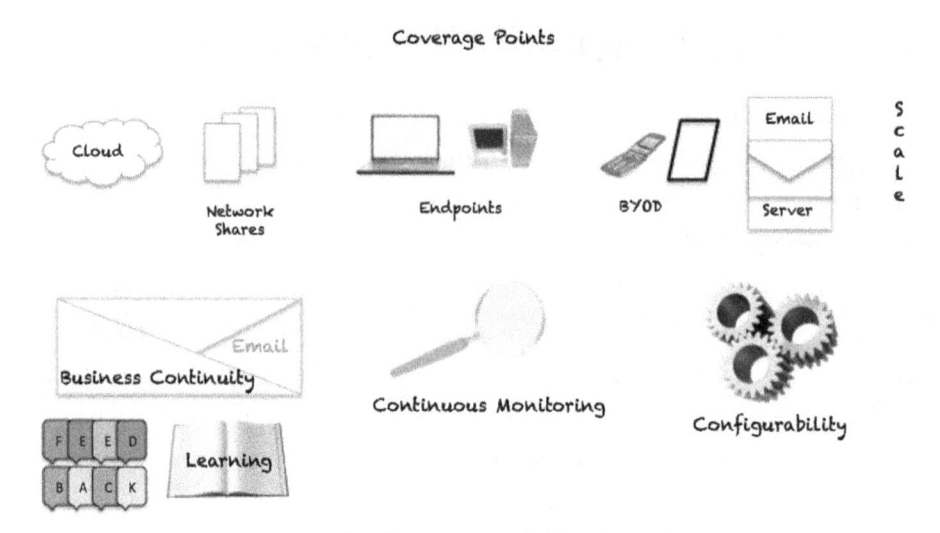

CHAPTER 1   DATA SECURITY FUNDAMENTAL REQUIREMENTS

Figure 1-8. *Overall Requirements for Our Data Security Solution*

Identifying and Remediation of Confidential Data

Protecting sensitive data from leaving the organization is our primary goal. Theoretically, if we know all the sensitive data in the organization—its locations and who needs access—we can effectively protect it. The fundamental challenge here is determining whether the data contains confidential information and if it is in the hands of or exposed to unauthorized employees within the organization. The context determines if data needs to be protected.

Figure 1-9 depicts the following scenario:

CHAPTER 1 DATA SECURITY FUNDAMENTAL REQUIREMENTS

It is acceptable when a CEO emails all executives regarding an impending merger, though the information is sensitive. However, if an employee were to send out the same information about an impending merger, it would be considered sensitive, and the context would not apply. Therefore, this action should be classified as a security violation.

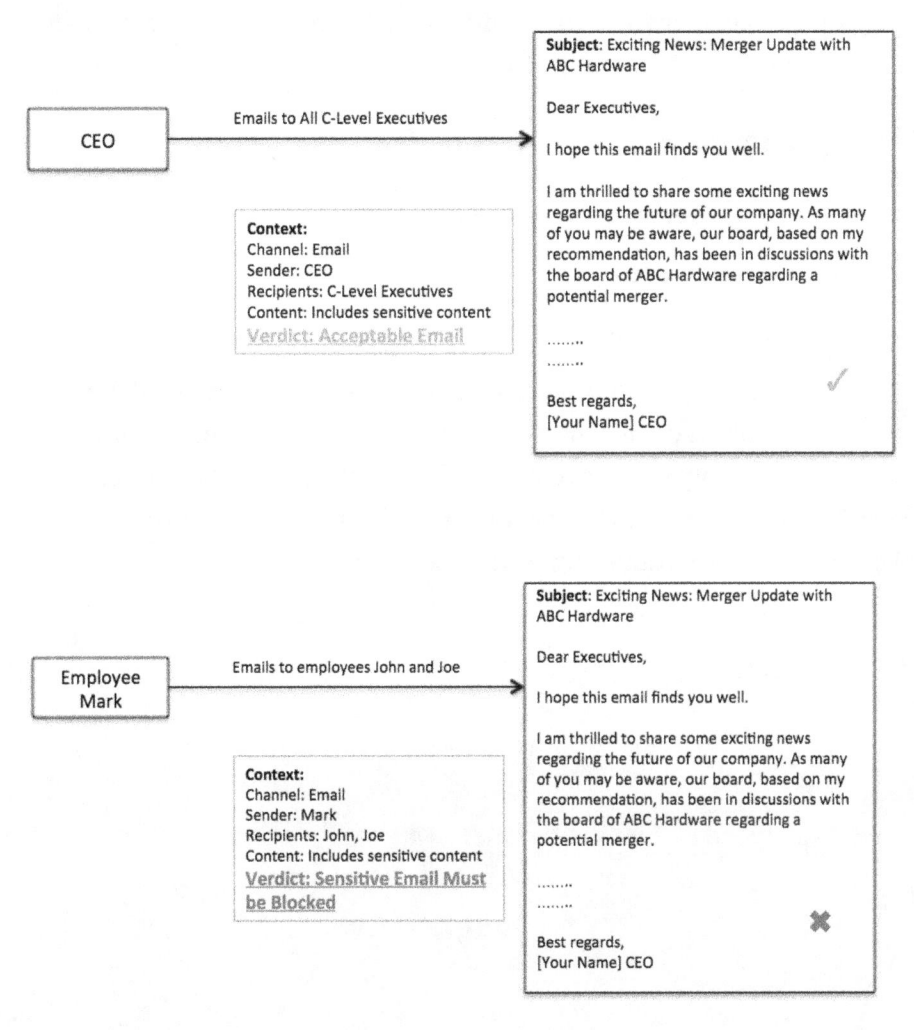

Figure 1-9. Sensitive vs. Non-sensitive Based on Context

At this juncture, I understand you would be considering security policies that dictate whether data is confidential. However, let's not jump ahead of ourselves. I would like to guide you through the intricacies of these requirements so that you fundamentally grasp the core knowledge and can develop your ideas.

Protecting data involves two fundamental stages: data inspection and remediation.

Data Inspection

Data inspection comprises two sequential steps:

1. Contextual Analysis
2. Content Examination

The second step, scrutinizing the data itself, can be skipped if the contextual analysis deems the data trustworthy and non-suspicious. Essentially, security software can expedite the data inspection process when the contextual match is deemed reliable. Figure 1-10 illustrates high-level steps for examining content sensitivity.

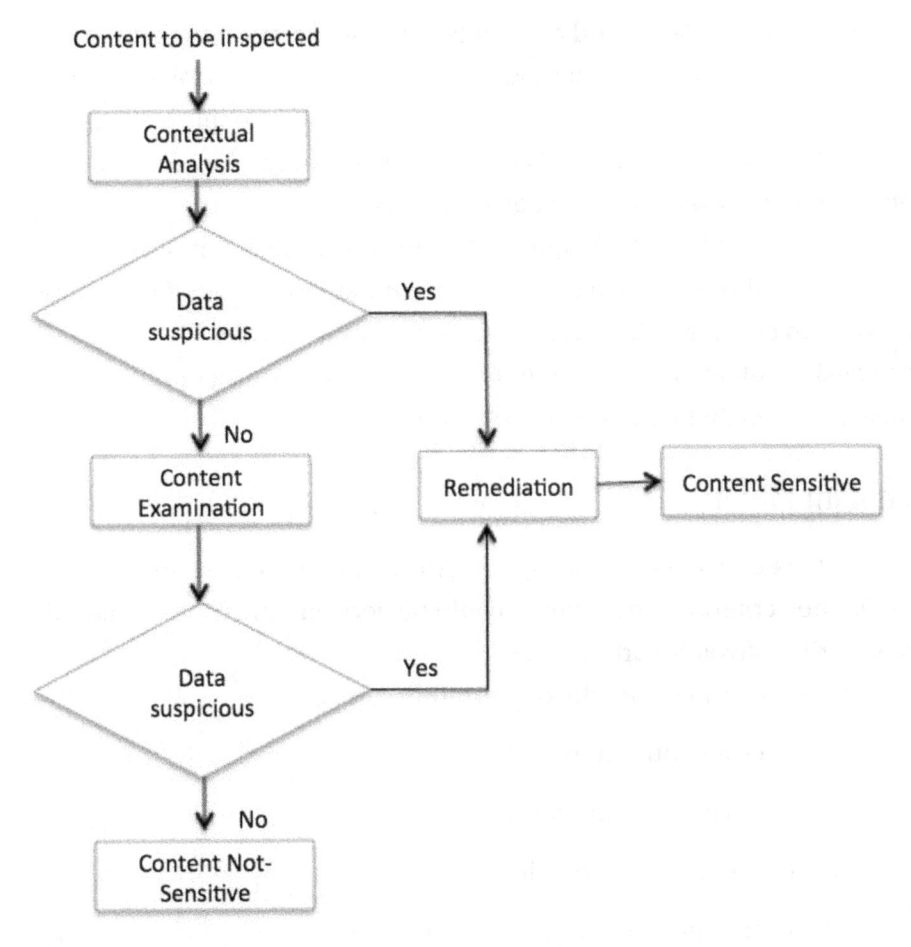

CHAPTER 1 DATA SECURITY FUNDAMENTAL REQUIREMENTS

Figure 1-10. *High-Level Steps in Content Examination*

Contextual Match

Contextual matching involves examining diverse factors such as the source, recipients, potential collaborators, data format, data type, data size, data location, and sometimes even the access time.

23

CHAPTER 1   DATA SECURITY FUNDAMENTAL REQUIREMENTS

Verifying the source and recipients may entail confirming the originator of the data, the method of access, and potential collaborators. Examples of this would include an email sent from an employee's laptop connected to the corporate VPN to a group of other employees' corporate email addresses, or a file stored on a shared network drive created by Employee A, modified by Employee B, and accessible to Employee C.

Data attributes need to be checked if they are suspicious. For example, let's say an email attachment consists of many picture files that are screenshots of different customer profiles of a banking organization; in that case, it might be considered a security violation.

Content Match

Content matching involves comparing the actual content against a set of predefined criteria. These criteria could be derived from pre-defined rules or security software-learned rules.

Predefined rules from the organization can include

- Access control rules
- Data classification rules
- Content sensitivity rules
- Regulatory and compliance law rules
- Auditing rules

The security software strengthens over time, autonomously crafting rules as it familiarizes itself with the customer's setup. But here's the real deal: Within this process, the confidence threshold becomes key. Imagine the software making a call, saying, "I'm X% sure this content is fishy." That X? It's the confidence threshold, a crucial element in the software's decision-making.

CHAPTER 1 DATA SECURITY FUNDAMENTAL REQUIREMENTS

Remediation

Remediation is the process of resolving and mitigating issues at hand. A more detailed description of remediation involves taking appropriate actions to address any breaches, weaknesses, or non-compliance with security policies or standards. The goal of remediation is to restore the integrity, confidentiality, and availability of data and systems, thereby reducing risks and ensuring ongoing protection against potential threats.

For example, let's assume we discover suspicious content shared in a network drive accessible to employees who shouldn't have access. Remediation could involve either revoking the data access for unauthorized employees or removing the data from that location. We will explore various types of remediation options in Chapter 2.

Now, here's the real deal: the effectiveness of Data Inspection and Remediation holds the key to keeping confidential data safe and sound within the organization's walls. Those in charge of deploying security software must grasp this fundamental truth to configure and uphold security solutions effectively. While many organizations tend to cut corners when it comes to remediation, let me tell you, it's non-negotiable. Remediation is the crucial step you can't afford to skip.

Data Security at Coverage Points

A crucial consideration lies in how effectively a data protection solution integrates with an organization's network infrastructure and ensures data security across all integration points. Let's delve into the journey of a newly established e-commerce company to illustrate this point. Initially, their operations were modest, processing just five orders per day for a handful of items, with a team of 25 employees who shared an intimate familiarity. Communication primarily relied on email and chat messengers, reflecting their minimal network infrastructure centered around a single business site.

CHAPTER 1   DATA SECURITY FUNDAMENTAL REQUIREMENTS

However, as the business gained traction, order volumes surged to a staggering 10,000 per day, accompanied by a vast expansion in product offerings. Scaling up to meet this demand required a significant workforce increase to 5000 individuals, resulting in the loss of the close-knit camaraderie among employees. Automation systems were introduced to streamline processes, necessitating a more robust network infrastructure to support multiple operational sites. Communication channels diversified to include platforms like Slack, Zoom, and cloud-based services such as Google Drive, each requiring stringent protection measures. With the rise in employee numbers, the need to safeguard confidential data stored on laptops became paramount, particularly for those traveling on business.

Despite the absence of a dedicated cybersecurity team in its infancy, management soon recognized the imperative of investing in robust data protection solutions as operations expanded. As the organization continued to evolve, its global footprint expanded, with order volumes skyrocketing to 10,000 orders per hour and an employee count reaching a staggering 300,000. The initial data protection solutions, adequate for the early growth phase, proved inadequate for the monumental scale and complexity of operations. Consequently, the organization had to invest in sophisticated, globally scalable data protection solutions capable of seamlessly managing terabytes, if not petabytes, of data. Data traversed their extensive global network infrastructure, spanning data centers, appliances, and a significant cloud footprint. Protecting data across all access points became crucial, considering the myriad ways data could be transmitted, copied, shared, and manipulated. This operational complexity underscores the necessity of robust data security measures across all coverage points, an essential component of our requirements.

Thus, if I had to define data security at coverage points, it refers to the protection of data at various access points within an organization's network infrastructure. These coverage points include any location or interface where data is transmitted, stored, or accessed.

CHAPTER 1   DATA SECURITY FUNDAMENTAL REQUIREMENTS

Data security at coverage points refers to the protection of data at various access points within an organization's network infrastructure. These coverage points include any location or interface where data is transmitted, stored, or accessed. Ensuring data security at these points is essential for safeguarding sensitive information from unauthorized access, manipulation, or theft.

We will be discussing elaborately about coverage points by channel in Chapter 2. Most of the coverage points in an organization that needs protection can be seen in Figure 1-11.

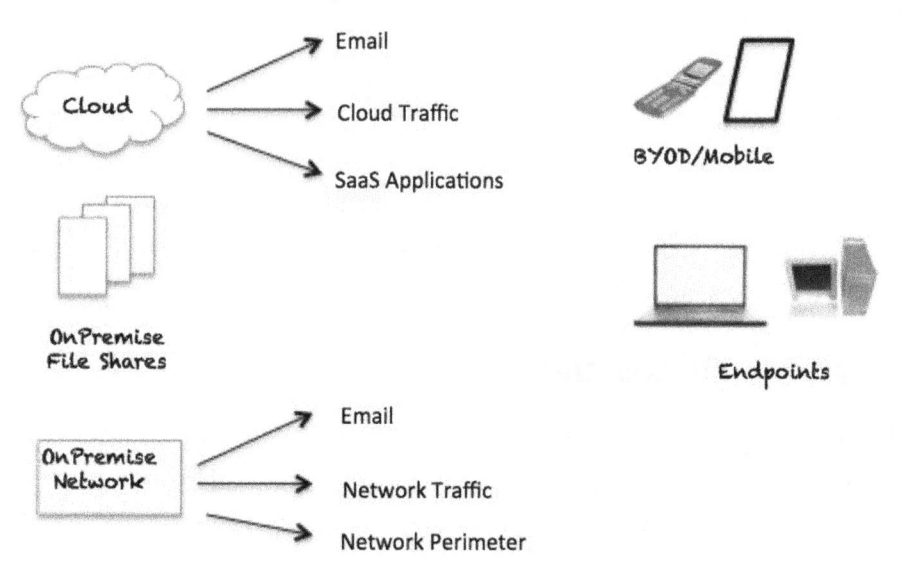

Figure 1-11. Coverage Points

Network Perimeters

Entry and exit points into the organization's network, such as firewalls, proxies, routers, and gateways, are where external threats attempt to gain access. Internal malicious users, with the knowledge of network infrastructure, can orchestrate an attack through a weak link.

CHAPTER 1　DATA SECURITY FUNDAMENTAL REQUIREMENTS

Data Centers

Data centers can be either physical or virtual and large organizations typically have multiple data centers to host servers that run various applications and storage systems. Ensuring HA/DR for these data centers is mandatory for large enterprises to maintain business continuity. Now security software not only has to protect the data in active systems but might also have to cover backup systems.

Endpoints

Devices such as laptops, desktops, smartphones, and tablets are used by employees to access and process data. Many organizations have common PCs for employee access and employees might use shared administrator credentials to log in to those systems. These systems are potential points of vulnerability. Malicious internal employees use generic Administrator accounts to execute their attacks a majority of the time.

Email and Messengers

Almost all organizations make use of emails and messaging applications to facilitate communication in their organization. Channels used for communication include email servers, messaging apps, and video conferencing tools.

Cloud Services

Many organizations use cloud services to store data. Microsoft O365 and Gmail services are popular email services adopted by many. Additionally, organizations could host their proprietary software in cloud platforms, and use their computing resources. All these are potential points of vulnerability that an attacker could take advantage of.

Remote Access Points

Connections are used by remote employees, contractors, or partners to access the organization's network, such as virtual private networks (VPNs) or remote desktop services.

Ensuring Business Continuity

Let's talk about business continuity—it's the heartbeat of any organization's day-to-day operations. Each company has its own unique set of processes, and sometimes, even different departments within the same organization operate differently. Preserving business continuity stands as a paramount goal for any security product, as discussed earlier in this chapter.

Now, let's take a trip down memory lane. Have you ever encountered or heard about a scenario where software installed on your computer suddenly became a resource hog, slowing down your machine to a crawl? You know, gobbling up CPU, Memory, and Disk Space like there's no tomorrow? Yep, that's the kind of intrusion we're talking about—when software disrupts your daily computer usage.

Sure, security software needs to keep an eye on almost every activity on your computer to ensure data protection. But here's the catch—it shouldn't come at the cost of turning your device into a sloth. When software behaves this way, users usually hit the uninstall button or start tinkering to make it stop.

Picture this: an employee is about to send a message with a mammoth compressed file attached. Security software needs to leap into action—uncompressing the file, and scrutinizing its contents, all in the blink of an eye, without causing any visible lag to the user interface.

Sometimes, security software needs to sift through terabytes of data every quarter, ensuring the organization stays compliant. It needs to be smart about—knowing what to scan, what's already been checked, and delivering those compliance reports without making organizations wait around.

CHAPTER 1   DATA SECURITY FUNDAMENTAL REQUIREMENTS

Last but not least, there's the cost of ownership. Security software shouldn't demand high-end hardware that breaks the bank for organizations to procure and maintain. After all, the bottom line matters, and excessive costs could put a strain on the business's financial health. Organizations then tend to take shortcuts missing the comprehensive security.

Security Solution Configurability

The way a security solution is deployed and configured plays a crucial role in shaping its overall performance, directly impacting the security stance of an organization.

The flexibility of a security software's configuration can significantly influence its usability. In my experience, some organizations prefer a ready-to-go solution, requiring minimal setup, while others prefer to have full control over the configuration. It's like driving a car with a manual transmission vs. an automatic one. Those who prefer hands-on configuration want all the knobs and whistles at their disposal, constantly fine-tuning the security software to squeeze out maximum efficiency. Therefore, configurability becomes a fundamental requirement for any security software.

As we discussed earlier, data coverage points can vary widely, and security software must offer tailored configuration options for each point. Remediation rules may differ depending on the situation. Configuration also involves how the security software integrates with other business tools used by the organization, such as Jira, Splunk, Service Now, and Active Directory. Successful integrations are key to ensuring business continuity. This interconnectedness among our requirements indicates that we're on the right track toward achieving a common goal.

Improperly configured rules or those created with malicious intent can directly compromise the security posture, posing a significant vulnerability. Therefore, organizations regularly review their security configurations to identify any irregularities and address any gaps.

Configurability encompasses a broad range of features for security software, including the following. Don't worry if some of these concepts are unfamiliar to you; we'll discuss each one in more detail over the next two chapters.

- Security rules that define context and content-matching criteria
- Remediation configuration
- Security violation generation configuration
- Continuous monitoring configurations
- Configuration for coverage points
- Encryption, Classification configurations
- Business tools integration configuration
- Compliance reporting configuration
- Data retention configuration
- Analytics setup
- User and usage settings for the security software

Feedback and Learning

Every security software must be able to learn and adapt from its deployed environment. While some may overlook this aspect, I consider it fundamental, as comprehensive security cannot solely rely on configuration rules. Without this capability, organizations would constantly find themselves tweaking security settings. Whenever new data emerges, the security software must be informed whether it's confidential or not. By default, software assumes that data not meeting sensitivity criteria is non-confidential.

Let's consider a real-life scenario. Imagine a marketing organization launching a new campaign and wanting to survey products introduced in the past year along with their adoption metrics. This information may be highly proprietary, but if the security software's configurations don't include these adoption metrics—such as a new Excel sheet as shown in Figure 1-12, with columns for product name, maximum discounted price, and sales numbers in millions—the software wouldn't recognize this data as sensitive because it hasn't been defined as such yet.

Period	Best Selling Product	MSRP	Max Discounted Price	Sales in Millions
Jan 2023	Phone	370	310	10
Feb 2023	Tablet	600	500	7
Mar 2023	Phone	350	300	9
Apr 2023	Laptop	1200	1100	4
May 2023	Watch	200	175	2
Jun 2023	Tablet	550	490	9
Jul 2023	Laptop	1100	1000	12
Aug 2023	Desktop	1700	1200	4
Sep 2023	Phone	380	330	12
Oct 2023	Printer	150	100	2
Nov 2023	Laptop	1100	1000	5
Dec 2023	Phone	370	300	20

Figure 1-12. *New Excel Spreadsheet for an AD Campaign in an Organization*

With the benefit of feedback and learning, the security software must recognize that the organization handles the sales of various products, such as phones and laptops. It should deduce that safeguarding sales data is crucial and automatically prevent any illegal handling of spreadsheets, should such a situation arise. Customers should not need to create policies for each piece of sensitive data they possess.

Imagine your security software as a cautious guardian, always on the lookout for trouble. Reactive security is like having this guardian spring into action only when a threat is detected, following predefined rules and addressing suspicious events as they happen. But in today's fast-paced world, where technology evolves at lightning speed, relying solely on reactive security isn't enough.

Think of it this way: modern cars come equipped with sensors all around, constantly scanning the environment to prevent accidents before they even happen. Similarly, we need our security software to go beyond reacting to threats and start anticipating them proactively.

That's where the heart of this book lies—in exploring how to develop software that breaks free from the confines of rules and takes security to the next level. We're talking about Autonomous Data Security—a future where our software anticipates and prevents threats before they have a chance to strike. It's about building a smarter, more intuitive security solution that stays one step ahead of the game.

Proactive Security

In this chapter, I'd like to introduce the concept of proactive security at a high level. I encourage you, dear readers, to keep proactive security in mind as you read through the next couple of chapters. In Chapters 4 and 5, we'll explore this topic in detail and discuss how we can achieve the golden state of protection before threats or data leaks occur.

The textbook definition of proactive security goes like this. Proactive security refers to the approach of anticipating and preventing security threats before they occur, rather than reacting to them after they've already happened. It involves actively identifying potential vulnerabilities, implementing measures to mitigate risks, and continuously monitoring systems to detect and address any suspicious activities or emerging threats.

At this juncture, let's briefly touch upon the pros and cons of proactive security to understand better.

Pros of proactive security

- Proactive security measures help prevent security breaches before they occur, reducing the risk of unauthorized access, data leaks, and other cyber threats.

- Proactive security allows organizations to identify and address vulnerabilities in their systems before they can be exploited by attackers.

- By continuously monitoring systems for suspicious activities, proactive security enables organizations to respond quickly and effectively to potential threats, minimizing the impact of security violations.

- Proactively addressing security risks helps organizations maintain compliance with regulatory requirements and industry standards.

Cons of proactive security

- Proactive security measures can only work effectively based on feedback. If no feedback then there will be more false positives leading to spamming and unnecessary panic in organizations.

- The cost of implementing and maintaining proactive security might be expensive for customers as it is resource-intensive.

Through feedback and continuous learning, security software can proactively thwart threats. Although we focused more on learning and monitoring in this section, you might have questions about feedback—"What is feedback?", "Who should provide the feedback?", and "Who is it for?"

Feedback

In simple terms, feedback is the user input given to a system to assess its performance. In our security software, feedback is received whenever an administrator interacts with the system. For example, let's say an administrator tries to remediate a security violation marked as a false positive. That serves as instant feedback. The system can then trace back to the context and content that triggered the violation and learn from the feedback, recognizing it as a false positive despite the initial determination by the matching engine.

When building continuous monitoring systems, guidance is crucial—what we refer to as supervised learning in AI. With supervision, systems can improve, resulting in fewer false positives and increased accuracy. Without supervision, a system may not even recognize genuinely suspicious events. Therefore, security software should always seek feedback and learn from it.

Feedback, along with learning from it, can be constructively utilized to achieve the following in organizations:

- Reduce false positives of security violations
- Improve security posture by automatic remediation
- Reduce operational overhead
- Reduce configuration tuning of security software
- Aid forensic analysis

Continuous Monitoring

A way to look at maintaining organizational data control is continuous monitoring. It is the process to make sure all data is always in the control of the organization. Only authorized users have access and everything stays compliant. However, continuous monitoring doesn't stop at inspecting all data access-related events that are occurring in an organization. It is much more!

Tracking User Behavior

Continuous monitoring involves observing and analyzing how people behave. It's like paying attention to the way individuals act in different situations. Continuous monitoring is closely linked to proactive security because understanding patterns can help identify potentially risky events before they happen. One of the key aspects is tracking the behavior of users. For instance, if someone tries to log in multiple times without success, it raises red flags. Let's consider a more complex scenario. Imagine a user, let's call them User A, who logs into an application using their credentials from New York at 2 pm GMT. Then, just an hour later, they attempt to log in from Sydney, Australia. That's quite suspicious, right? How could someone travel from the US to Australia so quickly? It prompts us to question the legitimacy of these events. Perhaps the employee is on vacation in Australia, and the login from there is genuine, while the one from New York could be the work of a hacker. The hacker might not be aware that User A is on vacation. Tracking user behavior patterns can involve various methods, including comparing how different users behave within an organization to spot unusual activities. We will discuss this in subsequent chapters in more depth. This approach of not trusting anyone and always validating for legitimacy is the core principle of the zero trust approach.

Monitoring of Storage Systems

Continuous scanning for data exposures in storage systems ensures compliance while maintaining organization. In large systems, these scans may last for days. Therefore, during continuous monitoring, security software must employ intelligence to avoid scanning unchanged data repeatedly. And these types of incremental scans should run across all repositories to maintain coverage.

Monitoring Network Traffic

This involves analyzing network traffic to track user interactions with network resources, applications, and services, and identifying any unusual or unauthorized access attempts.

Scaling

Often, one of the most disregarded and underestimated aspects of any effective data protection solution is the sheer scale of the data it has to manage and safeguard. There are two aspects when considering the scale. The sheer vastness of the network infrastructure that a security solution needs to cover and the amount of data that the security solution needs to safeguard. A security solution deployed to cater to 500,000 employees constantly monitoring their actions would be different in terms of scale when compared to a deployment environment of 1000 employees. Protecting multiple coverage points with an expanded scope of global monitoring across data centers, cloud solutions would have to be done by a sophisticated solution. When developing a security solution, the scale at which it can operate is an important parameter to measure. The hardware and software configurations needed by the security software and the breadth that it can support in terms of scale have to be documented clearly for organizations to adopt the right software.

CHAPTER 1   DATA SECURITY FUNDAMENTAL REQUIREMENTS

Storage systems and associated technologies have improved to support huge volumes of data. Did you know that in 2000, a 1 terabyte (TB) hard drive was not even available for consumer use? Hard drives were only a few gigabytes at most. Now, in 2024, we can buy a decent 1TB external hard drive for about 100 USD or less. I remember articles, even in the later part of the 2000s, discussing how anyone could have more than 1TB of data to store. Look at us now. A small percentage of organizations now need to store petabytes of data. Given our incredible technology growth trajectory, I'm sure that most organizations will need to store petabytes of data in a few years.

Did you know that storing just 1 petabyte (PB) of data for five years could cost an organization hundreds of thousands of dollars? And if they decide to store it in the cloud, we're talking millions! It's mind-boggling numbers, isn't it?

The growth of data storage needs necessarily implies one thing to us: our data protection solution needs to scale from supporting a few gigabytes to now supporting petabytes of data.

Scaling is not all about huge data volumes but also means scaling the solution across the globe. Today, most medium to large enterprises operate in multiple locations, maintaining a global presence. A security solution should be able to protect the entire organization across all business operational sites of that organization, including cloud applications. Automatic inventory search in the cloud is not feasible without customer input; therefore, the organization's participation is equally important.

Summary

Data protection is indeed critical for everyone, not just large enterprises. In this chapter, we examined the importance of data protection and why both small and large enterprises prioritize it. We distilled the requirements for a data protection solution into the following:

CHAPTER 1   DATA SECURITY FUNDAMENTAL REQUIREMENTS

- Identification and remediation of confidential data
- Data security at coverage points
- Ensuring business continuity
- Security solution configurability
- Feedback and learning
- Continuous monitoring
- Scaling

We emphasized the critical need for safeguarding business operations in the face of potential threats and highlighted the role of feedback and continuous learning in enhancing security measures. However, it's important to note that while we've delved into the core requirements for a robust autonomous security solution, we still need to delineate the specific use cases each organization might require. Remember, requirements outline the system's overall capabilities and features, while use cases offer concrete examples of user interactions. As we move forward to address various use cases, we'll rely on these fundamental requirements to shape our solutions effectively.

In the upcoming chapters, we'll explore traditional approaches to data protection by security vendors, their limitations, and how to design a top-tier data security solution that fulfills these requirements. Finally, we'll work together to develop a solution that can operate autonomously.

CHAPTER 2

Traditional Data Security

In this chapter, we will discuss how security vendors have approached and solved data protection by first understanding the security fundamentals behind any data protection solution. Our primary focus will be more on their methods of preventing internal attacks and analyzing their complexities, rather than external attacks. Throughout the remainder of the book, we will predominantly pivot our attention to internal attacks, as they are the most complex and require creative solutions to solve. Organizations can and should actively evade external attacks by employing robust network security methods, leveraging threat intelligence, and deploying effective Endpoint Detection and Response (EDR) solutions capable of detecting malware attacks.

Building upon the discussions in the first chapter, we will progress ahead similarly, covering the basics of how vendors initially designed data protection solutions and how they have developed using the tools and options available. We will explore the possibilities and outcomes of designing the solution differently given various scenarios while examining the common pitfalls and why the solutions wouldn't work in the real world. To remind everyone, business continuity, scaling, and performance are crucial for a good data protection solution. Most of the solutions available overlook these fundamentals and focus on addressing specific use cases for customers, rather than addressing the overarching problem.

CHAPTER 2　　TRADITIONAL DATA SECURITY

It's akin to applying a band-aid solution, instead of adopting a holistic approach to address the root cause of the problem.

By the end of this chapter, you will possess the necessary knowledge to analyze any data security solution in the market and enumerate its pros and cons. You will be capable of suggesting solutions to common problems that they face. Let's not linger too long; let's dive right in. I take great pride in sharing these methods, as I have accumulated this knowledge over years of working and gaining experience in this field.

Security Background

At this juncture, we need to understand a few important concepts and tools that are available to us. These concepts and tools will help you better understand our options in specific scenarios. All security vendors need to familiarize themselves with these concepts and tools before building a robust solution.

User Personas

Let's begin with the user personas of a data security system. In a large organization, there are many users with varying profiles seeking to safeguard data. Understanding the motives of these personas is crucial for designing our solution effectively.

- **IT Administrator**: In small to medium-sized companies, the IT administrator is the individual responsible for all IT operations, including maintaining data security solutions. They monitor for security violations and handle reporting and remediation themselves.

CHAPTER 2   TRADITIONAL DATA SECURITY

- **Policy Administrator**: In a large organization, there is typically a separate team of administrators responsible for security policies. They author and configure data security systems with appropriate policies.

- **Violation Manager/Incident Manager**: This persona applies to a group of individuals in large companies. Their primary responsibility is to address security vulnerability violations or incidents and remediate them. Their motivation is solely to safeguard the organization from potential data threats or leaks.

- **Security Analyst**: This person analyzes and evaluates security threats. The distinction between the Violation Manager and Security Analyst lies in their focus—while the Violation Manager addresses violations after they occur, the Security Analyst assesses future threats and evaluates the organization's overall risk status.

- **Compliance/Audit Manager**: This individual ensures the organization complies with relevant data protection laws and regulations, such as GDPR or HIPAA. They oversee data privacy policies and procedures, conduct audits, and ensure alignment with regulatory requirements.

- **CISO or Executive**: This person or group of executive-level employees hold ultimate responsibility for the organization's security posture. They make strategic security decisions and rely heavily on reporting capabilities, security analysts, and other personas responsible for maintaining security solutions.

CHAPTER 2   TRADITIONAL DATA SECURITY

Common Security Configurations

In any data security solution, you will find the following common security configurations that are necessary to safeguard data.

Secure Network Infrastructure

Though this is not part of the security solution itself, the network infrastructure takes precedence before installing any security software. All servers, coverage points, and services that are exposed to the Internet are carefully evaluated. Installation of firewalls, proxies, VPNs, and intrusion prevention systems is planned out meticulously. In large companies, data centers are typically properly segregated, and servers are appropriately provisioned. Backup software is installed, and backup locations are predefined. HA/DR scenarios are properly thought through and appropriate provisioning would be done. Data regulations are carefully considered, and if the organization operates globally, measures are taken to ensure compliance with local laws across the entire infrastructure. Generally, servers have standard images with appropriate antivirus software installed. Communications between servers occur through secured channels like TLS or encryption. Laptops are provisioned appropriately for end users with standard images. Nowadays, all data on laptops or PCs is encrypted, so even if an employee loses their laptop, extracting data from it is not easy.

Approved applications are only allowed and installed on end-user machines and only corporate-approved applications are allowed to store data let alone confidential data. Then there would be a list of applications that are okay to use but not corporate-approved. Those are used to make sure business processes are smooth and employee needs are appropriately taken care of. Identity management rules are properly defined.

CHAPTER 2   TRADITIONAL DATA SECURITY

All the above configurations, as you can imagine, can't be achieved overnight. It takes a long duration and typically large organizations spend millions if not billions in setting up and maintaining their infrastructure securely.

Access Control and Management

Identity and access management are crucial aspects of securing data. All security solutions allow administrators to configure access controls, ensuring that only authorized users have access to sensitive data. This involves defining roles and permissions for each role, assigning users to roles, and accommodating any exceptions that may arise. The term Role Based Access Control (RBAC) denotes access controls based on roles.

Integration with authentication providers also falls under this category. For example, an organization may mandate all users to Single Sign On (SSO) through their preferred Identity Provider (IDP) before allowing them access to their corporate applications. Identity providers may use passwords, biometrics, and multi-factor authentication (MFA) to verify the identity of the users.

Access and deny lists can be used by security solutions, restricting access to certain URLs based on roles or groups. Whitelisting and/or blacklisting properties are available to seal data vulnerabilities. For example, traffic to a certain server without a proxy may be whitelisted. Continuous access monitoring settings may be utilized to periodically scan servers and shared drives containing sensitive data.

Policies and Rules

Security policies are at the core of any security solution. These policies can range from simple to complex, depending on the number of rules attached to them. Security solutions typically allow you to specify any Boolean operator to combine these rules. For example, you can "AND" two

45

CHAPTER 2   TRADITIONAL DATA SECURITY

rules together, "OR" them together, or complement a rule using the "NOT" operator, among others. Boolean operations can involve multiple rules simultaneously, leading to complex configurations. Consider the following example:

$$Policy\ P1 = \left(\left(Rule\ 1\ or\ Rule\ 2\right) OR \left(RULE\ 3\ AND\ RULE\ 4\right) OR\ !RULE 5\right)$$

These rules, known as matching conditions, determine the criteria for the matching process. For instance, suppose you want to block all outbound emails containing an attachment with the word "Important." In this case, your security solution would scan all outbound emails with attachments, searching for the keyword "Important." These rules are often referred to as keyword rules, but security solutions may include various other types of rules as well. These could involve identifying patterns in documents, specifying sender or recipient criteria, or even utilizing rules based on file properties. I understand this is barely even scratching the surface of policy configurations in security solutions, but my main point is to make you aware that there could be security policies which are a combination of rules.

Coverage Points or Channel-Based Configuration

The network perimeter, integration points, or boundaries are the primary targets of most attacks. Therefore, security solutions typically offer security configurations to protect based on channels. Here, the term "channels" refers to logical groupings of certain modes of access. For example, if an organization utilizes cloud-based O365 email, the channel could be labeled as "Cloud Email." Similarly, organizations often assign computers to their employees, and the corresponding channel might be labeled as "Endpoint Users" or "Computer Users." Additionally, shared drives within a company could be grouped under a single channel named "Network Share."

There could be channel-based configurations. For example, the download file size limit of channel "Network Share" is 1GB at a time and if any user downloads more than 1GB then raise a violation. As you can see, I sort of defined a policy combining a channel configuration setting. That's how modern security solutions provide ways for security administrators to configure the security products to safeguard the data.

The definition of a Channel in a security solution can be wide or narrow. For instance, a security solution might say all Network Shares are one channel vs. another security solution might say "Shared Drives" are a channel, "Sharepoint servers" are another channel, and so on.

Remediation Actions

For you to become familiar with different data protection methodologies, you need to understand the various types of actions that can be taken to prevent security violations. Although you may already be aware of many, a few may surprise you here.

- **Notify**: This is the most common and, in my opinion, the most useful action. Notifying the originator, sender, or other concerned stakeholders about a detected violation allows us to educate users. As we now know, most internal data leaks are accidental. Education is crucial for preventing users from committing the violation again. Proper and continuous education is key to ensuring protection. This action can be combined with other actions and is commonly done. For example, Block and Notify.

CHAPTER 2   TRADITIONAL DATA SECURITY

- **Block**: This is a basic type of action that can be taken when dealing with DIM. Blocking a data transfer can immediately prevent the violation from occurring at that point. Though we block, future violations can occur from the same source and our solution might have to block the same user.

- **Data Access Revocation**: Access revocation is an action commonly done to remove unauthorized users from accessing the data. Removing share access is a common thing that gets done in cloud platforms. DIM and DAR revocation can mean different things when you think about security risks for a company. I'll let you think about it.

- **User Access Revocation**: This is more intrusive where we have the option to revoke the access of the user. This is typically done in the cases of repetitive offenders. Removing access to a cloud application for a user, for example, could mean that the user will not be able to log in to that application anymore.

- **Add Note**: This note is intended for administrators who are investigating these security violations. Let's assume you've encountered a security breach involving leaked credit card numbers from a shared drive. You can take action to alert the administrator with a message like "Unauthorized Customer PII," for example.

- **Encrypt**: This action involves encrypting the data in question. The encryption keys and location must be configured beforehand for this to work. The encrypted data can remain in the same location or be moved to a new one. Typically, when moved to a new location, security solutions create a marker file in the original location to indicate that the data was relocated.

- **Quarantine**: Quarantine entails moving the data in question to a new location. This action is typically performed in DAR, and a marker file is left in the original location, similar to encryption.

- **Delete**: This action simply involves deleting the data in question. Most organizations would avoid using this type of action, but in extreme cases, it may be necessary.

- **Pop-up**: This action is common for DIM, where a pop-up message is displayed to the user when they commit a security violation. For example, if a user is uploading a file to a cloud drive with broader access, a pop-up can ask, "Do you really want to upload this sensitive file to the specified location?"

- **User Explanation**: This is in addition to the pop-up message discussed earlier. Along with the pop-up, it might be necessary for the user to provide a business justification before taking the action. Using the same upload example as mentioned in the pop-up action above, users could be prompted to provide a business justification. If no valid business justification is provided, then the protection strategy might simply be to block the upload.

- **Classify**: We can tag files with classification tags as a response action. For example, let's say the organization has a classification system to tag files as confidential vs.

non-confidential; then, they can appropriately tag the file in question. Later, these tags can be used to detect confidential content.

- **File Operations**: All file operations can be used as remediation actions to protect the data. Other common operations include move, zip, anonymize, etc.

- **Send Alert**: This is a type of escalation where alerts are sent to notify concerned stakeholders. Stakeholders could be administrators, managers, the head of the unit, security personnel in the organization, etc. Alerts can be phone messages, pager alerts, emails, Slack notifications, and so on.

- **Raise Severity**: The severity of the security violation can be raised to denote that it is more serious now. For instance, the first few violations from a user could be seen as medium severity, whereas repetitive violations could result in high severity violations.

- **Custom Actions**: There can be a script or a program that the security program can execute to carry out a customized action for an organization. For example, a custom action could include raising a Jira ticket in their system and notifying the manager about it. Any workflow can be attached to the remediation actions.

EDR Configurations

Though I mentioned earlier that EDR solutions primarily apply to external attacks, it's important to understand the basics. Any EDR solution would have threat detection rules. These rules may include detecting suspicious processes, network communications, file changes, or unauthorized access attempts. Typically, an EDR solution would monitor for specific malware signatures, user/machine behaviors, and any indicators of compromise (IOCs). These settings could also include logging, event capturing at specified sampling rates, or generally capturing all occurrences of a specific event.

Reporting

Often underestimated requirement by all security vendors is Reporting. Reporting is so important for all the stakeholders in an organization to gain visibility. Here stakeholders refer to the people who are security liable for the whole organization and it can be all C-level executives, security analysts, and administrators. There can be different kinds of reports that security solutions offer but all solutions don't make it convenient for organizations with all reports that they need. Some organizations prefer customized reports and most solutions don't prioritize and address those use cases.

There are various types of reports and they are as follows:

- Violation Reports
- Remediation Reports
- Threat Intelligence/Assessment Reports
- Regulatory Data Compliance Reports (HIPAA, GDPR, SOX, etc.)
- Security Training Reports
- Organization Vulnerability Assessment Reports
- Organization Risk Reports
- User Risk Reports
- Audit Reports
- Penetration Testing Reports

CHAPTER 2   TRADITIONAL DATA SECURITY

Each of the above reports can be scheduled or generated on demand with a different set of criteria. Reports provide visibility to higher management, and they might be mandatory for organizations in certain verticals to pass compliance/audit checks.

Alerting

Security vendors may provide "alerting" services to notify administrators about specific security events. Alerts can have different levels, with Low, Medium, and High being the most common. They can be delivered via email, text messages, or pager alerts. Sophisticated security systems can integrate with applications like Jira or Splunk and execute workflows based on these alerts. Because these workflows can be customized and proprietary to each organization, the IT department may develop and integrate them with alert receivers based on their specific needs. Below are some examples of alerts to help you visualize:

> **Low Alert**: Threshold of 1000 violations received on the DIM channel.
>
> **Medium Alert**: Unable to quarantine in the shared location \\shared server\quarantine\.
>
> **High Alert**: Malware threat detected on servers in the East data center.

Security Software Patching

Applying vulnerability patches is a routine task for IT administrators. Threat intelligence and penetration testing reports frequently reveal vulnerabilities in software and network access points, making it crucial for security administrators to take necessary actions to safeguard systems. Security solutions assess the risk level of software and update risk scores once patches are applied. Testing these patches before deployment is beneficial for organizations to avoid disrupting regular business operations.

Security Software Deployment

IT administrators are responsible for deploying security software within the infrastructure. First and foremost, they need to design and plan thoroughly to cover both depth and breadth. They must consider various entry and exit points, address high-traffic routes, and work with existing appliances and software to determine the best possible coverage points. Once they have gathered all the necessary details, they proceed with deploying the software. Deployment can be entirely on-premises or a hybrid approach that covers both cloud and on-premises infrastructures. For on-premises deployment, they need to start by specifying hardware configurations, operating systems, and library versions like Python and Java required for the software. This is followed by the deployment itself and ongoing maintenance. For cloud deployments, IT administrators need to work with security vendors to appropriately provision and run the software.

Encryption

Security solutions may offer integrations with third-party software to encrypt and decrypt data. For example, integration with Microsoft Azure (Microsoft Information Protection Purview) is quite common these days, where organizations can store their encryption keys in Azure and use them for encryption and decryption. Microsoft takes care of everything, and all that needs to be done is to invoke APIs to carry out encryption-related operations. Some solutions might offer encryption out of the box or integrate with other encryption solutions from vendors like Microsoft, McAfee, Symantec, IBM, Dell, etc.

CHAPTER 2 TRADITIONAL DATA SECURITY

In large organizations, there may be overarching standards dictating the level of security for all intranet communications. For instance, it might be a requirement for all server or software communications to adhere to TLS 1.3 using AES 256 keys. This standard applies to all software, including the security protection software itself, which must be configured to meet these requirements.

Classification

Classification of documents is critical for some organizations as it allows them to track confidential and sensitive documents effectively. They prefer to classify every document and email within the organization under specific categories. Typically, they use a tree-like structure to organize document classification. A sample classification hierarchy illustrated in Figure 2-1 shows that there can optionally be sub-classifications under the main classification category.

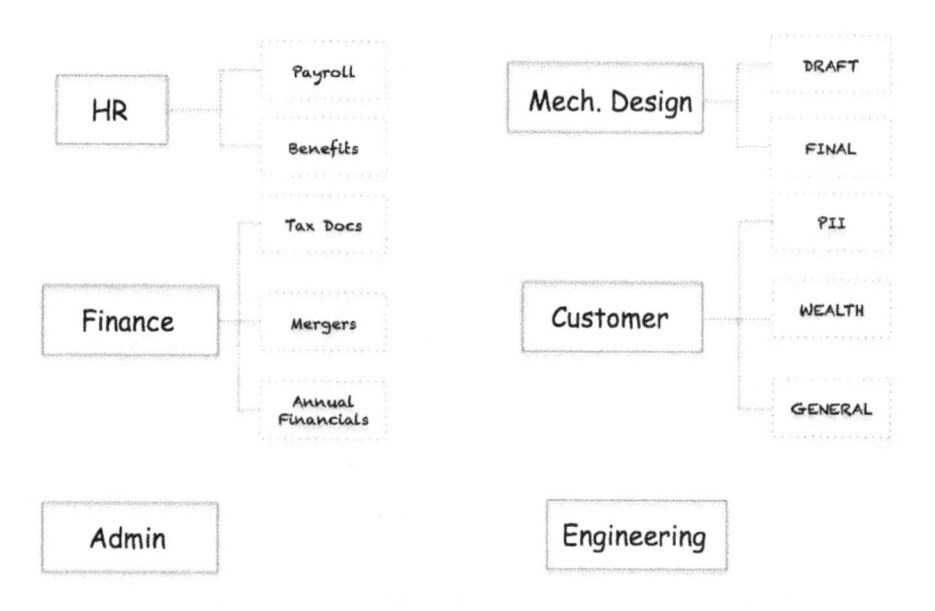

```
HR ---- Payroll
        Benefits

Finance ---- Tax Docs
             Mergers
             Annual Financials

Admin

Mech. Design ---- DRAFT
                  FINAL

Customer ---- PII
              WEALTH
              GENERAL

Engineering
```

Figure 2-1. *A Sample Classification Hierarchy*

Several security vendors provide classification services and offer tracking and violation reporting based on document classification. Alternatively, some vendors choose to integrate with classification software such as Titus and Azure Information Protection systems, allowing third-party software to store their classification hierarchy and classify documents. Classification can be likened to tagging, where all digital assets in an organization are tagged. Based on these tags, as depicted in the figure, organizations can create policies or rules to match against the tags and protect classified information.

Posture Management Configurations

In any organization, there is a clear demarcation between the infrastructure and applications running on top of it, along with distinctions between Cloud and On-premise hosting. Managing the risk posture of both these components is critical. There are two broad types of Posture Management solutions available:

CSPM—Cloud Security Posture Management: CSPM is specifically designed for cloud infrastructure and cloud security. It covers both homegrown private cloud infrastructure and the infrastructure provided by cloud providers. CSPM deals with misconfigurations, manages cloud infrastructure, and reports threats on them. Common CSPM use cases include continuous monitoring of cloud resources, configuration management, compliance assessment, threat detection, incident response, and risk management in cloud environments.

SSPM—Security Service Posture Management: SSPM focuses on misconfigurations in applications deployed on top of the infrastructure. It can operate on the cloud, hybrid cloud, and even on-premises environments. SSPM use cases vary widely and may include network security management, endpoint protection, identity and access management (IAM), data protection, security policy enforcement, vulnerability management, and security analytics.

The most important aspect to understand is that both CSPM and SSPM solutions allow you to configure services and manage configurations. They track configuration drift and report any risks associated with the current configurations. Additionally, they report on the compliance aspect of applications regarding various regulatory requirements.

User Risk Configurations

This user risk-based configuration, although rare, is supported by a few security solutions available. These solutions allow for configuring reporting based on user risk scores. User risk scores might be calculated based on various parameters, including repeat violations, the number of uploads/downloads within a measured time interval, accessing certain locations, and deviations from normal behavior patterns.

There are broadly two types of security solutions: those that follow the data and those that follow the user. Data breaches can be mitigated by either or both approaches. Following users may lead to the identification of the actual root cause of the problems. While it is rare to identify attackers in the real world, user risk-based configurations allow security administrators to configure systems and restrict access for risky users. This makes it very difficult, if not impossible, for internal attackers to launch an attack. Following data is essential as malicious users might transform the data. For instance, if they rename the file to a zip file format, most of the solutions might not be able to examine the content as they go by file extensions for extracting the data.

These configurations, which track behavior patterns, also provide coverage if an external attacker attempts to impersonate an internal user and tries to exfiltrate data. More on the line of zero trust, this has become popular in the recent times.

Data Retention

Data retention configurations are necessary for compliance, audits, and investigating security violations later on. Security laws may mandate that all security violations be stored for a period of up to seven years. Additionally, there may be internal regulations within the organization requiring the retention of the original content that caused the violation for the same duration. These settings are configured within the security solution itself to ensure that old violations are not deleted. Organizations may also back up this data in case of future compliance or audit requirements.

Cyber forensics, also known as digital forensics or computer forensics, is the process of collecting, analyzing, and preserving digital evidence from electronic devices and systems to investigate cybercrimes or security incidents. Tracking user behavior patterns that lead to violations may reveal whether the user was acting maliciously.

Security Incident Severity

Security solutions enable administrators to specify the severity of violations detected in various cases. This severity aids administrators in understanding incidents and prioritizing them accordingly. It serves as a clue for them to assess the severity of the situation. Incident severity can be automatically adjusted based on repeat offenses, although few security solutions effectively implement this feature. One reason for this is the lack of close monitoring of user behavior and the failure to correlate data across different channels. Incident severity-based workflows for remediation is a well-desired feature among all organizations.

CHAPTER 2   TRADITIONAL DATA SECURITY

Data in Motion vs. Data at Rest

Having analyzed all the different concepts and tools available, let's shift our focus to data and data protection methods. There are two large categorizations of any data in any system. They are Data In Motion and Data At Rest. Data security is all about how you identify, examine, and protect this data while ensuring business continuity at all times. Let's learn about this in detail.

Data In Motion (DIM) refers to the data that is literally in motion. The data could be in the process of being actively transferred or transmitted between different locations, devices, or systems. This movement of data can occur over various communication channels, such as wired or wireless networks, and can involve different protocols and technologies. Cloud data can also be in this bucket when sending cloud emails, uploading or downloading files from or to the cloud. I would be referring to this type of data as DIM throughout the rest of the book.

Examples of data in motion include email transfers, uploading/downloading files from a system/server, transferring data between computers, online web traffic when browsing through a website, streaming videos, and so on. Essentially, any instance where data is being transferred from one point to another in real-time or near real-time falls under the category of data in motion.

Protecting this type of data in motion is crucial for organizations, as confidentiality and integrity are paramount to them. I know your gears are turning now. Is it that hard to protect this? Did I catch your thought? As I could guess, you are thinking that protecting this type of data would involve implementing encryption, secure communication protocols, firewalls, intrusion detection systems, and other security measures to safeguard data as it travels across networks and devices. You are right! These are good ways to protect data in motion.

CHAPTER 2   TRADITIONAL DATA SECURITY

Data At Rest (DAR) refers to the data that is sitting, or resting, if you will, somewhere on the disk. This is the data not actively being transmitted or processed. In other words, it is data that is stationary or "at rest" within a storage medium, such as a hard drive, solid-state drive, or tape backup system. This data can include files, databases, archives, or any other form of digital information that resides in storage devices. Also, do remember to include cloud repositories too. I would be referring to this type of data as DAR throughout the rest of the book.

Examples of data at rest include files stored on a computer's hard drive, database records stored on a server, archived documents stored on a backup tape, virtual machine images stored on a cloud storage platform, and so forth. Similar to DIM, protecting DAR and ensuring that only authorized people within the organization have access becomes crucial for organizations, as you can imagine. The larger the organization, the larger the data store, the larger the threat surface, and, in general, the larger the scale. Similar security measures for DAR typically could include encryption, access controls, authentication mechanisms, and regular data backups. All these measures for both DIM and DAR help prevent unauthorized access, tampering, or data breaches.

Though at the outset, it might seem that the protection methods for DIM and DAR are almost the same, there are differences. There are variations in the ways you treat them when there are violations. We are going to analyze the attributes and characteristics of DIM and DAR in detail where you will be able to see that the protection strategies needed are different.

CHAPTER 2 TRADITIONAL DATA SECURITY

Characteristics of DIM vs. DAR

Characteristic/ attribute	DIM	DAR
Time	Time-bound. They are available in transit for a short period.	Not time-bound. Usually stored on drives where they have been sitting for days if not months or years.
Access Risk	It is accessible to anyone, as there can be malicious interceptors.	Only those who have access or can gain access can read/update the data.
Awareness	If the data is lost or tampered with during transit, the recipients might realize it immediately.	If the data is lost or tampered with, no one would even realize it, as there is no real-time monitoring of them.
Size	The size of the data can't be big. Mostly, there are limitations on how much data can be transferred in an instant. For example, emails have attachment size limitations.	There are no size limitations. Data can be as large as it can be. Few Bytes to GigaBytes are pretty normal.
Context	The data can be a partial transfer—chunked in a network—and there might not be any context associated with it.	The data is wholesome. This is the whole file and that is the maximum context there ever can be.
Type	Depending on the transfer, there might be type limitations. For example, these days most email servers don't allow transfer for executables.	There is no type limitation. The file might be of any type.

CHAPTER 2 TRADITIONAL DATA SECURITY

Characteristic/ attribute	DIM	DAR
Audit/ Compliance risk	The data transferred is gone and auditors don't consider this an active risk.	The data sitting over a shared drive can be viewed as an active risk and might fail the audit.
Violation response	When a confidential data leak is happening, a data protection solution should prevent it (block the transmission).	When a confidential data leak is happening, i.e., the data is exposed to unauthorized people, then restricting access or quarantining or deleting the data are possible options.

Now, with these characteristics, data protection strategies have to be developed in a customized fashion. Have you realized that your data protection strategy has to be superfast and efficient for DIM rather than DAR, as DIM is time-bound?

Monitor vs. Prevent

Since we touched up ever so slightly on violation response, we must understand the difference between monitoring and prevention when we are developing data protection strategies.

Monitoring refers to the act of simply inspecting the data and reporting whether there was a data violation or not. Alternatively, monitoring can be thought of as a camera—observing everything that is happening, both the good and the bad, without taking any action other than collecting statistics and reporting.

CHAPTER 2　TRADITIONAL DATA SECURITY

Prevention, on the other hand, refers to the act of inspecting and preventing a data leak if it were supposed to happen. Prevention is more comprehensive, as it includes monitoring and ways to thwart an active attack. However, not all recovery mechanisms are always available. For instance, you can't encrypt a file in real-time if all the data might not be available to you, or if you are dealing with data accessible via a cloud service and the service doesn't provide options to encrypt the data.

Monitoring or prevention can be applied to both DIM and DAR. Why would you need to monitor if prevention can include monitoring, too? Can't I get everything done by always using prevention? What are the scenarios in which I just need monitoring? Take a few minutes to think about this.

Okay! Let's see if our thinking matches.

Scenarios Where Monitoring Is a Necessity

While prevention is crucial for proactively stopping security violations, monitoring still plays a significant role in a comprehensive data protection strategy. Here are some scenarios:

Detection of Advanced Threats: Prevention can only block known threats and may not detect sophisticated zero-day attacks. Monitoring allows us to observe everything that is happening and identify patterns and behaviors that may indicate a threat. While a single action may not raise suspicion, a combination of activities could constitute a threat. Analyzing the data gathered through monitoring could reveal advanced threats.

Incident Response: As it is impossible to prevent every security violation, monitoring provides organizations with the opportunity to record ongoing activities and address them later. Monitoring serves as a form of incident response that can aid in future investigations.

Compliance/Audit Requirements: Many organizations are required to implement continuous monitoring of their systems and data to evaluate risk status continuously. Monitoring assists in meeting these requirements by continuously observing and inspecting activities. Audit reports are generated based on the output of monitoring software.

User Behavior: Monitoring user behavior is fundamental for building an effective data protection solution. Without monitoring, it is impossible to develop effective solutions. Monitoring serves as the "eyes" of the security system, allowing organizations to learn and adapt. This concept is a central theme of this book as well—exploring how monitoring can be efficiently utilized to prevent security violations and gain valuable insights.

Improving Security Posture: Continuous monitoring of all systems, software, and data enables organizations to identify vulnerabilities that attackers, both internal and external, may exploit. Therefore, monitoring helps organizations enhance their security posture and become more resilient to attacks.

I want to discuss monitoring and emphasize it over prevention because better monitoring could yield a much more secure future. Building reliable monitoring systems is quite a challenge. Just capturing data isn't sufficient; effective monitoring needs to explore the uncharted and unknown territories. It requires digging deep into correlations and analyzing data to uncover meaningful insights. To summarize, **prevention is for the known and monitoring is for the unknown.**

What Actions Can We Take in Prevention?

Please review the "Remediation Actions" under the "Security Background" section—if necessary—to gain a better understanding. I want you, my dear readers, to consider how each of the remediation actions, such as "Block," "Notify," etc., applies to DIM and DAR. In which cases would monitoring work better? Remember the requirements that we summarized in the first chapter. It's all about efficiently and effectively satisfying those requirements with the tools at our disposal.

CHAPTER 2   TRADITIONAL DATA SECURITY

All the actions that we discussed earlier can be implemented in prevention, but some actions might not apply to certain scenarios. For example, for a DIM Email channel policy, a remediation action of removing access to data might not have any significance, but it could be crucial for a DAR Network Share Channel policy.

Data Security by Channel

Building on the foundational knowledge we've acquired, we will now explore the channels that require protection to ensure data security. It is crucial to understand the data flow within an organization to identify the limitations of existing security practices. By analyzing these data flows and studying the current security gaps, we aim to develop a more robust data protection solution. This comprehensive understanding will enable us to design and implement enhanced security measures that effectively safeguard sensitive information.

Email Security

Let me take you back to the 1990s, the dawn of the Internet and email. I still remember the day when I first created an email account and sent a message to my friend. I was so excited that a message could be transferred from one person to another via a computer. The first email message that I sent was instantaneous. My friend received the message, and there was astonishment and excitement all around, to say the least. There can be multiple recipients for a single message, and we can attach files to an email. It all seemed so miraculous during that time.

With every technological innovation, amidst all the promising advancements it brings, there are inevitably negative aspects as well. Email, the single most powerful medium of communication at the time, could be used as a potent weapon to attack people. A harmful message could be sent to one or more people, and the greatest advantage is that the attack can be instantaneous. Email was a great gift to attackers, I would say, as they didn't have to wait. Attacks could be carried out with little to no time, and they could witness the effects as well. The immediacy of the attack is staggering, isn't it?

Imagine an attacker, a faceless coward lurking behind, sending out a barrage of emails loaded with viruses to innocent people with the sole intention of causing harm. The attacker doesn't have to physically go anywhere; it's easy to carry out, instantaneous, and what more could an attacker ask for? Upon opening and downloading the email, there would usually be an executable that would attack the target computer. This was causing great havoc in those days. The ability to distinguish genuine emails from malicious ones became the ultimate goal. Every security vendor like McAfee, Symantec, and F-Secure in the initial days focused on protecting against these emails—an external malware attack. Little did they know about internal attacks and how much worse an internal attack could turn out to be.

The primary aim of these security solutions was to thwart malware attacks that could infiltrate an organization, leading to unforeseen consequences such as data loss and disruptions in business activities. Spamming emerged as a prevalent issue in the late 1990s and early 2000s. Even today, spamming remains a nuisance, but thanks to advanced spam protection filters, its impact has been mitigated. However, during the early days of the Internet boom, email spamming posed a significant threat. Internet Service Providers (ISPs) were vulnerable to hacking, necessitating urgent measures to safeguard them. Security vendors worked with ISPs and then they started working with organizations to protect the email. Security vendors began scanning emails for any threats, both incoming and outgoing, although enterprises were solely focused on incoming emails. It was only later that they realized data could be leaked out of the organization similarly.

CHAPTER 2   TRADITIONAL DATA SECURITY

Most of the data leaks that were preliminarily discovered were unintentional. It was during this period that even those with malicious intent were unaware that data could be exfiltrated in this manner. Though it seems obvious now, it wasn't back then. This led to the birth of email data protection. All emails were scanned for accidental exposures and reported. Since data could be transported in an email message, everyone with a genuine interest in the company was emailing data that needed to be shared. They were emailing to clients, to themselves, to co-workers, and it turned out to be much easier and quicker. Everything in the world is about time. If someone could save time, we call it efficiency, then everyone would adopt and use it, no matter what it is. Look at the rise of telephones. No better example can exist.

Organizations deployed email security products to protect their emails so that they could intentionally or unintentionally expose sensitive data. Common practices that were followed were allowing security administrators to define rules based on senders, recipients, and content of the email itself starting from the subject, to body and attachments. The security product would be effective based on detection technologies they use behind the scenes to spot a data breach. Most of the detection technologies were basic during the initial days like keyword match and pattern-based match. Once a match was found the remediation steps were to either notify or block and notify. As days progressed, the effectiveness of the matching improved.

Security solutions typically connect to the organization's on-prem Active Directory (AD) server. However, nowadays, they also connect to Azure AD servers in the cloud to synchronize user hierarchies, roles, and groups. This results in better protection, and remediation steps can be improved. Today, some solutions can track users constantly violating defined policies, and then escalate the user's risk score. Remediation steps may include notifying the manager of the violation creator and requesting an explanation from the violator.

CHAPTER 2   TRADITIONAL DATA SECURITY

Many organizations now adopt Microsoft O365 or Gmail as their email provider, placing the responsibility on security vendors to protect the data. A typical security configuration for an email solution is outlined below in Figure 2-2. The email application forwards the message to the source MTA, which determines the appropriate destination MTA, and relays the email appropriately. However, when a security product is integrated into this process, the source MTA can be configured to route the traffic to the security product first. Based on the security product's assessment (whether to block or forward the message), the source MTA will forward the email to its intended destination.

Akin to the growth and evolution of promising things in this world, attackers grew as well. They became shrewd in their practices, always thinking ahead to wield crafty, devious schemes to attack. Their next target was the network. If they could attack one individual via email, they could also target the entire organization's network. It was a progression. More serious than email, if a network is hacked, then all the data flowing within an organization can be compromised.

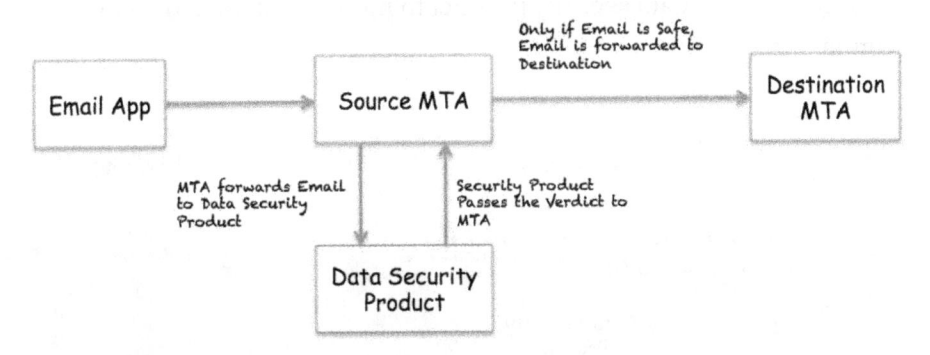

Figure 2-2. Email Security Solution Configuration

CHAPTER 2   TRADITIONAL DATA SECURITY

Network Security

The Network Channel can involve packet sniffing at a low level or website traffic analysis at the application level. Moreover, there are messages transmitted via various protocols such as FTP, SCP, etc., for certain applications. Therefore, thorough inspection is necessary to protect the network from insider threats, which can exploit any of these avenues. Furthermore, when applications are hosted in the cloud, it becomes essential to intercept traffic to and from cloud applications. This interception of cloud application traffic is typically performed by security vendors, and the specialized solutions that handle this task are known as Cloud Access Security Brokers (CASBs).

Let's now examine the Network channel and consider Cloud Application Data Security as a separate channel. All of the Network Channel is DIM and there is no DAR here. Figure 2-3 illustrates a network security solution in which all requests and responses from a client machine to the Internet pass through a web proxy. The web proxy collaborates with a data security product to monitor for data loss and potential threats.

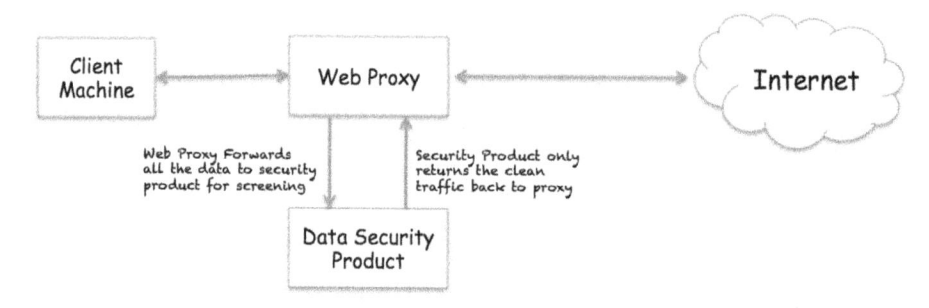

Figure 2-3. Network Security Solution Configuration

As you can see here, the network channel is broken down into two main categories: (1) Packet Sniffing at L3 and (2) Application layer protocol traffic at L7.

Packet Sniffing

Data security solutions typically integrate high-speed network capture cards capable of capturing and analyzing packets. These packet capture cards are leveraged to detect potential sensitive data leaks. They allow security solutions to analyze various types of threats effectively. By inspecting all packets, security solutions can apply their rules to identify any security breaches.

Application Layer Data Protection Using ICAP

ICAP—Internet Content Adaptation Protocol—is a protocol used in computer networking to enable web servers or other proxy servers to offload the analysis of certain tasks to specialized servers known as ICAP servers. These tasks typically involve content transformation, modification, or analysis, such as virus scanning, content filtering, data loss prevention, and content caching.

ICAP works by allowing a web server or proxy server to send content to an ICAP server for analysis or processing before delivering it to the client. The ICAP server can then perform various operations on the content according to predefined policies or rules set by the administrator. Once the ICAP server has processed the content, it sends it back to the web server or proxy server, which then delivers it to the client.

Network Shares

During the scanning of these shares, continuous monitoring is required to ensure that ACL permissions are always correct. All data in all folders within shares need to be swept through at least once, and then incremental sweeping is necessary. A single sweep in a large organization with several terabytes or petabytes of data could take days.

CHAPTER 2   TRADITIONAL DATA SECURITY

Endpoint Security

Endpoint security addresses data protection on endpoints, where data is stored on employee machines and accessed both internally and externally, making it relevant for both DAR and DIM use cases. Scalability and performance are crucial considerations when dealing with endpoints, especially in large organizations with hundreds of thousands of employees and machines. Solutions must scale and perform effectively to ensure business continuity while protecting confidential data, taking remediation actions as needed, and generating security violations and reports.

Employees may use their laptops in various locations, including home or public networks, and access the organizational network via VPN. In such cases, data protection solutions must adapt and provide appropriate protection. Additionally, security solutions on endpoint machines must seamlessly integrate with proxies and load balancers.

Endpoint DIM involves monitoring all activities on endpoint devices, from user logins to logouts or shutdowns. This includes monitoring actions such as USB drive connections, CD writing, screen captures, messenger communications, accessing shared drives, and more. Handling drivers and browsers on endpoint machines adds complexity, especially considering the variety of operating systems. All data must be inspected and decisions made instantaneously to avoid impacting system usability. For example, delays in sending messages via internal messenger services can disrupt communication. Therefore, real-time processing is essential to maintain productivity and security. Figure 2-4 shows the steps that happen in an endpoint once the user performs a simple action like file copy.

CHAPTER 2   TRADITIONAL DATA SECURITY

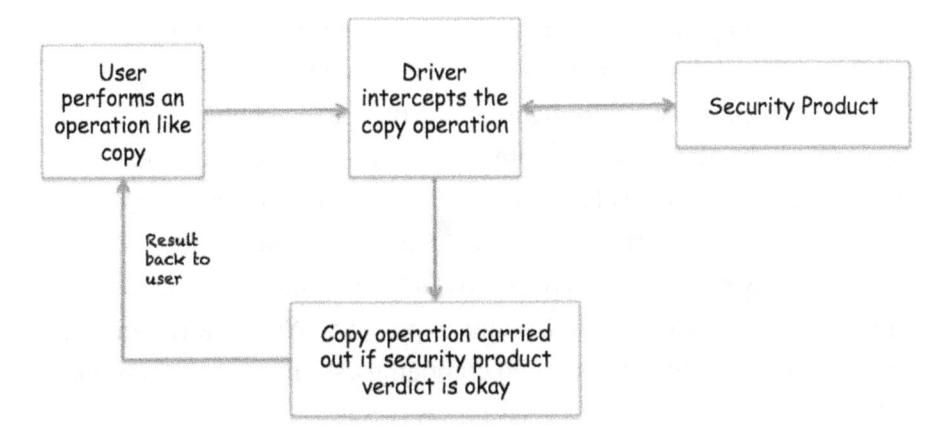

```
┌──────────────┐      ┌──────────────┐      ┌──────────────────┐
│    User      │      │   Driver     │      │                  │
│ performs an  │─────▶│ intercepts the│◀────▶│ Security Product │
│ operation like│     │ copy operation│      │                  │
│    copy      │      │              │      │                  │
└──────────────┘      └──────────────┘      └──────────────────┘
       ▲                     │
       │ Result              │
       │ back to             ▼
       │ user         ┌──────────────────────┐
       │              │ Copy operation carried│
       └──────────────│ out if security product│
                      │  verdict is okay      │
                      └──────────────────────┘
```

***Figure 2-4.** Email Security Solution DIM Use Case*

Endpoint DAR entails scanning the data stored on endpoint machines. The scanning process can be targeted, focusing only on specific endpoints, or a full sweep, encompassing all endpoints. By scanning files, confidential data stored on these systems can be revealed, necessitating access control checks. In certain scenarios, exceptions may apply. For instance, if a laptop belongs to one of the C-suite employees, having confidential data stored on their machine might not be ideal.

BYOD Security

This is one of the most challenging tasks, given that Bring Your Own Device (BYOD) policies allow employees to utilize their personal phones, iPads, and laptops for work purposes. These devices pose potential vectors for data loss, and there's a risk that employees, as internal users, might unwittingly introduce threats along with their devices. Therefore, security solutions must be robust enough to identify BYOD devices brought onto the organization's network.

Device management is crucial in this context. Organizations should implement robust device management solutions and, on top of that, utilize security products to configure security policies, such as encryption, password requirements, and remote wiping capabilities, on employees' devices. This ensures a level playing field between employees using BYOD and those who work on computers provided by the organization.

The security risks associated with BYOD are significant, prompting many security-conscious organizations to prohibit BYOD entirely on their networks. In fact, in highly classified companies, such measures may be mandatory.

Deploying endpoint security solutions offered by security vendors, such as mobile device management (MDM) and mobile threat defense (MTD) software, helps detect and mitigate security threats on personal devices. These solutions can identify malicious applications, detect suspicious activities, and enforce compliance with security policies.

CASB Security

Security can be provided by vendors by acting as Cloud Access Security Brokers (CASB) to snoop into cloud application traffic. Cloud applications could also include DIM and DAR. CASBs offer threat detection software coupled with prevention mechanisms to detect and mitigate cloud-based external and internal threats. This may involve real-time monitoring of user activities and network traffic to identify suspicious behavior patterns indicative of security threats.

One of the big use cases for CASB is shadow IT. CASB solutions offered by security vendors help detect and manage shadow IT by discovering unauthorized cloud applications and services being used within the organization. This enables IT teams to assess risks associated with unsanctioned cloud usage and take appropriate action to mitigate them. This falls rightly under the purview of CSPM and SSPM.

Customer Environments

We've discussed a wide array of concepts, tools, and options available to security vendors, examining data protection across various channels. Now, let's explore different customer environments. Our goal is to develop a solution versatile enough to operate effectively in any environment and across all types of channels. Currently, there are products tailored to specific channels or environments, some focusing solely on one aspect like SSPM. I aim to provide you with an overview of these diverse environments and channels, setting the stage for a fresh perspective in the upcoming chapters.

On-Premise

On-premise refers to the customer's environment, typically comprising their own data center and office spaces, where they exercise full control. Their IT administrators are responsible for setup and maintenance, owning everything from routers and switches to large server infrastructure. A security solution designed for on-prem environments must possess specific characteristics and features.

First, product installation and updates are solely managed by the customer and their IT team. Any databases or third-party software used must operate within the customer's environment. Security vendors cannot release updates expecting immediate customer adoption. Additionally, customers with globally distributed data centers and offices require scalability and performance across their global presence.

Consider how an on-premises Network Security or Endpoint Security solution would operate. For instance, think about deploying Endpoint DAR across thousands, if not hundreds of thousands, of laptops. The aim here is not to propose a specific solution but to encourage critical thinking about implementation strategies.

However, on-premises solutions come with their own challenges. Security vendors cannot actively monitor the product, necessitating resilience to failures and the ability to handle challenges independently. The solution must accommodate variations in customer bandwidth, multiple Active Directory servers, and the desire for centralized policy management across different channels.

Moreover, the security product needs to adapt to the customer's network infrastructure, including compatibility with reverse proxies, load balancers, and custom encryption methods. Special customer scenarios such as acquisitions and mergers pose unique integration challenges. The solution must facilitate seamless integration of new user bases, servers, and email systems, perhaps even automating the discovery of new network shares during mergers.

Addressing these diverse use cases underscores the importance of an on-premises security solution in preventing internal attacks.

Cloud

There are two types of clouds to consider: public cloud and private cloud.

Public cloud involves utilizing cloud resources from providers such as Amazon, Google, and Microsoft. Cloud providers charge based on usage, allowing customers to host their environment (servers and applications) on the cloud. In contrast, a private cloud may be established and maintained by the customer itself or by a cloud provider exclusively for that customer's use, without sharing with other clients.

In public cloud environments, resources are shared among multiple users, who access them over the Internet on a pay-as-you-go basis. While users share the infrastructure, their data and applications remain logically isolated. Public clouds offer scalability, flexibility, and cost-effectiveness, enabling users to scale resources according to demand and pay only for what they use.

Private cloud, on the other hand, provides a dedicated environment solely for one organization. Offering greater control, security, and customization options, private clouds are preferred by organizations with specific compliance requirements, sensitive data, or legacy systems that cannot be easily migrated.

As a security vendor or organization aiming to protect confidential data in the cloud, considerations must be made for the cloud infrastructure and application operations. How do we secure services that can be spun up or down at a moment's notice? Protection for cloud application data, cloud email, and cloud web traffic (such as ICAP in the cloud) becomes crucial.

Typically, small-scale companies opt to host everything in the cloud, foregoing on-premise hardware altogether.

Hybrid

Hybrid environments represent a blend of both on-premise and cloud infrastructure. In these setups, certain hardware and resources reside on-premise, while others are hosted in the cloud. This configuration reflects the reality for many organizations, especially those in transition or those with specific data requirements.

For some customers, transitioning entirely to the cloud might be a goal, but they are currently in a transitional phase. However, for many organizations, a complete shift to either on-premise or cloud infrastructure is impractical. They need to leverage cloud applications while retaining large volumes of data on their on-premise servers.

Addressing data protection in such hybrid environments poses unique challenges. For instance, cloud-based services can be updated seamlessly, but on-premise systems may lag behind. Ensuring seamless compatibility between upgraded and non-upgraded components becomes essential. Additionally, employees often utilize both on-premise and cloud resources, raising questions about how data protection measures can be consistently applied across all environments.

In essence, navigating the complexities of hybrid environments requires forward and backward compatibility within the security solution to ensure seamless integration and data protection across all platforms and resources.

Limitations of Data Security Solutions

Now, let's examine the limitations of current data security solutions. With the foundational knowledge gained from the previous sections, you will be well-equipped to understand the analysis of existing product solutions discussed in this section.

Lack of Comprehensive Coverage

First and foremost, comprehensive coverage stands out as the single most crucial expectation from any security vendor by small to large organizations. However, many security solutions fail to cover all channels and environments comprehensively. Often, these solutions are tailored for specific purposes, resulting in a lack of integration with other components of data protection solutions. For example, a user behavior analytics solution may excel in monitoring user behavior and reporting usage patterns but may lack integration with other essential components. This closed-box approach makes it challenging for organizations to configure and maintain separate solutions to cover all channels and environments effectively, especially on a global scale. While organizations are willing to invest in comprehensive security solutions, they seek unified solutions that can address their diverse security needs.

The depth of coverage, even within a single channel, is often questionable in certain data protection solutions. For instance, a CASB solution might cover only a few of the cloud applications used by a customer, leaving others unprotected. This limited coverage renders the deployed solution ineffective, potentially leading to the leakage of sensitive data through overlooked applications. The rapid growth of cloud applications exacerbates this issue, as security vendors struggle to keep pace with the multitude of applications, each with its own API and upgrade cycles. While maintaining parity with every cloud application is costly and challenging, security vendors must recognize that medium to large organizations typically adopt new cloud applications over an extended period, providing ample opportunity for vendors to adapt and provide adequate coverage.

Organizations often deploy multiple solutions to address security gaps, leading to a suboptimal experience. They must interact with different security products for each channel, each of which implements security measures differently, resulting in heterogeneous violations. This situation causes significant concerns for organizations, as it leads to poor reporting, a challenging experience for administrators, and generally unfavorable outcomes.

Detection Gaps

Security vendors and most importantly organizations should be cognizant of detection gaps. A detection gap can be defined as a period of operation of the product when internal or external circumstances force content detection not to happen fully. There can be a multitude of what I call "circumstances" but the most common ones are as follows:

Content Extraction Failure

When a document is submitted for content violation detection, the initial step in a security solution's process is to crack open the document and read its contents. This document could be of any file type, such as ZIP, PDF, image, embedded file, and more. The security solution then proceeds to read and convert the content, typically in a standardized format like UTF-8. This phase, formally known as content extraction, is the foundation for subsequent content matching.

However, complications may arise because of format discrepancies, leading to potential content extraction failures or prolonged processing times. As I've consistently emphasized, maintaining business continuity is key. Therefore, if content extraction becomes excessively time-consuming or unattainable, the security solution may resort to a fail-open approach. In simpler terms, this leads to no content detection, and the message passes through unchecked. This is termed "content extraction failure," and there can be detection gaps when this situation arises.

Cloud Service Failures

Today, most security vendors rely on a microservices architecture in the cloud, where each service is defined with clear responsibilities and can be independently scaled as needed. These services can be either single-tenant (handling only one customer) or multi-tenant (handling multiple customers). However, there is a possibility of downtime when services crash, and it takes time to bring up new instances of the same service. This downtime is purely based on how the solution is implemented. Poor implementations could result in cloud service failures, where no content detection service is available, and the content up for detection could slip through undetected. This presents another scenario of a detection gap.

Policy Loading Failures

There could be issues with distributing security policies to all content detection engines, or there could be delays in loading all the security rules and their dependencies. Once more, this is purely based on implementation. In my experience, I have observed many vendors encountering some form of policy loading failure, leading them to resort to fail-open approaches when such situations arise. This also results in a detection gap.

Security Solution Timeouts

A security solution may have implemented timeouts to protect itself from spending too much time processing content and evaluating potential threats. However, these timeouts could lead to detection gaps. Once again, it depends on the preferences of the solutions and organizations involved in these timeout scenarios—whether they opt for fail-open or fail-closed approaches.

Content Sizes

The sheer size of content alone can create gaps in detection. Let's assume the security solution can only process file sizes up to 10 MB. Then, any content beyond 10 MB is exempt from scrutiny, leading to a loss of comprehensive coverage and thus, a detection gap. This poses a considerably challenging issue to address. While a security vendor could increase the processing limit to gigabytes, doing so compromises the time taken to process each file of that size vs. maintaining comprehensive coverage. One other important note here is that for the content extraction to properly work from the original format to standardized UTF-8, the whole of the file needs to be there. There may be limitations where the solutions fail to function altogether. All of these scenarios represent detection gaps.

Lack of Unified Policies

The next significant concern from any organization to security vendors is the lack of unified policies across the system. Let's consider a scenario where a security vendor offers five different applications for threat protection, data protection across all channels, and reporting solutions. Unfortunately, there is no single pane of glass where a customer can survey everything. Even if such a user interface is provided, the policies or rules may be incompatible.

CHAPTER 2   TRADITIONAL DATA SECURITY

Let's picture ourselves as a banking institution entrusted with safeguarding sensitive customer data, including credit card numbers. Within our organization, we manage various channels like Email, Network, Endpoint, and Cloud CASB, each needing robust protection. Ideally, our data security solution should offer the flexibility to craft a unified policy that detects and prevents credit card number leaks across all channels. However, the reality is quite different.

Most security solutions on the market today mandate the creation of separate policies for each channel. While managing a few policies may seem manageable, envision the complexity that arises when dealing with over 1000 policies, each with its own set of rules and exceptions and version control in place. Maintaining this extensive array of policies quickly becomes a daunting challenge. Remediation actions may not be available for each channel and the organizations have to manually remediate violations.

Poor Matching Technologies

Matching technologies to detect whether content is a genuine violation or not must be top-notch. However, not all security vendors provide a content detection engine that is effective. They may produce too many false positives or false negatives. While false positives are problematic, false negatives are even more concerning as they allow actual violations to go unnoticed. Additionally, content detection engines may not be able to detect all types of content. For example, some engines cannot scan zip files, embedded files, picture files, video files, or files larger than a few megabytes, leading to an ineffective matching engine.

The efficacy of the matching technologies available in a security product, including threat detection capabilities, predominantly differentiates a good solution from a bad one. Some solutions have different detection capabilities for different channels, leading to varied results.

CHAPTER 2   TRADITIONAL DATA SECURITY

Resiliency, Scalability, Performance

Scale and performance are paramount for any security solution. Without them, the fundamental requirements of data protection, such as keeping confidential data safe and not affecting business continuity, cannot be satisfied. The solution as a whole, starting from UI, infrastructure, reporting framework, content matching engine, and remediation action processor, to channel-specific components, everything needs to perform cohesively and scale. There can be a million security violations in an hour if the policies aren't configured properly. Hence, the system should scale and perform robustly for runaway policies.

Some security vendors don't even promise to support scale as it is very difficult to design solutions, operate, and maintain for a large scale. In those cases, they would only support small and medium businesses with less than 1000 employees per se.

Another crucial aspect of a security solution in terms of resiliency is its ability to auto-tune based on the environment. Currently, no solution available in the market offers this capability. Auto-tuning is an essential feature for organizations of all sizes, addressing aspects such as memory usage, scale, and processing power. By auto-tuning, I do not mean the auto-scaling available in cloud solutions, but rather the internal adjustments of a security product. For example, if most files undergoing content inspection are relatively small and can be quickly evaluated in milliseconds, the solution should adapt to process multiple content inspection requests simultaneously, thereby producing faster outputs.

Organizations highly desire auto-recovery from failures, such as content inspection crashes or process memory errors, as they prefer security products to handle these issues autonomously. They expect the security product to monitor its health, recover from failures independently, and maintain optimal performance without manual intervention.

Weak Configuration Options

By lacking comprehensive flexibility in configuring the security product itself, many potentially great security products fall short. Configuration options are crucial, but having too many can make the product overly complex. Thus, finding the right balance is essential. Not all configuration options need to be available to all organizations. It's something worth considering.

Configuration options will encompass settings tailored to various organizational use cases. For instance, certain organizations prioritize inspecting very large files, even if it extends the inspection time. Others may require the security product to decode all foreign language text and scan for content loss in images and videos. Such settings can be numerous. Larger clients typically demand a plethora of adjustable parameters, including certificate-based authentication for integrations. Configurations are not an aspect security vendors should treat lightly, yet many do.

Poor Usability

Many enterprise security solutions available in the market are notoriously difficult to deploy. While having limited configuration options is one challenge, a more significant issue arises when the deployment process itself is overly complex. Even cloud-based products, often touted for their ease of use, can present usability challenges. A complicated onboarding process can create barriers for organizations, and poorly designed workflows or defects can further exacerbate these issues.

Additionally, some solutions are incompatible with certain operating systems and hardware configurations, severely restricting deployment options for customers. The lack of robust recovery options and inadequate support for databases can also contribute to the difficulties organizations face, leading to increased frustration and inefficiency. Overall, poor usability in enterprise security software can significantly hinder its effectiveness and limit its adoption.

CHAPTER 2 TRADITIONAL DATA SECURITY

Bad Monitoring and Reporting

As we discussed earlier, continuous monitoring is essential to track user behavior patterns. The lack of monitoring across all events and channels leads to a weak product that doesn't function to its full potential. Effective detection cannot occur without continuous monitoring, undermining the entire product. Monitoring each channel individually and correlating events across all channels for a user or source is crucial. We discussed two approaches earlier: one following the user and the other following data. Whichever path a security solution takes, correlation is necessary. We need to stitch events together to gain a comprehensive view. It all boils down to the fact that better monitoring leads to better solutions. Zero trust solutions require continuous monitoring and authentication capabilities as they trust no one.

Reporting is crucial for executives to evaluate the risk status and maintain compliance to satisfy regulatory requirements. Reports need to be available on-demand, scheduled, and in the formats that executives require. However, most solutions lack robust reporting capabilities. They may lack essential reports or fail to cover all channels effectively. Auditors periodically require organizations to submit these compliance reports to make sure the organization obeys all data security and privacy laws. Cross-border data flow is another important aspect that reporting needs to cover.

Poor Upgrade Options

Forward and backward compatibility options are essential when an organization is hybrid. Not all software can be upgraded simultaneously without disrupting business continuity. If protection is left unattended for a few days, there is a potential risk of a data breach. Hence, compatibility between versions is a necessity.

Upgrading software, especially for on-premise solutions, should be effective and easy. This depends on how the solution operates. Some solutions work with an agent installed on each server or endpoint machine, while others operate entirely from the cloud. Regardless of the approach, upgrades are crucial. Large organizations invest significant resources in upgrading their data protection software and associated infrastructure. For example, some organizations take upwards of a year to plan and roll out upgrades. They conduct extensive user testing to deploy security policies, thus they need to ensure that when upgrading environments, all their security policies and settings remain intact to prevent any data breaches.

Organizations typically have a global presence, being spread across different locations around the world, and they interact with various cloud application providers. During upgrades, the solutions should be able to maintain the quality of content detection technologies both before and after the upgrade. For instance, upgrades shouldn't have defects that may cause false positives and false negative security violations. Most of the security solutions have inferior quality upgrades resulting in bad experiences for organizations.

Inadequate Integrations

The data security solution is deemed an excellent fit only if it can seamlessly integrate with other business tools that organizations might use. These integrations include systems such as Jira, Service Now, Splunk, Active Directory, encryption systems, classification systems, threat intelligence systems, and appliances like proxies, load balancers, and analytics solutions if used separately, as well as reporting solutions if used separately. As you may have already surmised, many security solutions fail in this regard. They overlook the crucial fact that the ease of adoption by customers significantly influences their longevity. It serves as a key factor for customer retention.

Too Expensive for the Value

Security solutions need to be priced right for the value they provide. Many security vendors do a poor job of pricing, either leaving money on the table or setting prices too high. Pricing needs to be appropriate for the value a solution offers. I'm not advocating for security vendors to price their products low; rather, they need to assess how effectively their solution covers the use cases for a customer and price it accordingly.

Today most of the security vendors offer subscription-based pricing in terms of users in an organization. Even if the security product gets used or not, vendors charge organizations. They don't charge based on usage.

Poor Customer Support

For any enterprise product, customer support is indispensable, especially. A proficient support team can engage with customers and grasp their true use cases. Given the diversity of customer environments, product teams cannot create a one-size-fits-all solution. Instead, they must prioritize and develop features that deliver genuine value to customers. When a customer reports a problem, the support team should not merely aim to superficially close the case. Instead, they should delve into the true root cause of the issue, understand the underlying business process, compare it to similar cases from other customers, and devise a solution that benefits the majority.

Organizations require guidance during upgrades, integrations with their business systems and security products, threat monitoring, and forensic investigations. A proficient support team that delivers exceptional service will not only enhance customer satisfaction but also generate a steady stream of requirements for the product team to enhance the solution's comprehensiveness and effectiveness.

CHAPTER 2   TRADITIONAL DATA SECURITY

Summary

You, as readers, must feel confident in evaluating data security solutions using a wide range of parameters. Assess the overall product, consider which market segment it caters to, and evaluate the comprehensiveness of the product along with the functionality supported in each component. Evaluate against the key requirements we distilled in Chapter 1. When assessing the involvement of artificial intelligence in a data protection solution, examine the test data, training methods, and whether it employs unsupervised learning. Look for the false positive and false negative rates. Simply incorporating AI does not make a security solution great; you must consider the business value AI brings to the table.

Great security solutions have the following characteristics: comprehensive coverage, scalability, performance, effective content detection systems, wonderful configurability, great reporting capabilities, flexible integration capabilities, proper versioning support, and great threat monitoring systems. Most importantly, they adapt to the deployed environment, provide suggestions and options to IT administrators, and do not always mandate organizations to configure every single aspect of the product. Self-recovery and autonomous operation are much desired by organizations.

In the next chapter, I will introduce you to strategies for thinking beyond the usual norms to build a great solution. Your imagination is key, as possibility and success lie within the bounds of imagination. We will discuss how to overcome the pitfalls we discussed earlier by adopting a strategic mindset toward solving this security problem.

CHAPTER 3

Thinking Outside Norms

In this chapter, I aim to expand your understanding of creating an effective data protection solution. Instead of offering a single solution, I encourage you to approach the problem from different perspectives. Drawing on the knowledge you've gained from the first two chapters, I'm confident you now have a solid grasp of the issue and available options. However, it's crucial to not feel limited by these options. To illustrate this, I've structured this chapter to review in detail what you might already know, and then explore creative alternatives. Using scenarios commonly encountered in the field, I've employed a sample organization to make the concepts easier to grasp. For security analysts and IT administrators reading this, you'll discover new ways to frame your questions and address challenges. Sometimes, all it takes is a clear description of your problem to guide a conversation with a security vendor.

Certain aspects of designing a data protection system are essential and cannot be overlooked. If your organization is grappling with how to safeguard its data, it's vital to consider these components. As you progress through the following sections, consider how they relate to your organization. Where do you fit into the equation? Do these descriptions align with the situations your organization encounters? With that in mind, let's get started.

CHAPTER 3   THINKING OUTSIDE NORMS

Sample Organization and Use Cases

Consider a fictional scenario involving a healthcare organization known as "*Good American Hospital*" (GAH) which is in the process of procuring a data security solution. We'll examine various use cases to understand how the security solution should be designed.

Let's define some terms and use cases that would be used in the sections below.

National Drug Code: This is represented by a 10 or 11-digit number matched by the following regex.

$$\wedge(?:\backslash d\{4\}-\backslash d\{4\}-\backslash d\{2\}|\backslash d\{5\}-(?:\backslash d\{3\}-\backslash d\{2\}|\backslash d\{4\}-\backslash d\{1,2\}))\$$$

Prescription: This can be described by any email body or a document containing all of the keywords in the list {"date, dosage, patient, age, doctor, pharmacy"} and has to encompass a combination that matches the regex of the National Drug Code.

Drug Names: This is a proprietary document of GAH containing names of all the drugs the doctors in GAH can use.

Dosage Identifier: Dosage is identified by matching the following pattern

$$\{\backslash d+:\backslash d+:\backslash d+\}$$

Drug Usage Procedure: This is a proprietary resource document of GAH that contains detailed information about various drugs, prescription dosages, and usage procedures like diet restrictions. A handful of such documents are identifiable by keywords in the drug names list and dosage identifiers.

Hospital Domain: @gah.org would be the hospital domain.

AD groups: Active Directory groups used in the hospital system: Executives (hospital management includes chief doctor only and C-level executives of the hospital who are not doctors), Doctors (doesn't include nurses), Non-doctors (doesn't include executives), Billing Department, All Employees, All Nurses.

Bill Receipts: Bills can be identified by documents containing the Patient name, SSN, Date of Birth, Payee Name, Credit Card Details, Address, Insurance Covered Amount, Bill Date, and Amount owed.

Revenue Details: Revenue details are represented by content containing at least two keywords in the list {"revenue, gross profit, operating profit, sales"} and keyword matching the year {2024}

Fictional Use Cases

These are some of the use cases we'll discuss in this chapter. I've broken them down into sub-elements. Don't worry if you don't understand any of this right now; we'll go into detail later in the subsequent sections of this chapter.

Use Case 1: GAH wants to keep track of all employees who print out a prescription or drug usage procedure.

Sender: All Employees
Channel: Print from any Endpoint
Match Criteria: Prescription or drug usage procedure
Remediation Action: Monitor

Use Case 2: GAH wants to block all outgoing emails containing prescriptions in the body or attachments from non-doctors to external email address domains.

Sender: Non Doctors
Recipients: Any email address that has an external domain. i.e. not "@GAH.org"
Channel: Email
Match Criteria: Body or Attachment containing prescription
Remediation Action: Block

CHAPTER 3   THINKING OUTSIDE NORMS

Use Case 3: GAH wants to ensure patient information doesn't get into shares that have access to employees in the group "Non-doctors."

Recipients: Accessibility of folders that are shared with Non-doctors
Channel: Network Share, Cloud Applications—Storage
Match Criteria: Drug names, Prescription, Drug usage procedure, Bill Receipts
Remediation Action: Block, If already present Quarantine.

Use Case 4: GAH wants to restrict emails with unreleased hospital revenue details only among executives.

Recipients: Not Executives
Channel: Email
Match Criteria: Revenue details
Remediation Action: Block

Use Case 5: GAH wants patient bills over $10,000 to be authorized by the Chief Doctor and not shared with anyone other than patients and the billing department.

Recipients: Patients, Billing Department, Chief Doctor
Channel: Email, Network Share, Cloud Storage, Endpoint
Match Criteria: Bill Receipts
Remediation Action: Block/Delete as appropriate

Policy Language

The language we use to set rules in security systems needs to be super flexible, and able to handle all sorts of conditions and logic. You might wonder, among all the things in security, is the language for setting rules really that important? Absolutely! Picture this: if the language can't do certain things, like say, use the NOT operator to create exceptions, then we're stuck. We can't make rules that say something isn't part of a group

CHAPTER 3 THINKING OUTSIDE NORMS

or isn't in a list of keywords. We're left without the tools we need to express ourselves properly. I've seen systems where the language is so limited that administrators have to resort to messy workarounds, leading to a nightmare of policy maintenance. Let's consider the following fictional use cases from GAH and see how the policy language should address these scenarios.

Policy Context Rules

Context Matching is crucial for filtering out messages that the security solution doesn't need to analyze, ensuring scalability, performance, and business continuity. Refer to the events that are listed in Table 3-1 and compare them with the use cases above to determine whether they require attention.

Table 3-1. Context Matching Examples

Events happening in hospital	Context match	Inspect further
Dr. Harry prints out a prescription	Endpoint Print Channel—Use Case 1 Match	Yes—Inspect to see if it is a prescription or drug usage procedure
Nurse Alice copies the drug usage procedures to her personal Box-folder	Copy to Cloud Applications Storage and Personal Box—Use Case 2 Match	Yes—Inspection needed to see the content that is being copied
Chief Doctor accesses Drug List on his laptop	No	No

(continued)

Table 3-1. (*continued*)

Events happening in hospital	Context match	Inspect further
Dr. Abby uploads prescriptions to a corporate Box folder in the cloud. This folder is accessible to nurses.	Copy to Cloud Applications Storage And Accessible by Nurses—Use Case 3 Match	Yes—Inspection needed to see the content that is being copied
Employee Andy emails prescriptions to the patient's email—sally@newmail.com	Non-doctor Andy, Outside Domain—Use Case 2 Match	Yes—Inspection needed to see the content that is being copied
Employee Mike sends drug usage procedure documents from a common system using a doctor's login and sends them to his corporate email. Downloads and stores it later.	Not a Match—But should have been a match as it is an impersonation of a doctor login	No
CEO sends unreleased revenue details to all executives	Not a match as there is no policy covering the use case between the CEO and executives	No

As you can see in Table 3-1 for the context match, we need to consider the sender, recipients, and destination, specifically the endpoint, which could include a laptop, shared drive, or cloud storage. Additionally, we need to differentiate between whether it is a corporate application or not, as well as the login credentials for that application, as we have to distinguish between corporate Box and personal Box accounts.

The context match determines whether we need to allocate additional computing power to this task or not. Chapters 4 and 5 delve deeper into determining when to conduct further scans and when to refrain, even if a context match hasn't occurred, to facilitate system learning.

Policy Matching Rules

A policy rule, as discussed in Chapter 2, denotes a condition. A policy can contain multiple rules, and each rule should be joined to another rule using an AND or OR Boolean operator. Additionally, the NOT operator can be applied to any rule to denote the complement of the condition. Any number of rules can be joined together, and the policy language shouldn't limit organizations to a fixed number of rules that can be used in a policy.

Check out the following sample rules:

Rule 1 OR NOT(Rule2)
Rule 1 AND (Rule 2 OR Rule 3)
Rule 1 OR (Rule 2 AND Rule 3) OR NOT(Rule 4)

As you can see there can be compound rules where multiple rules are joined and of course, there is priority (rules inside parenthesis). It is like evaluating a prefix or postfix expression. Each rule can undergo conversion into a postfix expression, ensuring that priorities are correctly met during evaluation.

Now, let's explore how to write conditions for the fictional use cases we discussed earlier. Please note that we're currently setting aside concerns about remediation actions, such as "Block." Our primary focus will be solely on defining the conditions.

Use Case 1: GAH wants to keep track of all employees who print out a prescription or drug usage procedure.

The "Match Criteria" we saw earlier for this use case is prescription or drug usage procedure. Here two conditions can be further broken down into rules as follows:

CHAPTER 3   THINKING OUTSIDE NORMS

Prescription Match: Drug Keyword List AND National Drug Code

Drug Usage Procedure Match: Drugs in drugs list AND Dosage Identifier AND Diet Restrictions

Drug Keyword: Keywords in {"date, dosage, patient, age, doctor, pharmacy"}

National Drug Code: Regular Expression $^\wedge(?:\d\{4\} - \d\{4\} - \d\{2\} | \d\{5\} - (?:\d\{3\} - \d\{2\} | \d\{4\} - \d\{1,2\}))\$$

Drugs in Drug List: Drugs in Drugs Keyword List

Dosage Identifier: Regular Expression $\{\d+ : \d+ : \d+\}$

Dietary Restriction: We don't have any way of determining it as of yet.

So the final policy match condition rules can be written as below:

```
(
    (
        Rule 1 (Keywords in {"date, dosage, patient, age,
        doctor, pharmacy"} )
            AND
        Rule 2 (Reg Ex ^(? : \d{4} - \d{4} - \d{2}
        |\d{5} - (? : \d{3} - \d{2}|\d{4} - \d{1,2}))$)
    )
    OR
    (
        Rule 3 ( Drugs in Drugs Keyword List )
            AND
        Rule 4 (Reg Ex {\d + : \d + : \d+})
    )
)
```

The above example should give you an idea of how the policy rules are constructed. There were only four rules here, but you can imagine real complex use cases having more than ten rules with complex Boolean logic in them.

CHAPTER 3   THINKING OUTSIDE NORMS

Better flexibility in rule construction will lead to better policies and ultimately better protection. Imagine if you didn't implement the "AND" operator, then the above use case example could have been impossible to implement.

Exceptions

Exceptions essentially serve as "NOT" conditions, instructing the security solution not to generate a violation if the condition specified in the exception is met. Let's take use case 4 and focus only on exceptions.

GAH wants to restrict emails with unreleased hospital revenue details only among executives

Is there an exception here? This use case can be interpreted as GAH wanting to raise a violation and then block the content if it involves access to Non-Executives.

So the exception class can be executives. The policy can be structured with Match Criteria and Exceptions as follows.

Unreleased Hospital Revenue: At least 2 keywords in {"revenue, gross profit, operating profit, sales"} and keyword matching the year {2024}

Policy match condition rules are:

```
(
    Rule 1 (At least 2 Keywords in  {"revenue, gross profit,
    operating profit, sales"})
        AND
    Rule 2 ( Keyword in {2024})
)
```

Exception rule conditions are:

Rule 3 (Recipient in Executives AD Group)

Here the recipient is the end user who is receiving the content. The content can be an email, a file that is given share permissions, or a file that is downloaded onto a laptop that belongs to the end user.

CHAPTER 3   THINKING OUTSIDE NORMS

The final policy is:

```
(
    (
        Rule 1 (At least 2 Keywords in  {"revenue, gross profit,
        operating profit, sales"})
            AND
        Rule 2 ( Keyword in {2024})
    )
    NOT
    (
        Rule 3 (Recipient in Executives AD Group)
    )
}
```

Exceptions may become intricate with compound rules, meaning there can be multiple rules combined using AND, OR, or even complemented with the NOT operator. To optimize efficiency, security solutions prioritize evaluating context rules first.

Creative Policy Language

In this section, we've covered the basics of expressing policies using context rules, matching rules, and exceptions—standard forms of representation. But let's push beyond these boundaries. Imagine with me for a moment: How can we get creative with policy language? While the requirements for policy language remain unchanged—to safeguard sensitive content as defined by use cases within an organization—let's explore innovative ways to achieve this goal.

In our hypothetical scenario, we have GAH describing their use cases in plain English, which we then translate into a language our security solution can comprehend. You might wonder: Why can't our security solution understand English directly? Why do we need to translate it into

CHAPTER 3 THINKING OUTSIDE NORMS

rules? Can't the security product autonomously interpret English (or any chosen language) internally, allowing users to interact solely in their preferred language? Let's explore this further.

Imagine if your security product could understand plain English commands—wouldn't that be convenient? While building a full Natural Language Processing system might be beyond the scope of your current setup, you can still incorporate some action words to simplify policy creation. Remember how we broke down the use case into "Remediation Action," "Sender," "Recipients," and "Channel"? We can prompt policy authors with specific action keywords, making it easy for organizations to grasp what's being done. The challenge lies in defining reusable rules based on these terms, rather than relying solely on match criteria like keyword lists or regular expressions.

If you and your security team are up for the challenge, consider a creative approach using classification. Start by classifying sensitive documents and then create policy rules to protect them. Continuous monitoring will help keep up with classification over time, though it may be more challenging for larger organizations due to evolving criteria and diverse departments or regions. Remember, there's no one-size-fits-all solution here—I'm simply broadening your perspective on what's possible.

Another option to consider is using Large Language Models (LLMs). Think of LLMs as super-smart text analyzers, like GPT-4 or BERT, that have been trained on tons of text to understand and generate human-like language. They're great at sifting through security logs, emails, and alerts to spot potential threats or unusual patterns that might signal a security issue.

For security software developers, understanding what LLMs can and can't do is key. They excel at interpreting and analyzing text but may have limitations in context and accuracy. It's also important to keep in mind the ethical side of using LLMs—like making sure they don't perpetuate bias and that they comply with legal standards.

When it comes to using LLMs, you have a couple of choices: you can either build your own model tailored to your needs or use a pre-trained one. For instance, if you're focused on cloud protection, you could customize an LLM to generate policies based on specific keywords related to your domain. This approach helps you create policies that are both relevant and aligned with your organization's goals, without getting bogged down by the complexities of a massive model.

Dependency on Policies

Having explored policy language in the preceding section, let's address a fundamental question: why do we place such heavy reliance on policies? While I'm not proposing the outright elimination of policies, we should aim to diminish our dependence on them needing to be flawless for optimal solution performance.

Every security company says the following. At the heart of any security setup are the rules and guidelines it follows. Imagine it like building a strong fortress: if the rules for guarding it are weak, even the best walls won't keep out invaders. They're saying that if the rules aren't set up right, the security system won't do its job well. I believe it's not just about the rules; the security system should be smart enough to ask for help from the people running it even if the rules are weak.

Now, I bet you're wondering: if our rules aren't up to scratch, how do we keep things safe? Take a moment to ponder on that. You might have jumped to the conclusion that weak rules lead to either too many false alarms (things flagged as issues that aren't—false positives) or worse, some real problems slipping through undetected (false negatives). Before diving deep into false positives and false negatives, let's review some shortcomings of the security policies.

CHAPTER 3   THINKING OUTSIDE NORMS

Shortcomings of Security Policies

In the preceding section, we discussed enhancing the creativity of policy language to facilitate greater expressiveness, assisting policy administrators in building more effective policies. Now, let's revisit the policy structure. Figure 3-1 depicts the structure of a class policy, including all its elements.

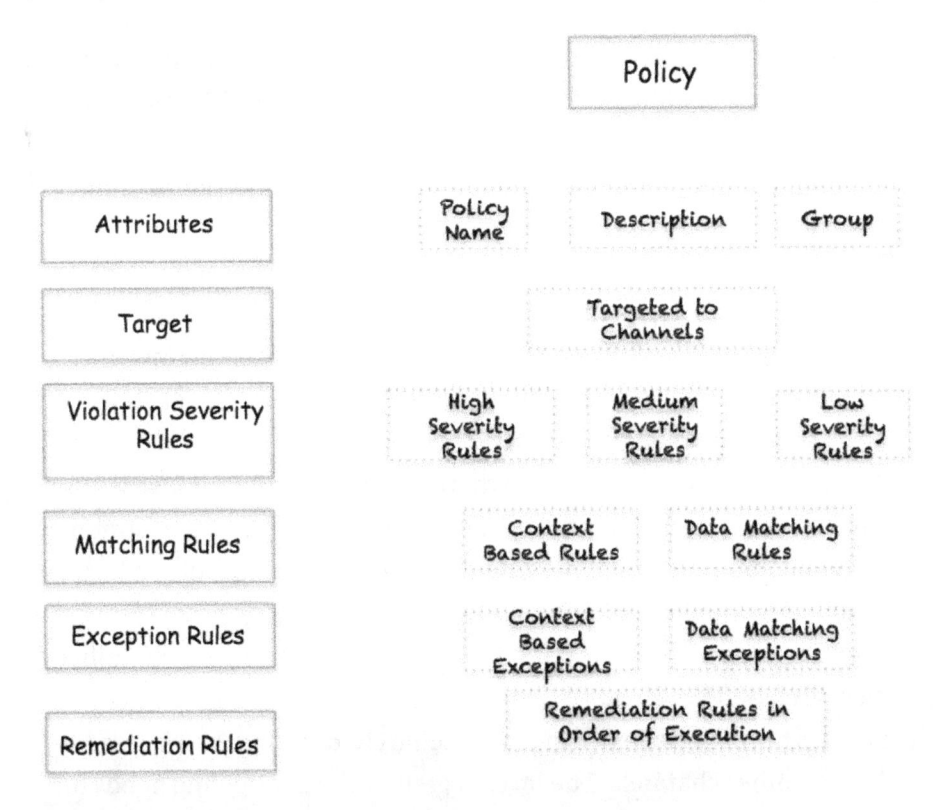

Figure 3-1. Policy Structural Elements

In Figure 3-1, the right column represents the various elements within a policy, each of which can be further detailed as specified in the rows. For example, every policy must include matching rules, which can be categorized into two types: context-based rules and content-based rules.

99

Can you pinpoint what is lacking in the structure? Consider how a policy author in an organization can create a policy by filling in all the details. What would they lack? It's not solely about the structure itself; rather, when we think beyond the structure, several issues come to light, including the following:

Improper Policy Targeting

The fundamental problem is policy not targeted uniformly to all channels. Let's assume you say that policy is targeted to the "Network Share" channel. How do you know that the sensitive data is only in the corporate shares? Well from an organizational perspective, security administrators might challenge us claiming that they have restricted sensitive content never leaving the corporate share folder. How can you guarantee that? Let's assume a malicious user writes a script or program to read the contents of the sensitive file and writes it to another file in a USB drive. Now the policy might prohibit users from manually copying the whole file but can it block a script that reads and transforms into another file in a different location? I want to present you with this extreme example to make you understand what a malicious script can do. Since a policy administrator in an organization will never imagine this scenario, there wouldn't be any possibility to prevent it.

Another issue with policy targeting contradicts the concept of unified policies discussed in Chapter 2. Once the targeting field is designated, the policies become exclusive to that specific channel and are not readily available to other channels. The level of granularity in targeting needs to be clearly defined. For instance, suppose we want a policy to specifically apply to cloud applications. In that case, the security solution should offer options such as all cloud applications, all corporate applications, all non-corporate applications, and so forth. This hierarchical grouping should encourage policy administrators to avoid individually selecting applications unless necessary. In another instance, when applying policies to the endpoint channel, it is preferable not to differentiate between Data-in-Motion (DIM) and Data-at-Rest (DAR) on the endpoint.

Static Rules and Inherent Complexity

Policy rules are essentially static directives devoid of inherent intelligence. For instance, consider a keyword list comprising "credit card," "user name," and "address." Now, imagine the content containing fields for Street, City, State, and Zip, but lacking the specific keyword "address." Although the intent was to identify addresses, the security solution would not flag this discrepancy because the address was segmented into individual components. Therefore, it becomes imperative to grasp the underlying intent behind the rules. In Chapter 2, we delved into the policy administrator's intentions, and now we must examine them from the policy perspective.

Creating rules can become quite intricate, especially when dealing with multiple compound rules, exceptions, and diverse content detection technologies. I've encountered policies containing 20 matching conditions and 50 exceptions, making them difficult to modify and upkeep. Due to this complexity, policy administrators often resort to repeatedly creating similar policies to address similar conditions with minor variations. As a result, reusability is neglected, reminiscent of a software codebase burdened with significant technical debt.

Limited Availability of Response Actions

The execution engines for response actions must possess the intelligence to discern the intentions of the policy administrator when carrying out response actions. Often, response rules in security solutions offer a limited range of potential actions, and even when they do, administrators may not configure actions for all channels, despite applying the policy universally. For instance, let's consider a scenario where a policy author

CHAPTER 3   THINKING OUTSIDE NORMS

intends to prevent sensitive content from being sent via email. In this case, they would create a policy and associate it with a block response action. However, if the same policy is applied to network share scanning in the Network Share channel, the "block" action may not be applicable. It is imperative that the underlying intent is understood, and appropriate actions, such as deletion or quarantine, are taken for sensitive files.

Typically, the policy structure offers an abundance of options to the policy administrator, aiming to provide precise control over their requirements. However, this approach often causes the administrator to overlook the broader, holistic perspective. While some situations call for fine-grained control, the administrator must exercise this level of control only when necessary. Instead of prioritizing flexibility in policy structures, let's focus on enhancing the intelligence of the detection engine.

Let's return to false positives and false negatives for a moment. You've probably already considered how to reduce false alarms but maybe haven't given as much thought to the stuff that's slipping by unnoticed. If you're still pondering those missed issues, you're thinking beyond the usual. And that's exactly where I want to guide you—let's tackle those missed problems head-on.

Why is there a false negative? Something was sensitive but we missed it because our security system with weak policies discerned that it wasn't sensitive. How can we make the policies stronger while maintaining business continuity? For example, let's say there was a file demo.txt in a folder in the corporate network share. Now an employee who has access to this file downloads it to his laptop. Is this event suspicious? How do we determine that? First of all, let me tell you that your system is not going to be intelligent in a day. It is going to learn and adapt based on all the events that are happening in the deployed environment across all channels.

CHAPTER 3 THINKING OUTSIDE NORMS

Learning from Partial Content Matches

Can we pick up insights from partial content matches and offer policy suggestions to our authors? Even better—what if we could prompt authors to automatically apply our suggestions, or at the very least, obtain their approval before implementing them? You may be pondering how organizations can approve policies without conducting thorough reviews. It's indeed a valid concern! Mere suggestions aren't enough; we must practically demonstrate the same violations observed in the system. This way, they can consider the recommendation and fine-tune it as needed. Another approach is to put recommended policies in a test mode. I'll delve into policy feedback and test mode policies in the following sections. But first, let's circle back to partial content matches. What exactly are we talking about here?

Let's take our hypothetical scenario use cases one by one. Each use case offers data that is something valuable.

Use Case 1: GAH wants to keep track of all employees who print out a prescription or drug usage procedure.

From this use case description, any of us can easily say that prescription or drug usage procedures are important to GAH and they consider it sensitive and worth tracking. However, they know that the business practice is to print them so they don't want to block the print operation but just monitor. Again let's summarize our learnings:

Sensitive: Prescription and Drug Usage Procedure documents
Who can do it: Any employee
Business Practice: Printing Prescription and Drug Usage Procedure documents

Now armed with these insights, our security solution can designate prescription and drug usage procedure documents as sensitive. Since these documents are accessible to all employees, they may not be ultra-sensitive but rather fall into the categories of low or moderate sensitivity. If our security solution comes across prescription or drug usage

103

procedure documents anywhere within the organization, can't it offer policy recommendations? For example, if these documents are put on a website and uploaded, the solution could suggest that it's likely sensitive information and shouldn't be allowed. Just because there isn't an explicit policy in place doesn't mean our system should turn a blind eye. I envision our system making reasonable assessments and recommendations, rather than scrutinizing everything. By providing such feedback, policy authors can refine policies and enhance their coverage.

Use Case 2: GAH wants to block all outgoing emails containing prescriptions in the body or attachments from non-doctors to external email address domains.

Continuing along the same path, let's review our second use case. What insights can we draw from this scenario? It appears that at GAH, it's standard practice for employees in the "Doctors" Active Directory (AD) group to send prescriptions to external domains—likely to patients or pharmacies. Our security solution needs to recognize this practice. Building on the previous use case, we now understand that while all employees can handle prescriptions, not all can send them via email. Specifically, members of the "Non-doctors" AD group can print and handle prescriptions within the hospital premises; they're not permitted to take them outside. Granted, it's impossible to physically prevent someone from carrying a printed prescription off-site, but monitoring all print activities helps enforce this policy. Perhaps the hospital should consider tightening printing restrictions in the first use case. We could ask policy authors whether we should adjust the policy to only allow printing for the Doctors AD group. Policy authors might suggest expanding printing permissions to include the Nurses AD group as well, but not all employees. This is the kind of flexibility I'm advocating for. Our security solution can provide valuable insights to refine policies based on these learnings summarized below.

Sensitive: Prescription

Who can do it: Doctors in the AD Group

Business Practice: Email prescription to external domains

We need to examine the underlying intent of the policy and then learn from it. Let's now explore other use cases and see what we can learn from them.

Use Case 3: GAH wants to ensure sensitive information doesn't get into shares that have access to employees in the group "Non-doctors."

Sensitive: Here, the sensitive information includes prescriptions, drug usage procedures, and so on.

Who can do it: Doctors and Executives (Non Doctors)

Business Practice: Doctor's AD group has access to the network share folders or cloud share folders where sensitive information may be present.

Like the previous use cases, partial learning indicates that sensitive information is limited solely to the Doctors AD group.

Use Case 4: GAH wants to restrict emails with unreleased hospital revenue details only among executives.

The underlying intent behind this use case can be summarized as follows:

Sensitive: Unreleased hospital revenue details are only viewed by Executives.

Who can do it: Executives

Business Practice: Hospital revenue details are shared among executives via email.

The fact that unreleased hospital revenue details are exclusively accessible to executives via email suggests that GAH aims to limit access to this revenue detail information across all communication channels. However, they haven't accounted for every possible scenario, such as Network Share, Cloud Storage, Endpoints, and BYOD channels.

CHAPTER 3   THINKING OUTSIDE NORMS

A recommendation can be proposed to the policy administrator to reassess the policy to ensure comprehensive coverage across all channels. The administrator can then make exceptions as needed and fine-tune the policy accordingly.

Use Case 5: GAH wants patient bills of over $10,000 to be authorized by the Chief Doctor and not shared with anyone other than patients and the billing department.

As evident from this use case, the established business practice dictates that the billing department must obtain authorization from the Chief Doctor for patient bills exceeding $10,000 before releasing them. Therefore, the bill receipts are considered sensitive information. The use case itself is broad enough to warrant a policy covering all channels. Therefore, the partial learning that the security solution can glean is that patient bills are overseen by the billing department and tightly regulated by other employees.

Sensitive: Patient bills
Who can do it: Chief Doctor, Billing department
Business Practice: Patient bills are managed by the billing department and the Chief Doctor.

Hence, if patient bills are found in other channels, we can recommend to the policy administrator to create or modify the breadth of the existing policy to ensure comprehensive coverage.

The insights gained from partial learnings derived from policies and matches, stemming from discovered business intentions, have the potential to elevate a good security solution to greatness. Organizations should interpret their policies with clarity of their business intent, thereby refining and broadening them more comprehensively. Even if your security solution doesn't automatically perform this task, you can continuously enhance and fine-tune your policies.

Policy Feedback

Policy feedback is vital for any security solution, serving as an effective method to minimize both false positives and false negatives. While many organizations may tolerate false positives, false negatives are a major concern. However, let's think outside the box for a moment: false positives aren't ideal either. They flood the system with numerous security violations, discouraging remediators from analyzing and addressing them. Naturally, humans are inclined to invest their time only when there's value to be gained. Sorting through countless violations, only to find most of them are false positives, also leads to a poor customer experience.

When a violation is flagged as a false positive, it should promptly trigger feedback to the policy and offer suggestions for remediation. We'll delve into violation remediation feedback in the upcoming section. For now, let's concentrate on policies. Consider what insights we can glean when a security violation is identified as a false positive. The policy administrator authored policies based on specific use cases, yet we encountered false positives in the system. How did this occur? Let's examine one of our hypothetical scenarios involving GAH. Meanwhile, I want to let you know that false positive violations are pretty common in a security system deployment. Always remember that it is better to have false positives rather than false negatives.

Consider the following email from a nurse working in GAH to a patient:

CHAPTER 3   THINKING OUTSIDE NORMS

To: Mark.Walls123@gmail.com [Fictional email. No impersonation intended]

Subject: Request to Reschedule Your Appointment with Dr. Abby Dated March 15, 2024

Date: 03/15/2024

Dear Mark,

I hope this email finds you well.

Our records indicate that you, Mark Walls, aged 56, are a patient of Dr. Abby and were scheduled for an appointment on March 12, 2024. It appears that you missed this appointment, and Dr. Abby would like to follow up with you regarding your prescription dosage of Sumatriptan [55700-899]. Your health is important to us, and you must attend your appointments regularly.

Please feel free to give us a call or reply to this email at your earliest convenience to reschedule your follow-up appointment with Dr. Abby.

Warm regards,

Alice Cooper, RN
Good American Hospital
alice.cooper@gah.org

This email violates **Use Case 2: GAH wants to block all emails containing prescriptions in the body or attachments going out from non-doctors to external email address domains**.

When our content detection engine in our security solutions runs, it would tag this email as a prescription, whereas this email is in no way related to a prescription. It matched the prescription because it contains all keywords in the list {"date, dosage, patient, age, doctor, pharmacy"} and has a drug code "55700-899" as well. This email will be blocked as per our policy. Setting aside the fact that it would be blocked and the consequences of it, this is a false positive violation.

Violation remediators, upon encountering this violation, would immediately label it as a false positive. Since it hinders business practices, they might update the remediation action from "block" to "monitor." However, as you can see, this approach is fundamentally flawed.

When violation remediators identify this issue, their instinct might be to mark it as a false positive. However, this action, aimed at mitigating the problem, actually disrupts essential business practices. Changing the remediation action from "block" to "monitor" might seem logical, but as you know, it's not the right solution.

A significant aspect of psychology and stereotyping influences this situation. Additional monitoring software, such as a security solution, is often perceived as the problem. In such cases, there's a natural inclination to adjust remediation measures or, in extreme cases, disable the policy altogether, intending to revisit and rectify it later. Unfortunately, the anticipated review of policies often doesn't materialize, perpetuating the issue.

How should GAH proceed in this case? The initial step they could take is to enhance the policy by including the Nurses AD group, thus restoring business continuity with minimal disruption. Given the circumstances, this alteration minimizes potential damage. Subsequently, if GAH wishes to strictly maintain the original policy, the definition of "prescription" needs updating. Alternatively, if they opt to modify the policy, they can update it to incorporate customer communication rules and specify the sender as a nurse from the Nurse AD group.

How can our security solution support the aforementioned process? Once a violation remediator marks the violation as a false positive, we should promptly initiate the feedback process by posing a few questions regarding why it was labeled as such.

Should the definition of the prescription rule be revised?

Should Nurse Alice Cooper, or an AD group involving Alice Cooper, be added as an exception?

CHAPTER 3   THINKING OUTSIDE NORMS

The responses to these inquiries should be integrated into the policies, and an updated policy should promptly appear on the policy administrator's screen for modification. Further, similar violations that have not yet been flagged as false positives can be grouped and presented to violation remediators to be marked accordingly.

Now, we ought to commence partial learning from the content matches derived from the updated policy, and thus, the cycle persists. This ongoing enhancement, as underscored numerous times in this book, will culminate in a comprehensive security solution.

Please review another authentic example of a false positive use case below:

While the Chief Doctor is on vacation, the billing department sends a patient bill to Assistant Chief Doctor Sean Yaton for authorization.

This scenario presents a genuine false positive that GAH did not anticipate, as it would violate the following use case:

Use Case 5: GAH requires patient bills exceeding $10,000 to be authorized exclusively by the Chief Doctor and not shared with anyone other than patients and the billing department.

To resolve this issue, the policy needs to be enhanced to include Assistant Chief Doctor Sean Yaton in the exception list.

Therefore, providing feedback on the policy is crucial for continuously fine-tuning the security solution for optimal performance.

Test Mode Policies

Test mode policies differ from real policies in that they do not generate actual security violations. For any robust security solution, enabling organizations to test their policies in a production environment is essential. Many organizations, specifically large ones, maintain a separate testing environment where they deploy the security solution to evaluate it before implementing changes in the real production environment. Similarly, cloud customers often have distinct test and production environments where they assess configuration and policy alterations. However, it is crucial to acknowledge that the test environment may not accurately replicate the complexities of the real production environment, such as traffic diversity and user volume.

Therefore, test mode policies serve a vital purpose. Organizations can modify existing policies or create new ones and test them in a controlled test mode environment before deploying them in full production mode. These test mode policies do not include any remediation actions to prevent any impact on the production environment.

Using our hypothetical sample case in this chapter, consider a situation where GAH wants to author a new policy that prevents employees from storing patient information (PII data) on their laptops. To execute this directive, the security solution administrator could create a blanket test policy that covers the endpoint channel for all employees. This test mode policy would get active for a few days (let's call it a week) and be used in both DIM and DAR on the endpoint channel. A sample set of test violations gets reported and the policy author and violation remediator can review these violations.

Let's say a sample set of violations has revealed that nurses store patient information on their laptops for appointment scheduling purposes. This poses a risk for GAH, as nurses have access to personally identifiable information (PII) of patients. The test policy has highlighted a potential vulnerability in their hospital processes that needs addressing. Initially, the test mode policy would include an exception for laptops belonging to nurses. Subsequently, as rules are implemented to prohibit the storage of patient information, this exception can be removed. Without this test mode, GAH would have faced hundreds, if not thousands, of violations, which may have gone unnoticed by violation remediators.

Additionally, test mode policies aid in fine-tuning certain matching criteria. For instance, if regular expressions or keyword lists are used as part of the matching criteria, the test mode policies enable organizations to refine these criteria until optimal results are achieved.

CHAPTER 3   THINKING OUTSIDE NORMS

Match Rule Types

The examples provided in this book thus far have utilized regular expressions or keywords as matching conditions. This choice was made to ensure simplicity and clarity in explanation. However, it's important to note that there is a vast array of rule types available for use. The possibilities are virtually limitless. Although there are standard rule types commonly employed by popular security vendors, organizations have the flexibility to define custom rule types as well.

In addition to predefined rule types, users can also create custom rule types by writing scripts or programs for matching purposes (see Table 3-2). When the content detection engine runs, it can invoke these custom scripts to determine if a match occurs. However, it's crucial to exercise caution when allowing users to write custom scripts, particularly in terms of performance. These scripts must execute swiftly, ideally in sub-milliseconds, to avoid disrupting business continuity.

Table 3-2. Content Matching Rule Types

Content matching rule type	Description
Context-based rules	Sender, recipients, email domains, channels, etc.
Context-based AD rules	Active Directory-based rules including hierarchies, groups, dl's, etc.
File attributes rule	Match files by type or extension, size
Keyword rules	Matching all keywords specified or partial number of keywords in the list. Distance between keywords can also be specified for some advanced use cases.
Regular expression rules	Matching defined regular expression
Device location rules	Endpoint location on the corporate network or an external public network

(continued)

CHAPTER 3 THINKING OUTSIDE NORMS

Table 3-2. (*continued*)

Content matching rule type	Description
Device OS rules	Endpoint OS—Windows, Mac, or Linux
Indexed data rules	Used for matching unstructured data. Index a set of documents and match them against that index. An index is usually a rolling hash of the contents of the documents.
Exact data rules	Used for matching structure data. Any data in a tabular format like in spreadsheets or databases can be matched.
ML rules	Train the system with a positive set and a negative set to match against the content.
Channel feature rules	Using features of the channel could lead to a violation. For example, printing any data; storing in USB; copying data to a shared folder, etc.
Bulk operation rules	Large download/upload/copy/move of files
Popular unique identifiers rules	There are unique identifiers that are used by each country like SSN, ITIN, Passport No, and Indian Aadhar Card to uniquely identify people.
Classification-based rules	Detect previously classified documents by their classification tags
Common file format rules	Tax statements, W2 statements, driving license, etc.
Malware or threat rules	Detection of malware or viruses
OCR based rules	Using OCR to detect image contents and rules to detect violations based on the contents. Can be used in conjunction with other rules.
User behavioral rules	Like copying a file, or sharing a folder (though covered in the channel there can be extensive options here)
Custom script rules	Allow policy authors to write custom scripts

CHAPTER 3   THINKING OUTSIDE NORMS

As a developer of a security solution, you have the freedom to devise your matching algorithm and rule types. The quality and diversity of rule types directly correlate with the flexibility and effectiveness of the solution.

In our running example, we could use the following rule types for various use cases given some conditions are met.

Use Case 1: GAH wants to keep track of all employees who print out a prescription or drug usage procedure.

- Channel feature rules to detect print
- Keyword-based rule to detect keywords in prescription keyword list as defined
- Regular expressions to identify drug code identifiers
- Popular Identifier-based rule to identify drug code identifiers
- Prescription and drug usage procedure documents if classified, then the classification-based rules can be used
- OCR-based rule if the prescription is scanned as an image and printed out
- Custom script rules to detect prescription and drug usage procedure documents
- Indexed data rule assuming prescriptions are unstructured documents
- If prescriptions are in a standard format used by GAH then a structured document matching rule or ML-based rule type can be used.

Use Case 2: GAH wants to block all outgoing emails containing prescriptions in the body or attachments from non-doctors to external email address domains.

CHAPTER 3   THINKING OUTSIDE NORMS

All the rules specified in the above use case can also be used here to detect prescriptions. In addition, the following can be used.

- Context-based rule to detect sender, recipients, and email domains
- File attribute-based rule to detect prescription as an attachment

Use Case 3: GAH wants to ensure sensitive information doesn't get into shares that have access to employees in the group "Non-doctors."

To detect sensitive information, all the rules specified under use case 1 can be used. In addition, the following can be considered.

- User behavior rules such as upload, copy, and move to detect data moving into shares
- Specific rules for Cloud Applications and Network Share channels to detect data movement

Use Case 4: GAH wants to restrict emails with unreleased hospital revenue details only among executives.

- Context-based rule to detect sender, and recipients
- Keyword-based rule to detect keywords in hospital revenue details as defined
- OCR-based rule if revenue details are scanned as an image and sent out in email
- Custom script rules to detect unreleased hospital revenue details
- Indexed data rule assuming revenue details are unstructured documents

115

- If revenue details are in a standard format used by GAH then a structured document matching rule or ML-based rule type can be used

- Common file format rules, if the revenue details follow a standard press release format

- Classification-based rules if revenue details document is pre-classified

Use Case 5: GAH requires patient bills exceeding $10,000 to be authorized exclusively by the Chief Doctor and not shared with anyone other than patients and the billing department.

- Context-based rule to detect sender, and recipients

- Keyword-based rule to detect bills

- OCR-based rule if bill details are scanned as an image and sent out in email

- Custom script rules to detect patient bills

- If bills are in a standard format used by GAH then a structured document matching rule or ML-based rule type can be used

- Classification-based rules if bills are pre-classified

- If the bills have specific file format extensions then file attribute match can also be used

Security Violations

In this section, we dig into the fascinating world of security violations, examining their lifecycle from inception to resolution purely from an analytical perspective. We'll dissect the structure and stages that each

CHAPTER 3   THINKING OUTSIDE NORMS

violation undergoes, weighing the pros and cons along the way. What improvements can be made? This chapter challenges you to expand your thinking and explore beyond traditional boundaries, encouraging a fresh perspective on security analysis.

Security Violation Remediation

More than just generating security violations, remediation and assisting businesses in remedying their violations are crucial. What is the lifecycle of a violation? Let's understand from Figure 3-2.

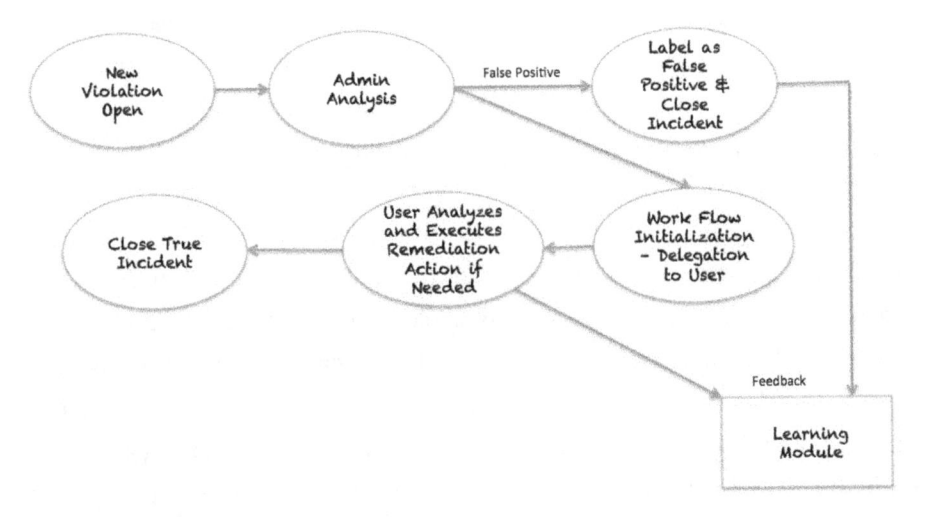

Figure 3-2. Violation Lifecycle

After a violation is generated, the next step is for it to appear in the UI, be available via an API, or be accessible through reports for the persona "Violation Remediator." Remediation involves analyzing the violation to determine if it is a false positive or a true violation. If it's a false positive, it should be marked as such or tagged in a manner that the security system understands. The solution should learn from the feedback given by the remediator, as false positives can occur due to diverse parameters.

For example, if it's an email violation, the sender might be authorized to send that content or the recipients might be approved to receive it. Similarly, for a CASB channel DAR violation, it might be acceptable to have the data in that folder with appropriate permissions for shared users. Learning and adapting to the environment is a step-by-step process. With continuous feedback and analysis of patterns, the security solution should be able to automatically remediate false positives to lessen the load on the violation remediator. If necessary, the remediator can review the false positive violations.

If the violation is genuine, the remediator needs to analyze its severity. Has remediation occurred? By remediation, I mean actions like blocking, quarantining, deleting, etc. Is the data safe? If no remediation has taken place, steps for remediation should be initiated. Policies should be modified if necessary, especially in cases of serious threats such as lack of coverage.

I would advise security vendors to auto-remediate violations as much as possible and not wait for violation remediators to take action. In many cases, the security solution may not have enough feedback to auto-remediate. In those cases, the security software can provide easy ways for remediators to group violations and remediate them. For example, if an email with financial data was remediated as quarantine, a suggestion could be provided to create or update a policy with a quarantine response rule so remediators don't have to remediate manually. If a remediation rule was already applied, another suggestion could be to auto-remediate and close the violation.

For enterprises, look at ways to automate violation remediation. Remediating violations is mandatory to prevent data breaches. If you are generating too many violations based on your organization-wide policy, then try separating those violations and tagging them. Having a way to mark those violations separately from the genuine violations is good for safeguarding data, as it is the most important job here. Delegating the work to multiple team members also reduces the workload.

Archive violations by date or type so you can easily look them up later. Continuous monitoring will lead to violations, and security systems will not notify of the same vulnerability multiple times. Hence, it is better to act immediately.

Before we dive deep into feedback, let's look at the scale and format of security violations that organizations have to deal with today.

Problems with Existing Violation Structure

It's quite astonishing, but large organizations usually amass millions of violations each month. Some even gather millions daily. When it reaches this scale, it's less about safeguarding and more about compliance. They gather such vast amounts of data to have evidence for potential future incidents. However, even managing a thousand violations daily can be extremely challenging and resource-intensive for remediation purposes.

Consider the immense scale and performance demands placed on security systems tasked with collecting a million violations daily. Your system must demonstrate robustness in handling violations, distributing updated policies and settings, and gathering system health information. It necessitates a substantial distributed system with resilience and robustness ingrained in every component.

The violations observed in the field typically adhere to a generic format, characterized by the fields outlined in Table 3-3. Violations are typically listed individually, each with its own set of fields. Violation remediators then need to address them one by one. This approach isn't very scalable. Some organizations attempt to streamline the process by delegating remediation tasks to various individuals, but it still takes considerable time and often yields no significant insights.

Table 3-3. *Violation Fields*

Violation field	Description
Violation number	A running number to keep track of violations
Violation event date	The date on which the event specific to this violation occurred
Violation persisted or received date	The date on which the violation was received by the administrative console for processing.
Violated policies	Policies this event violated. Note that information would be present on specific policy versions that were active when this event occurred
Violated channel	The channel on which the violation occurred
Violation proof	Matching snippets of information from the event that shows the violation
Remediation actions taken	Remediation actions that were taken
Sender and recipients	Sender and recipients if this is an email-related violation
URL	If this is a network-related violation then the URL
Cloud application	The name of the cloud application if this is a cloud violation
Endpoint device	The laptop, PC, or BYOD hostname on which the event occurred
Network share folder	If the event occurred on a network share
Collaborators of share	Network Share collaborators if applicable
User behavior suspicious event	Suspicious Event details on user behavior
User responsible for event	The user name of the user who was behind this event

(*continued*)

Table 3-3. (*continued*)

Violation field	Description
On the corporate or off the corporate	On corporate network or off the network
Violating content	The original content that caused the violation
Notes from violation remediator	Violation remediator notes
Violation remediation workflow	If a workflow is initialized after this violation then the details regarding that
Violation history	The history of this violation since the time the administrative console received the violation

Can you identify any issues with this structure? It seems to focus solely on violations, doesn't it? While having details about the violation is important, what about understanding its underlying intent or identifying correlations with other violations? How can we ensure that similar violations are prevented in the future? In some instances, the same violation might not recur because the security solution has implemented a remediation action to stop it. However, what about different scenarios?

For instance, in our hypothetical example, consider a situation where someone violates use case 3 by copying sensitive information into a network share folder accessible by non-doctors. The remediation action could involve disallowing that action or removing the document from the network share. However, this doesn't prevent any other employee from repeating the same action. In this context, we're not discussing how to educate employees on avoiding such actions, but rather what actions our security solution can take to prevent such occurrences altogether.

CHAPTER 3   THINKING OUTSIDE NORMS

Enhancement Options

False positive feedback is very critical to reduce the number of violations. Grouping and categorizing violations is the first thing a security solution should do as remediators can remediate incidents in bulk rather than dealing with them one after the other. When violation remediators perform actions to remediate—each action should be considered a learning opportunity. False Positive is not the only tag that they can apply to a violation. They can tag the violations with other statuses that are readily available or they can create custom statuses. Possible status options are resolved, auto-resolved, closed, false positive, known violation type, need to be analyzed, need to be triaged, analyzed, vulnerability exposed, triaged, and so on. By creating these statuses, the violation remediator sets a precedence of orderly remediation in the system with clear categorization of these violations. Auto-learning systems can learn this categorization and appropriately categorize violations. This level of categorization would be extremely useful during compliance audits.

Let me illustrate with a few examples from our hypothetical example involving GAH.

Use Case 1: GAH wants to keep track of all employees who print out a prescription or drug usage procedure.

Our security solution triggers violations for each instance of printing a prescription. As discussed earlier, prescription printing is standard practice at GAH, resulting in potentially hundreds or even thousands of prints daily, each generating a violation. When a violation remediator flags such a violation as auto-resolved, we can proceed to mark all print violations as auto-resolved after confirming with the remediator. Furthermore, new print violations can also be auto-resolved to prevent them from appearing in the remediation queue. Once a violation is marked as auto-resolved, it is considered remediated and reflected in our violation reports and compliance records as non-vulnerabilities.

CHAPTER 3   THINKING OUTSIDE NORMS

Use Case 2: GAH wants to block all outgoing emails containing prescriptions in the body or attachments from non-doctors to external email address domains.

When violation remediators stumble upon these violations, they might discover that they've already been resolved and promptly close them out. It's like a digital detective solving cases before they even hit the desk! The security solution can even take the wheel here, automatically marking similar violations as resolved. But hey, not every case gets a quick fix. If a violation needs a closer look, it's crucial to keep a watchful eye on previously resolved ones to see how they're being handled. Maybe there's a new twist in the tale that needs attention, like a secret note from the remediator saying, "Hey, these folks are cool to send prescription emails." It's all about fine-tuning the system's understanding of the business rules. Learning and evolving based on these insights are the secret sauce for an autonomous data security solution.

Now, imagine if our security solution could learn to fix things itself! By studying how violation remediators tackle issues and gathering enough insights, the system could start rolling out its remedies. Of course, it's not a one-bot show—feedback from the human experts is always welcome to keep things running smoothly. It's like having a cyber sidekick that learns from the best and becomes a pro in its own right!

There are other factors to think about when designing a masterful data security solution. They are covered in the subsequent sections.

Choosing Target Segment

I know it might be counterintuitive for many of you reading this book, but time and time again, I have seen many solutions fail because they were generically built and do not target a specific segment. The requirements are different for different segments, although data protection remains the common goal. Based on the amount of resources and time, building for a specific segment is better.

CHAPTER 3   THINKING OUTSIDE NORMS

So, how many segments are there? There are two broad divisions, but you can subdivide it further. For now, let's focus on the broad two. You can design a solution for Small and Medium Businesses (SMBs) or Large Businesses. When organizations choose to deploy security solutions, they should evaluate the target segment of the solution and match it up against their organization's size. Don't assume that a product designed for large organizations will work well for small and medium businesses. It won't and can be explained with a sample scenario below.

Let's consider the scenario where the security solution integrates with Azure AD. Azure AD provides six modes of authentication:

1. Username/password

2. Multi-Factor Authentication (MFA)

3. Certificate-Based

4. Federated Authentication (leveraging the organization's existing AD credentials to log in)

5. Single Sign-On

6. Conditional Access (based on device location, application, and compliance status).

A security vendor attempting to integrate with Azure AD might plan to implement username/password-based authentication and move on to the next requirement or integration. However, a large customer might have a policy in their organization that mandates the use of Federated Authentication or Certificate-Based Authentication for AD. These requirements are unlikely to be met by a vendor who built a solution for the SMB segment. Further, there are many nuances in each feature. To expand further, try answering the following questions. In certificate-based authentication—who manages the certificates? Should organizations deploy additional software to maintain their certificates, or should there be a built-in management system? How can we ensure the timely renewal of certificates? Is a simple alert enough to notify administrators if a certificate expires?

Solutions catering to large organizations should build integrations with detailed considerations on every option that is available to use. If you are still wondering about answers to the questions in the above paragraph, then a potential solution could be: The Security solution can notify solution administrators via email a month before a certificate expires. This must be done, even if external solutions manage third-party certificates. Timely reminders are a must as business continuity is paramount. Security solutions can perform basic certificate revocation checks to ensure validity.

Security vendors targeting SMBs aim to grab market share, as there are tens of thousands of businesses worldwide that need such solutions. Hence, they aim to satisfy every requirement a customer has, going wide rather than deep.

As a security vendor, how do you choose your target segments? You need to align your overall business goals and vision with the products you build. If you aim to expand globally and capture market share rapidly or if your organization has limited resources for development and maintenance, then focusing on SMBs should be your priority. Otherwise, targeting large enterprises might be more suitable if you are already a prominent player in the security industry and aim to expand with a data protection solution.

For such vendors who are targeting large businesses, customer retention and delivering enhanced value to existing clients would be paramount. This approach allows for a focus on product quality and thoroughness in the development process.

One question that has often arisen during my years of service at cybersecurity organizations is: "Can I design a solution for specific verticals?" The simple answer to this is "no." However, you can design certain elements specific to verticals. You can incorporate some pre-made policies and configurations specific to verticals, but not the entire solution.

CHAPTER 3　THINKING OUTSIDE NORMS

Many security vendors already offer point solutions and seek to expand into data protection by creating even more new point solutions. However, a key consideration during expansion is how well their existing solutions integrate with their new solutions. Managing different point solutions can lead to maintenance challenges for both the security vendor and the organizations adopting them.

Prioritization is the key to building solutions. Consider this real-world scenario: A medium-segment customer already using one of your solutions is interested in your newly developed data protection solution for the cloud. As a security vendor, you primarily support Cloud Email and Cloud Application Data Protection (CASB) channels and focus on SMBs. While you already support Microsoft O365 and Google Drive integrations, the medium-segment customer seeks support for the Salesforce application. Balancing the needs of various customers while prioritizing organizational goals can be challenging. There is no definitive answer; it depends on evaluating the asks by the medium-segment customer. If the feature request aligns with the needs of other SMBs, prioritize it; otherwise, focus on other customers.

Consider the same scenario where the medium-segment customer requests a new remediation rule for file quarantine. Here, focusing on other customers might be more appropriate, assuming that both supporting the Salesforce application and implementing the new remediation rule require similar resources.

Though this book isn't solely about prioritization, I wanted to discuss the above example to highlight the importance of choosing the right customer segment. The same principles apply if a large customer requests a new remediation rule—prioritize their needs, as they seek depth in solutions, and others may follow suit.

Choosing Deployment Environment and Channels

By deployment environment, I refer to On-premise, Cloud, and Hybrid environments. Most security vendors who are starting fresh aim to target the cloud use cases, as supporting on-premise installation is a significant commitment. However, dear readers, I don't want you to get bogged down by what other vendors do. What makes sense to your organization? Decide based on that.

You might have a couple of questions in your mind right now:

1. If I develop and operate a solution in the cloud, wouldn't I be able to provide support for all on-premise components if required?

2. Do most organizations eventually transition to the cloud?

Let me tackle both questions now.

Wouldn't I be able to provide support for all on-premise components if required?

Running a solution in the cloud and supporting all on-premise components is impractical. There are several reasons for this.

- Content detection at scale is not possible from the cloud if the data resides in on-premise servers.

- Highly expensive for customers to manage on-premise data assets from the cloud.

- Achieving comprehensiveness in coverage points is impossible from the cloud.

CHAPTER 3   THINKING OUTSIDE NORMS

Do most organizations eventually transition to the cloud??

This is a fundamental dilemma for organizations, security vendors, and everyone involved. The reasons are below:

- We will never be 100% cloud-based if you ask me until we have physical offices. There will always be components in the on-premise infrastructure. Perhaps the infrastructure maintenance may not fall under the onus of the organizations that use them, and it might be offered as a service, such as "On-premise as a Service" or "Data Center as a Service."

- Many organizations do not consider the cloud as secure, and they may never do so.

- Government organizations might opt for a hybrid approach but might never fully transition to the cloud. This situation is akin to saying we will never need to print again because everything is digital now. Despite the digital shift, we continue to print papers and documents, demonstrating the persistence of traditional practices alongside digital advancements.

Enterprises often end up evaluating the security of the data in their on-premise infrastructure vs. in the cloud. Consider Table 3-4 to decide the factors involved in installing and maintaining an on-premise organization-managed data security solution vs. a security vendor-managed hosted cloud data security solution.

CHAPTER 3 THINKING OUTSIDE NORMS

Table 3-4. *On-Premise vs. Cloud Storage Security Considerations*

Considerations for on-premise	Considerations for cloud
Installation and upgrades	Service availability
Licensing	Single tenant vs. multitenant
Maintenance and support	Public vs. private cloud
Resiliency, and robustness	Encryption and key rotation
Scalability	Play well with business workflows
Integrations to business tools	
Play well with on-premise appliances	

Security vendors should make the choice of supported channels based on the market segment that they are supporting. If you are targeting large customers, it is more likely that you should be on-premise and hybrid. If you are catering only to SMBs, you can get away with supporting only cloud-based solutions.

Some security vendors have only email protection or endpoint solutions, and they need to be more comprehensive and need to support all the channels that we discussed in Chapter 2. Getting to comprehensiveness is a long and committed journey for security vendors. Based on my observations, prioritizing channel support in the following sequence can effectively enhance revenue generation and expand the customer base. First, focus on implementing Email support (both Cloud-based and On-premise solutions). Next, integrate CASB (Cloud Access Security Broker) solutions. Then, address network support, encompassing both Cloud and on-premise environments. Subsequently, prioritize the Endpoint support, followed by Network Share support. Finally, consider implementing support for "Bring Your Own Device" (BYOD) scenarios.

129

CHAPTER 3   THINKING OUTSIDE NORMS

Mode of Usage

As a security vendor or enterprise administrator, the most crucial aspect in designing or selecting a data security solution is how the network architecture has been laid out and how organizations (customers) will configure and utilize the solution itself. Consider all the personas discussed in Chapter 2. How will each persona utilize the data security solution? At this juncture, let's review a few real-world scenarios so that you know how organizations use the security solution.

Scenario 1: An enterprise business has installed a data security solution to ensure compliance with data regulations.

Output Needed: Compliance reports every quarter.

If compliance reporting is the primary goal of an enterprise (as most enterprises indeed install data security solutions to meet compliance regulations and standards), the solution should offer robust options for generating various reports. Reports are generated based on violations that have been found in the past and also based on continuous monitoring results. If the organization doesn't meet compliance standards, then the report should expand on the vulnerabilities. Organizations will have additional resources to remediate the vulnerabilities to meet compliance standards.

These types of enterprises may not remediate security violations daily. This might be primarily because of resource constraints, or they would just like to collect all violations and review only if necessary. Occasional adjustments to policies may occur, but the primary focus will be on reporting. As a security vendor, your approach should prioritize breadth over depth. Enterprises require a solution capable of reporting on vulnerabilities across all channels. User analytics, risk scores, and compliance reports covering various data regulations such as GDPR, HIPAA, CCPA, PDPA, etc., need to encompass all channels.

CHAPTER 3 THINKING OUTSIDE NORMS

Scenario 2: An enterprise business has installed a data security solution to ensure all its Intellectual Property (IP) is safe.

Output Needed: No data breaches. Everything in control

All sensitive data specific to the enterprise must be kept safe. Therefore, policies must be robust and offer a wide variety of matching criteria to safeguard confidential data. IP could be in any format. For example, a manufacturing company could consider its designs IP, whereas a lab might consider all its formulae IP. Hence, as each vertical is different, IP could be a document, image file, video, etc. Content detection technologies should be advanced enough to capture all file formats. Remediation rules are essential. Continuous monitoring of data assets to maintain data control at all times is crucial. Rather than focusing solely on reporting and analytics, the enterprise business would prioritize data control and ensure there are additional resources available to remediate all security violations.

Security policy administrators would be constantly tuning policies, and comprehensive channel coverage, or at least coverage of channels where IP data can reside, should be ensured. In this mode, you would follow users with IP access rather than the data. Classification may be necessary to classify IP data, thereby preventing data breaches. Identity and access management, as well as encryption, could all be valuable.

Scenario 3: An enterprise business has installed a data security solution to ensure all its customer data is safe.

Output Needed: No leak of customer PII.

These are enterprises mostly in the banking, insurance, or healthcare sectors, where customer data confidentiality is paramount. Leaking customer Personally Identifiable Information (PII) could result in a damaged reputation and, more importantly, loss of trust among the enterprise's loyal customer base. Organizations will do everything to ensure customer data is safeguarded. Policies will be oriented toward customer information, and all employees with access to customer data will be closely monitored. Here, classification is not as important as continuous

131

CHAPTER 3   THINKING OUTSIDE NORMS

monitoring and tracking. Security vendors need to follow the data rather than the users in this scenario. Coverage is important but limited to customer data storage locations. For instance, if none of the customer data is ever supposed to be left on-premises, then cloud protection is not a priority. Reporting and a ton of configuration options are not needed, but pre-canned policies to protect customers' data might be necessary. We will focus on a model where policies can be system-generated as well in our next chapter.

Scenario 4: An enterprise has installed a data security solution to ensure that all its data is safe, whether it is internal or external.

Output Needed: No data breaches. All data is under control at all times.

Scale and performance are important here, besides the depth of policy coverage and continuous monitoring. This is a scenario involving a paranoid customer, particularly in the financial or federal defense sectors, where they are persistent about avoiding any leaks. Everything is kept confidential, making encryption crucial. Reporting and automatic remediation to protect data are expected. Channel coverage should be comprehensive, with absolute tracking of all users and data.

Scenario 5: An enterprise has installed a data security solution to ensure the safety of all its financial data.

Output Needed: No breaches of financial data.

This scenario is highly specific to safeguarding only financial information. It may pertain to a business operating in the financial trading sector, where confidentiality of all trades is paramount. The risk of a breach in financial data could lead to significant issues in the stock market for the enterprise. Pre-canned financial data protection policies are essential. Specific channel coverage is all that is needed.

Scenario 6: An enterprise has installed a data security solution to ensure all their data in the cloud is safe.

Output Needed: No breaches on cloud data

This is an enterprise that has recently adopted cloud technology and wants to ensure comprehensive protection for its data in the cloud. Comprehensive coverage of cloud channels with continuous monitoring and reporting is necessary. Classification and encryption may not be as important as ensuring support for all the cloud applications used by the enterprise.

Scenario 7: An enterprise is a consultant for many other organizations. They deploy their personnel to work on their client cases and all the data must be kept separate and no breaches are allowed.

Output Needed: No mix-up of client data and strictly no breaches

The business requires internal data segregation. Predefined policies and integration with Active Directory (AD) or user information for each project are necessary, likely using AD groups. Data within a client's domain should not be left externally while an employee is working with the client. Therefore, besides identity and access management, file cleanup after the client contract ends is essential. Whether on-premises or in the cloud, Network Share channel or CASB-DAR (Cloud Access Security Broker—Data at Rest) is required to ensure all files are properly cleaned up post-assignment. Reports specific to vulnerability and risk status for each enterprise's project are also needed.

All the above scenarios are not comprehensive, but tools to guide your mind to think toward how organizations perceive and use security solutions. The way described above might not be the only way to address their use cases.

Utilization Based on Personas

Each persona using the security solution has different goals and objectives. Hence, they expect a unique set of features too. We are reviewing how products are being used in depth both in the previous and the current sections to emphasize that feature adoption and customer retention are super critical for security products to drive business revenue.

CHAPTER 3   THINKING OUTSIDE NORMS

Features expected by the IT Administrator:

- Easy Setup and Maintenance
- Provisioning
- Add users' roles, provide access
- Generate Vulnerability Reports
- System Health Monitoring
- Overall Organizational Compliance
- Cloud Application Onboarding
- Scale and performance of the entire system

Features expected by the Policy Administrator:

- Easy Policy Authoring
- Extensive content-matching options
- Integrations to AD, classification, and encryption systems
- Policy audit logs and policy versioning
- Policy testing
- Policy coverage gap reports
- Policy import and export
- Customizable policies by channel
- Continuous monitoring policies
- Scale and performance of the entire system

CHAPTER 3 THINKING OUTSIDE NORMS

Features expected by the Violation Manager:

- Violation reports with customizable options
- Violation list and detail pages
- Violation remediation options
- Violation history options
- Integration of violation system with business workflow engines
- Alerting on violations
- Compliance reports
- Scale and performance of the entire system

Features expected by the Security Analyst:

- Threat/Violation/Policy reports
- Compliance reports
- Coverage gap analysis
- Organizational risk scores
- User risk scores
- Business continuity assurance

Features expected by the Compliance/Audit Manager:

- Compliance reports
- Organizational risk scores
- User risk scores
- Past compliance metrics and security gap drift analysis

CHAPTER 3   THINKING OUTSIDE NORMS

Features expected by the CISO or executives:

- Reports on overall deployment and health
- Report on policies/security violations/remediations
- Report on vulnerability/risk scores
- Business continuity assurance

Now, I'm going to categorize the feature expectations into major categories (categorization would be self-explanatory) and review them closely.

Setup, Deployment, and Maintenance

Cloud products have different setup and deployment concerns when compared to on-premise or hybrid deployment scenarios. The primary goal is to make sure it is straightforward to set up and maintain.

Installation/Upgrade of Security Software

This installation and upgrade applies to on-premise solutions and components. Security vendors usually maintain cloud components and they take care of upgrades/downgrades as needed. Installation of Security Software needs to be smooth, with flexible options to configure the product during and after the installation.

Configurations might include setting up of the following:

- Software usage language
- Server components
- Agent components
- Certificates for communication

- Credentials for Integration of encryption servers, classification servers
- Application Boarding Super User Credentials
- Proxies, Load Balancer credentials, and configurations
- Channel configurations—for example, email channel might involve MTA
- Traffic routing configurations
- Threat intelligence server configurations
- Database configurations—this is where policies and violations would be stored

Upgrade of software must be seamless, taking care of the following:

- Settings/configurations retained after upgrade of software components
- Forward and/or backward compatibility between various versions of security software
- Database upgrades
- Less downtime
- Roll back options in case of failures

Administrators need to receive alerts about the health of their security software systems, which include how well the security software is functioning. For instance, they should be notified if certificates are about to expire or if there are credential failures for servers. Additionally, if a policy generates an excessive number of violations, administrators should be alerted accordingly, and so forth. These health alerts and reports ensure the security software coverage duly exists and it can meet compliance and audit requirements.

CHAPTER 3   THINKING OUTSIDE NORMS

Onboarding Application

One of the most common tasks when setting up a cloud system is getting corporate and approved applications onboarded. Corporate applications are the ones given the green light by IT administrators and cleared by compliance and audit teams for organization-wide use. Approved applications, on the other hand, aren't corporate-sanctioned but are still permissible within the organization. For instance, Google might be a corporate application while Skype falls under the approved category. However, some applications aren't allowed within the corporate network because of the potential security risks they pose. For instance, all torrent file-sharing software might be blocked in an organization because of the inherent threats.

When setting up a corporate application, it's crucial to consider the users involved. We need to establish user identities in a way that allows us to connect their actions across various applications and channels. This correlation helps us understand user activities comprehensively. For example, imagine a user named Joe downloads several files from the corporate Google Drive and then sends them via Gmail to his personal email account. If we view these actions separately, it might seem like Joe simply transferred files and accessed Google Drive. However, when we link these actions together, it raises suspicion because it appears Joe is transferring potentially sensitive information to his email account.

In any analytics or UEBA solutions, it's crucial to evaluate user behavior and assign risk scores. To streamline this process, I suggest automatically categorizing the applications used in your organization as corporate, approved, or non-approved. This way, you can generate reports tailored to each category. Additionally, it's helpful to empower administrators with the ability to adjust these categorizations manually if necessary. These enhancements can significantly improve the effectiveness of the solution.

Even if you're using an on-premise solution, you can similarly implement application onboarding and still generate relevant reports automatically. To further enhance usability, consider incorporating application-specific policy options and remediation actions. As a security vendor, focusing on making the solution more automated can provide substantial benefits.

Onboarding Channels

Organizations typically start by installing the basic components of security software and then gradually expand support for different channels over time. Adding a new channel is a major enhancement to the security software. It's essential because it tests the scalability and performance of the software as workloads and coverage areas grow. All relevant policies should automatically apply to the newly added channel. Reports and configurations should also be applied automatically. Additionally, correlation and continuous monitoring systems need to be extended to cover the new channel.

Consider implementing automatic asset discovery. Here's what I mean: Suppose you've just added a new channel like "Endpoints." In that case, your continuous monitoring software should automatically identify all applications installed on each laptop. It should then generate a report highlighting any unapproved applications and assign a risk score to each user accordingly. Additionally, it should identify shared machines with generic logins and report them to the administrator.

On the flip side, if the new channel is "Network Share," the system should automatically discover repositories and identify the root targets for their content. This way, administrators can easily set up scans for continuous monitoring or for meeting audit and compliance requirements.

CHAPTER 3   THINKING OUTSIDE NORMS

Additional Solutions

In this section, let's discuss additional solutions you can build to complement the security software. Remember, the goal is to secure data, so you need to consider all use cases and situations that organizations face today. What supplemental solutions would aid the security software in performing better?

Analytics

By now, you probably recognize the indispensable role of analytics in the effective operation of a security solution. Developing an analytics engine is essential, and it's a straightforward decision that every security vendor should make. This investment serves dual purposes: enhancing the efficacy of their security solution and catering to a range of business needs, particularly in risk assessment for organizations. Let's dig deeper into this concept.

Enhancing the security solution

To establish a robust feedback loop concerning policies, violations, and system data, we need to gather a diverse range of statistics, cache sample data, and user information. This allows us to correlate data from various channels and feed it into an analytics engine. Think of it as a simple data mining solution that tracks and analyzes collected data over time. This process enables us to provide feedback to our own solution, detect anomalies, pinpoint data coverage gaps, and, most importantly, enhance visibility.

Let's illustrate the practical usage of an analytics engine to show what data can be collected using our hypothetical scenario involving Good American Hospitals (GAH).

Here's the type of data we can collect:

- User activities, categorized by roles like Doctors or Nurses
- Comparison of activities within each group
- Scanned data (with partial results)
- Feedback on violations
- Statistics from Data at Rest (DAR) scans on user devices
- Violations across different channels sorted by time
- Violation statistics over various periods, policy changes, data movements, and remediations

This data serves to refine policies, as discussed earlier in this chapter. Some of the advanced use cases that can be built are the following: A system that can learn data movement patterns to optimize performance during peak workloads. Even without complete data classification implemented by organizations, the system can identify sensitive documents and tag them internally, create an index to locate similar documents and offer visibility to policy administrators and violation remediators. By analyzing data and activity patterns, we can detect user intent and prevent certain actions. We are going to see more of this in Chapter 5. This overview demonstrates the importance of innovative thinking when integrating analytics and intelligence into our security solutions.

User Risk Assessment

Comprehensive visibility into suspicious user activities is paramount for administrators in any organization. They need to be able to scrutinize and thwart potential threats, whether they arise from deliberate malicious actions or unintentional behaviors that inadvertently expose sensitive data or create entry points for hackers. A robust analytics solution plays

CHAPTER 3   THINKING OUTSIDE NORMS

a pivotal role in identifying such activities, allowing for the calculation of risk scores that provide administrators with a clear understanding of the level of risk posed by specific actions or patterns. These risk scores serve as valuable indicators that administrators can use to assess the severity of potential threats and take appropriate measures to mitigate them.

The risk patterns and anomalies can be computed by employing a diverse set of heuristics. The analytics engine can dedicate initial time to learning (learning phase) and subsequently develop policies to track specific events or actions. These policies are not exposed to policy administrators but function more like internal rules, informing the content detection engine of what should be collected for analytics-related purposes.

Moreover, this risk assessment process holds significant importance in compliance-related audits. By accurately evaluating the risk associated with various user activities, organizations can ensure adherence to regulatory requirements and industry standards. Administrators can leverage the insights gleaned from risk assessments to demonstrate compliance during audits, thereby bolstering the organization's overall security posture and mitigating potential legal and financial liabilities.

As a cybersecurity professional tasked with designing security solutions, it's important to challenge yourself to explore unconventional approaches to risk assessment. Consider the following: Once risk scores are computed for each employee within an organization, policies can be proposed to policy administrators to detect activities based on these scores and determine whether to permit or prohibit certain actions. For instance, violations originating from a user with a high-risk score may consistently result in heightened violation severity compared to those from a user with a low-risk score.

Organizations can leverage risk scores to arrange appropriate training sessions for users, enhancing their awareness of the security risks they may pose. Implementing additional training and establishing separate tracking for high-risk users within the organization can strengthen overall resilience against threats.

Risk assessment can identify coverage gaps within an organization. For example, pinpointing a specific application as the primary source of violations could prompt policy administrators to devise tailored policies governing its use. Additionally, risk assessment, combined with peer comparison, can inform decisions to revoke access for certain users following significant security breaches.

In essence, visibility into suspicious user activities, enabled by robust analytics and risk assessment mechanisms, empowers administrators to proactively protect their organization's data and infrastructure against evolving security threats and regulatory scrutiny.

SaaS Security Posture Management

SaaS Security Posture Management (SSPM) refers to software that continuously assesses, monitors, and manages the security posture of all cloud applications used in the organization. It involves evaluating various aspects such as configuration settings, user permissions, data handling practices, compliance adherence, and overall security hygiene within SaaS environments.

SSPM software ensures the configurations of cloud applications are compliant and follow industry best practices. In some cases, organizations define configurations that are more restrictive than industry best practices to secure the data. For example, let's assume that the industry best practice for a cloud application user password is 12 characters, organizations may override with a value of 15 bringing more restrictions into the picture.

SSPM's primary features include the following:

- Configuration management
- Configuration drift management and prevention
- Cloud application compliance
- Cloud application risk assessment

CHAPTER 3   THINKING OUTSIDE NORMS

- Discovery of SaaS applications
- Continuous access control monitoring
- Policy configurability, and remediation

SaaS security posture management is something security vendors rarely think about when thinking about the comprehensiveness of a security solution. There are a handful of popular SSPM vendors in the market who support hundreds of applications.

SPM—Spend Management

Spend management involves monitoring the utilization of cloud applications within an organization. Despite investing significant resources and budget in procuring cloud applications for corporate use, many of these applications remain underutilized or unused. However, since licenses have been acquired for these applications, organizations are obligated to protect them, whether they are actively used by employees or not. Therefore, security solution policies must be tailored to safeguard the data that could potentially be accessed through these applications.

Our security solution, acting as a vigilant overseer, continuously monitors user activities, including application usage, and provides detailed reports. Armed with this information, administrators can make informed decisions regarding the necessity of maintaining existing application licenses. In many instances, they may find that certain applications are no longer essential, allowing them to streamline resources and reduce the overall threat landscape.

Summary

In this chapter, we broke away from conventional security norms, delving into the realm of innovative thinking to design robust security solutions. Through a hands-on example, we discovered the limitations of relying solely on traditional policies and regulations, realizing the power of leveraging insights from traffic patterns, violations, and stored data to craft dynamic security protocols. We emphasized the importance of establishing a feedback loop within our security solutions, recognizing its critical role in ensuring effectiveness. Furthermore, we explored the significance of tailoring security solutions to cater to diverse customer segments, recognizing their unique needs and preferences. Along the way, we uncovered how personas and various security scenarios play pivotal roles in shaping product adoption and usage patterns.

As we venture into the forthcoming chapters, we embark on a journey to craft a data security solution that exudes innovation, challenges norms, and deeply grasps business complexities. We aim to fashion a solution that is not only efficient and scalable but also operates autonomously, reducing reliance on rigid policies while maximizing coverage. With a keen eye on ensuring uninterrupted business operations and continuous data safeguarding, we prioritize the development of a solution that operates seamlessly around the clock.

In the next chapter, we delve into the design of the core components of our autonomous solution, drawing from the fundamental requirements outlined in Chapter 1 and acknowledging the limitations of existing solutions highlighted in Chapter 2. Our solution must avoid the pitfalls of its predecessors while integrating the sophisticated concepts discussed in this Chapter to achieve true autonomy and efficacy.

CHAPTER 4

Data Security Solution Design

Let's start our journey toward designing a great data security solution. After exploring the core security requirements and identifying the pitfalls of existing data security solutions, we're well-prepared to begin our design process. The preceding chapter should have provided insights into breaking limitations, a crucial skill for this and subsequent chapters. Without challenging traditional boundaries, we cannot achieve an optimal, forward-thinking solution. This chapter aims to enlighten security vendors and cybersecurity professionals on the essential elements of a data security solution that can be easily extended. I emphasize the importance of extensibility and maintainability; tightly coupled solutions often hinder scalability and adaptability without significant redesign efforts. Throughout this chapter, we will examine the core components that constitute a robust data security solution catering to diverse deployment environments.

Once we've outlined the security solution, subsequent chapters will delve into strategies for autonomy and leveraging AI models to enhance its longevity. It's important to note that this chapter and the next serve as a guide rather than advocating for a specific design approach over others.

For readers within organizations, this chapter offers valuable insights into how security solutions are typically conceived and their capabilities. Armed with this knowledge, you'll be better equipped to ask pertinent questions when engaging with security vendors. It's essential to recognize the limitations of security solutions in memory and CPU-constrained environments, such as mobile and endpoint devices, and to make informed deployment decisions and security policies accordingly.

Steps to Build a Data Protection Solution

Let's recall the security solution's core requirements from Chapter 1. They are

- Identification and remediation of confidential data
- Data security at coverage points
- Ensuring business continuity
- Security solution configurability
- Feedback and learning
- Continuous monitoring
- Scaling

Allow me to distinguish between core requirements and expected outputs. I advocate for keeping outputs like visibility and reporting distinct from the core requirements of a security solution. These outputs will be addressed within the defined use cases, rather than being directly incorporated into the requirements themselves. Put simply, the core requirements outlined here pertain to data protection, while organizational requirements will serve as our use cases.

Building a data protection solution is like constructing a house: you start with a vision of what you want to achieve, then carefully plan each step to bring that vision to life.

First, you need to define the overarching goal of your solution. Just like deciding on the type of house you want to build, whether it's a cozy cottage or a modern mansion, you need a clear idea of what your data protection solution aims to accomplish.

Next, you identify the primary use cases you want your solution to address. These are like the rooms in your house—each serving a specific purpose. Whether it's protecting sensitive data, preventing unauthorized access, or ensuring regulatory compliance, you need to clearly define what problems your solution will solve.

In the real world, once you have your goals and use cases in place, you set key metrics to measure the success of your solution. These metrics are like the milestones in your construction project—they help you track progress and ensure you're moving in the right direction. In this book, we will skip the success metrics and directly jump to the subsequent phase.

With the planning phase complete, it's time to start designing your solution. This is where you translate your requirements and use cases into a blueprint for your data protection solution. Just like designing the layout of a house, you need to create a modular design that is both effective and efficient.

A modular design breaks down your solution into manageable components, each with clear responsibilities. It's like dividing your house into rooms, each serving a specific function. By ensuring each component of your solution has a defined role, you can build a solution that meets all your functional and non-functional requirements.

Overarching Goal

Throughout our journey in the previous chapters, our primary goal has always been to shield sensitive data from falling into the wrong hands. However, putting this into action is far from simple. With data spread across various channels and devices, designing a comprehensive protection strategy requires meticulous planning and dedication.

CHAPTER 4   DATA SECURITY SOLUTION DESIGN

From pinpointing what constitutes sensitive data within an organization to tracking its whereabouts, identifying areas of coverage and potential vulnerabilities demands a significant investment of time and resources. We've emphasized the importance of relying less on rigid security policies, aiming for solutions that can operate autonomously without constant human oversight.

A key aspect of this endeavor is devising effective violation detection methods and implementing appropriate remediation measures to thwart potential threats. Additionally, ensuring comprehensive reporting and visibility of data security violations is crucial for maintaining a robust safeguarding process. Curating all these steps, let's define the overarching goal of an autonomous data security solution.

The goal of an autonomous data protection solution is to proactively safeguard sensitive information without the need for constant manual intervention, utilizing advanced technologies to detect, mitigate, and adapt to security threats in real time.

In this chapter, we'll delve into designing a versatile data security solution, setting the stage for our journey toward autonomy in the next. The key? Building a design that's not only robust but also adaptable.

Use Cases

The comprehensive data protection solution may encompass an array of use cases, yet our primary emphasis is prioritizing the essential and indispensable ones. Organizations, depending on their requirements, will prioritize core use cases. All the use cases below are crucial for any organization and are sufficiently generic to ensure easy relatability. As you review these use cases, dear readers, consider the situations you have encountered within your organization or as a cybersecurity professional.

Use Case 1—Generic Perimeter Protection: Protect confidential data from leaving the organization across various channels.

CHAPTER 4   DATA SECURITY SOLUTION DESIGN

Use Case 1a: Channel support should include both on-premise and cloud channels. On-premise channels should be Network Share, Email, Endpoint, BYOD, and Web. Cloud channels supported should be Cloud Email, Cloud Web, Cloud CASB, and Cloud Endpoint.

Use Case 2—Security Policies: Allow security solution administrators to define and modify security policies to identify sensitive content in the organization.

Use Case 2a: Every security policy should allow security administrators to associate context-matching rules, content-matching rules, exception rules, and in-built remediation actions.

Use Case 2b: Custom content matching conditions, custom remediation actions, and business integrations for triggering remediation actions should be supported.

Use Case 3—Security Violations: Allow security administrators to see security violations and the results of remediation actions when a content violation is detected.

Use Case 4—Reporting: Allow security administrators to generate violation reports, compliance audit reports, scan reports, vulnerability reports, threat reports, and risk assessment reports.

Use Case 5—Suspicious Behavior: Highlight risky users by continuous user monitoring to administrators.

Use Case 5a: Highlight risky channels and applications to administrators. Also, report suspicious user behaviors to the admin.

Use Case 6—Business Continuity: The solution has to be scalable and efficient to ensure uninterrupted operations within the organization.

Use Case 7—Zero Trust: The solution should be able to monitor continuously the threats and data leak attempts to prohibit them from happening and appropriately notify security administrators.

CHAPTER 4   DATA SECURITY SOLUTION DESIGN

Use Case 8—External Integrations: Integration with identity providers, classification solutions, encryption solutions, and business tools used in an organization should be possible across all channels.

Use Case 8a: Integrate with Azure AD to allow the following actions: Azure AD group-based policies and user rules enforcement, Azure AD-based logins to the solution, and Azure AD user hierarchy-based violation remediation workflows.

Use Case 8b: Integrate with the Microsoft Sensitivity Classification solution to classify all my documents in the organization based on the pre-defined labeling hierarchy.

Use Case 8c: Integrate with Microsoft Purview Information Protection solution to encrypt and decrypt content for remediation and content detection, respectively.

Use Case 8d: Integrate with Service Now for triggering incident remediation workflows.

Use Case 9—Auditing: Audit trails on all activities in a security solution should be available for security administrators to view on-demand.

Use Case 9a: Report the audit trail corresponding to all the policy modifications made on policies starting this year 2024.

Use Case 10—RBAC: The security solution should support Role-Based Access Control (RBAC) across various operations, such as policy authoring, violation remediation, and other related tasks.

The sub-use cases outlined above should provide clear examples of scenarios within the primary use case.

These use cases do not explicitly state that organizations are seeking autonomous solutions. As a security vendor, it is essential to anticipate the future needs of organizations and develop solutions accordingly. This approach mirrors Steve Jobs' method of innovation, as he did not rely on explicit user requirements when creating the iPhone.

CHAPTER 4　DATA SECURITY SOLUTION DESIGN

Core Components Identification

Now, we're diving into the heart of our mission: designing an autonomous data protection solution. A good design should always be based on both requirements and use cases. Requirements outline the overall capabilities and characteristics of the system, providing a foundation for the design. Use cases, on the other hand, offer specific examples of how users interact with the system to fulfill their needs or achieve their goals. Together, they inform the design process, ensuring that the final solution meets both the overarching objectives and the specific user requirements.

Let's start by pinpointing the essential functions required for each core use case. As we dive deep into these functions, we'll carefully consider their inputs and outputs, ensuring clarity and precision. We'll also evaluate who will utilize each function within the broader solution. Simultaneously, we'll gauge each function against our core requirements, ensuring alignment and effectiveness every step of the way.

At this juncture, defining our scope and outlining what this design will exclude is important. Firstly, we won't dig into UI interfaces and associated designs, as each security vendor has the flexibility to tailor their UI to complement the intricate backend. Additionally, we'll steer clear of discussions regarding deployment options, whether it be in the cloud or on-premises, and the specifics of cloud vendor tools or on-premises installations. Similarly, we won't delve into the intricacies of reporting interfaces or report formatting. To reiterate, our primary objective with this design is to establish clear responsibilities for the core components that underpin any robust data protection solution.

As you make your way through this first use case, you'll have a clear understanding of our intentions. So, let's get started without delay!

Use Case 1—Generic Perimeter Protection: Protect confidential data from leaving the organization across various channels

CHAPTER 4   DATA SECURITY SOLUTION DESIGN

To safeguard confidential data effectively, we require a robust content detection engine. This engine should have the capability to identify sensitive content by comparing incoming data against predefined rules or intelligent criteria. It's crucial that this engine can adapt and perform efficiently in both on-premise and cloud environments. Additionally, considering the endpoint channel, where shipping all data to the cloud for detection may not be feasible, the engine should be deployable on endpoints and even on mobile devices, despite the stringent requirements on memory and CPU.

Another essential component is the Channel Data Interceptors. These interceptors play a vital role in reading or intercepting data and forwarding it to the content detection engine for threat prevention. For instance, specific interceptors may be required for decoding endpoint channel DIM events or for reading data in the case of Endpoint DAR. Each channel may necessitate its own set of interceptors, tailored to its unique requirements.

Furthermore, we need a Policy Engine that allows policy administrators to author and implement policies effectively. This engine should support a flexible policy language, granting administrators the granular control needed to create specific or broad policies. It should also offer interfaces for building compound content-matching rules, context-matching rules, exceptions, and remediation actions.

Lastly, a Violation Processor is essential to manage security violations generated by the content detection engine. This processor should enable users to review violations and provide feedback. Moreover, it should facilitate external business integrations to streamline organizational workflows. These integrations may include a remediation engine, allowing violators to execute remediation actions manually, if required.

With the content detection engine, channel data interceptors, policy engine, and violation processors in place, we're well-equipped to tackle the first use case. As illustrated below in Figure 4-1, the inputs and outputs for each component are clearly defined.

CHAPTER 4   DATA SECURITY SOLUTION DESIGN

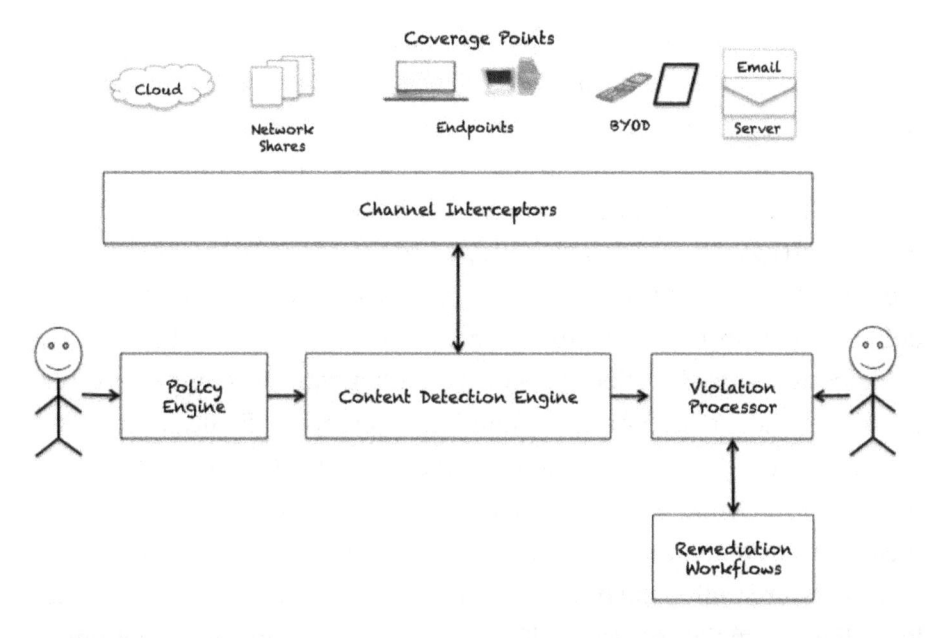

Figure 4-1. *Block Diagram of Basic Components in a Security Solution*

The basic components represented in Figure 4-1 will evolve, and the design specifics for each component will be elaborated on in the subsequent sections of this chapter.

Use Case 2—Security Policies: Allow security solution administrators to define and modify security policies to identify sensitive content in the organization.

In this scenario, the primary need is for security solution administrators to establish policies, a task facilitated by the policy engine component described in the previous use case. In addition to the policy engine, it would be beneficial to provide pre-built policies and rules as templates to simplify the process for policy administrators. These pre-built models can serve as ready-made solutions that administrators can either directly apply or customize based on their specific requirements. By offering pre-built models, compliance and data regulations such as

CHAPTER 4   DATA SECURITY SOLUTION DESIGN

HIPAA and Sarbanes-Oxley (SOX) can be translated into policy templates. This approach adds significant value to organizations, eliminating the need for them to create policies from scratch to adhere to these regulatory standards.

Just like the policy models, pre-built unique identifiers can also be provided to ease the burden on policy administrators. These identifiers are incorporated into the policy engine through user-friendly interfaces. They define specific formats and any additional rules associated with them. For instance, a standard US Social Security number typically comprises three digits, a hyphen, two more digits, another hyphen, and finally, four digits. However, exceptions exist; numbers can't start with 000, 666, or range from 900 to 999, and they must not end with 00. Rather than requiring organizations to manually define these parameters, pre-built unique identifiers streamline the process. Moreover, specifying exceptions to these identifiers is crucial as they significantly reduce false positive violations.

With a robust policy engine in place, we can tackle use case 2. Further details on the efficiency and effectiveness of the policy engine will be discussed later in this chapter.

Use Case 3—Security Violations: Allow security administrators to see security violations and the results of remediation actions when a content violation is detected.

For this particular use case, the essential component required is a violation processor. A critical aspect of the violation processor is its ability to swiftly receive and process violations in sub-millisecond time frames. As mentioned previously, many systems experience a high volume of security violations daily, reaching millions, thus necessitating efficient processing capabilities. Each violation typically entails additional remediation actions, such as administrator notifications, manager alerts, or integration with business systems like Jira and ServiceNow to initiate remedial workflows.

Another vital consideration pertains to the storage requirements for these violations and the duration of their retention. Violations can consume significant storage space, especially when retaining the original content responsible for the violation. Retaining this original content may be necessary for violation remediators' actions, compliance requirements, or audit clearance checks. Additionally, retaining original content can serve as forensic evidence for future investigations.

Use Case 4—Reporting: Allow security administrators to generate violation reports, compliance audit reports, scan reports, vulnerability reports, threat reports, and risk assessment reports.

For this particular use case, a reporting engine is essential. While we won't delve deeply into the specific requirements of the reporting engine here, the engine must support a variety of report types. These may include policy reports, policy audit reports, violation reports, threat reports, scan reports, continuous monitoring reports, user monitoring reports, compliance reports, audit reports, risk assessment reports, and more. Additionally, each report should offer extensive customization options, allowing users to specify date ranges and various criteria to tailor the reports to their specific needs.

Use Case 5—Suspicious Behavior: Highlight risky users by continuous user monitoring to administrators.

For effective continuous monitoring, it's crucial to focus on DAR use cases across all communication channels. However, some channels, like Email, might not have specific DAR use cases. Regular scans are necessary to detect any violations, which should be triggered by changes in policies, system updates (especially those informed by intelligent feedback), or data modifications.

All Data-in-Motion (DIM) events are monitored by default. To effectively manage DAR use cases, it's important to cross-reference user behavior to spot any unusual activities.

CHAPTER 4   DATA SECURITY SOLUTION DESIGN

For example, imagine you have a policy that restricts employees from accessing sensitive files outside of working hours. By cross-referencing user behavior, you can compare normal access patterns with current activity. If an employee who typically accesses files only during office hours suddenly tries to access sensitive data at midnight, this deviation from their usual pattern would be flagged as anomalous.

This approach helps in identifying potential security breaches or policy violations. The final step involves using an analytics engine that collects and connects this information to produce comprehensive risk assessment reports, helping you understand and manage risks associated with user behavior and system activity.

Use Case 6—Business Continuity: The solution has to be scalable and efficient to ensure uninterrupted operations within the organization.

This requirement is non-functional, ensuring the scalability, performance, and reliability of the solution. Business continuity remains a top priority. This use case demands efficient components and robust implementation capable of flexible scaling, whether in the cloud or on-premise. Fail-open and fail-close approaches are crucial for a content detection engine, ensuring uninterrupted operations.

Use Case 7—Zero Trust: The solution should be able to monitor continuously the threats and data leak attempts to prohibit them from happening and appropriately notify security administrators.

In use case 6, continuous monitoring within a security solution is vital for storing partial results and adapting to the environment. A reasoning module, capable of deducing from authored policies, partial results, violation processing feedback, and user activities, is essential for effectively addressing data exfiltration attempts.

Use Case 8—Auditing: Audit trails on all activities in a security solution should be available for security administrators to view on-demand.

Maintaining a history of entity modifications ensures the existence of an audit trail. This trail should encompass historical events, including timestamps and responsible parties. Additionally, providing the old and new values, where applicable, would be beneficial. Fulfilling this requirement necessitates the implementation of a statistics collection engine.

Use Case 9—External Integrations: Integration with identity providers, classification solutions, encryption solutions, and business tools used in an organization should be possible across all channels.

To meet this requirement, the system should be designed in a modular fashion and capable of interacting with external systems for tasks such as classification and encryption. While no specific components are mandated, the existing modules should be seamlessly integrate-able with other business tools. Typically, API-based communication would be employed, enabling the security solution to support various functions from authentication to data transfer.

Use Case 10—RBAC: The security solution should support Role-Based Access Control (RBAC) across various operations, such as policy authoring, violation remediation, and other related tasks.

A user role processing module is essential to establish role-based access control (RBAC) across different system entities such as policies, violations, configurations, analytics, reporting, etc. This module enables security administrators to define a variety of roles with distinct permissions. Subsequently, administrators can create users and assign them to their respective roles, thus ensuring the implementation of a robust RBAC system.

After examining all the requirements and use cases, we're ready to consolidate the component needs for a reliable and scalable data protection solution. The essential components encompass:

- Content Detection Engine
- Policy Engine

CHAPTER 4   DATA SECURITY SOLUTION DESIGN

- Violation Processor
- Remediation Execution Engine
- Analytics Engine
- Reporting Engine
- Statistics Engine
- Reasoning Module
- Feedback Processor
- User and Role Processor

Several of these identified components facilitate the autonomy of the solution. This chapter will concentrate on the core, with the autonomous aspect being addressed in the subsequent chapter. The interactions between these components are summarized in Figure 4-2.

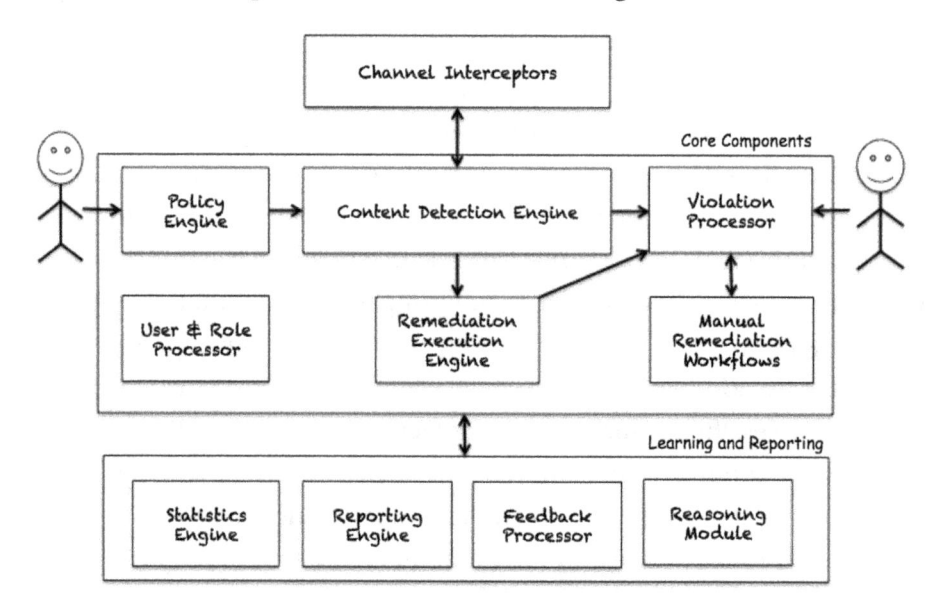

Figure 4-2. Block Diagram of All Components in a Security Solution

Design of Core Components

Now, we're venturing into the exciting phase of designing each component to meet our diverse needs. As we dive into the design process, we must keep a keen eye on both functional and non-functional requirements. Designing each component entails defining its responsibilities and how it collaborates with other components. Remember, our design should be adaptable, whether it's in the cloud or on-premises. Stay tuned for the next section, where we'll fine-tune and apply specific constraints, especially for endpoints and mobile devices. After completing the design of all our components, we will explore the entire layout in various configurations in the next chapter.

Content Detection Engine Internals

We'll start by exploring the inputs and outputs for the content detection engine, ensuring they align with the requirements we've previously defined. As we delve into these, we'll examine associated behaviors to ensure the coherence of inputs and outputs. The engine primarily depends on two crucial input configurations: engine settings and security rules. In subsequent chapters, we'll further augment these inputs with AI-based model inputs.

Inputs and Outputs

Engine configuration encompasses a range of primary settings crucial to optimize performance. These include advanced parameters, such as thread counts and message handling capacities. While specific parameters may vary depending on implementation, the engine can dynamically adapt to its deployment environment. We'll explore these advanced options in upcoming sections.

CHAPTER 4   DATA SECURITY SOLUTION DESIGN

Figure 4-3 shows the inputs and outputs of a content detection engine. Let's dive into the details.

```
                Policies    Message (Content to be examined)
                   |                |
                   v                v
   Settings for  ┌─────────────────────────┐  ──→ Violations to the violation
   Engine  ────→ │ Content Detection Engine │         processor
                 └─────────────────────────┘  ──→ Remediation Actions
                          ↑↓                        to the Remediation
                 ┌─────────────────────┐            Execution Engine
                 │ Content Standardization (to │
                 │        UTF-8)       │
                 └─────────────────────┘
```

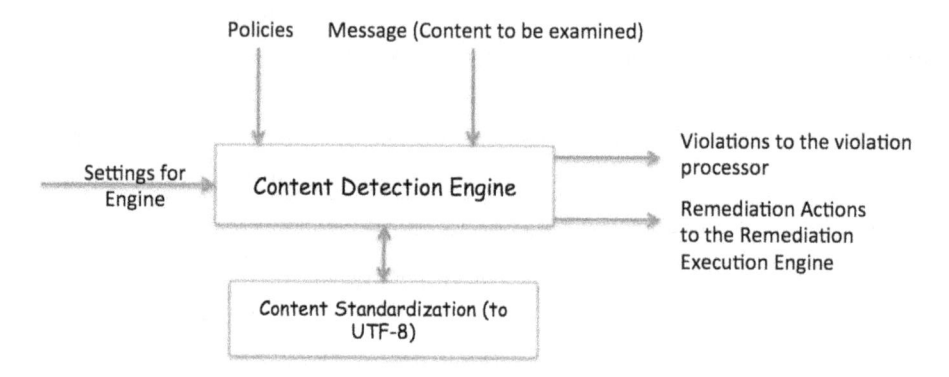

Figure 4-3. *Inputs and Outputs to a Content Detection Engine*

Security rules, or policies, serve as foundational inputs guiding the engine's operations. These rules enable the engine to distinguish confidential from non-confidential data. As discussed previously, each security rule comprises various components, including policy targets, context rules, data matching rules, exception rules, and remediation rules, sequenced for execution. The policy administrator establishes these ground rules or policies in the system and they are fed into the content detection engine.

Apart from configuration inputs, the other most important input that we should account for is data interceptor inputs. These interceptors play a vital role in providing data to the content detection engine. The inputs from various channel interceptors consist of raw files, whether intercepted network traffic, files read from a Network Share, and so forth. These files remain unparsed or, in other words, unconverted to a standardized format. It falls upon the content detection engine to fulfill this responsibility by parsing the original content and converting it into UTF-8 format for data-matching purposes. Let's refer to the content that is sent to the

162

CHAPTER 4   DATA SECURITY SOLUTION DESIGN

content detection engine as a message. A message gets transformed into a standardized format and then various configured rules are run on top of the message to determine security violations.

Two critical outputs from the engine include security violations when data breaches policies and the execution of remediation rules. The violation processor accepts these security violations as input, which is later examined by violation remediators. The remediation execution engine handles the execution of remediation rules. There are two methods by which we can design the execution of remediation actions: synchronous and asynchronous.

In synchronous processing, the content execution engine would initiate a synchronous call to the remediation execution engine. It would await a response from the remediation execution engine and then update the results of the action execution in the violation before forwarding it to the violation processor. Conversely, asynchronous processing would involve the execution of remediation actions asynchronously, with the content engine not waiting for the action to complete. The action's result is forwarded later to the violation processor, and the security violation gets updated accordingly.

Figure 4-4 summarizes the workflow for both asynchronous and synchronous processing of remediation actions.

CHAPTER 4   DATA SECURITY SOLUTION DESIGN

Asynchronous Remediation   **Synchronous Remediation**

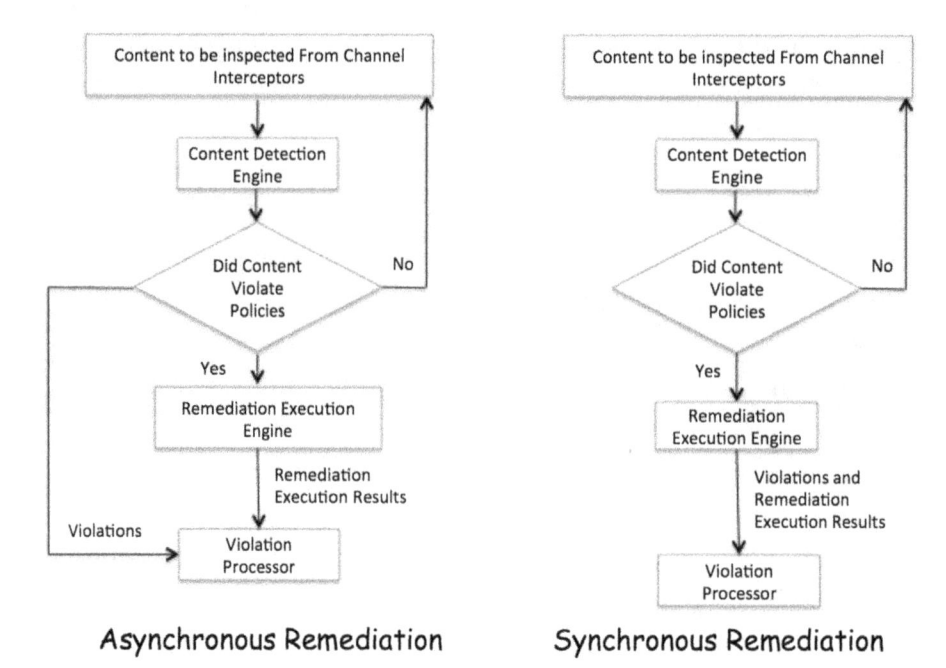

Figure 4-4. *Asynchronous and Synchronous Remediation Execution*

Usually, violation remediators won't address violations immediately, as soon as violation processors process them. Instead, they will wait until the remediation results for security violations get updated. Asynchronous execution provides scalability benefits for the content execution engine and is much desired over the synchronous method.

Now that we've addressed the fundamental inputs and outputs, let's revisit our essential requirements and consider any additional aspects relevant to the detection engine. Every security vendor must undertake this review process continuously throughout the design phase.

Ensuring business continuity for the content engine entails prioritizing its resilience and robustness. Firstly, we must ensure resilience to failures. But before discussing failure scenarios, let's recap what we've established thus far. In the diagram, you'll notice the inputs and outputs, with the centralized module referred to as "matching." Let's break down the steps involved when a message arrives at the content detection engine for matching.

Content Matching Message Lifecycle

The following Figure 4-5 illustrates the lifecycle of a message. As a reminder, dear readers, a message refers to the content received from channel interceptors for content examination.

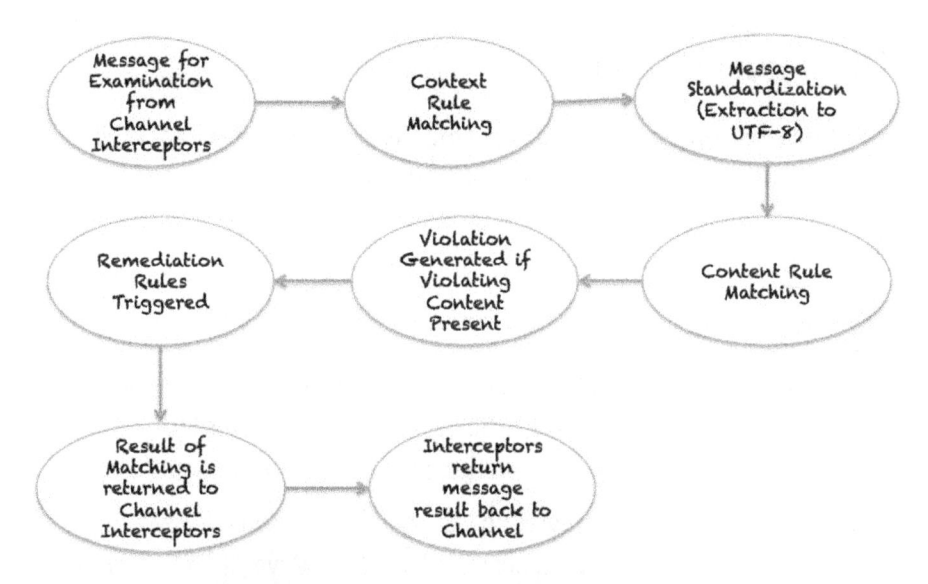

Figure 4-5. Lifecycle of a Message

At a broad level, the initial phase of the content detection engine involves context rule matching, as depicted in the above diagram. Upon successful completion of this step, the process proceeds to message parsing or extraction and message standardization. Messages typically consist of different components such as a message body and attachments, with each attachment possibly containing embedded files. Once all message components have been parsed and extracted, the standardized content undergoes evaluation against context-matching rules and exceptions. Should a match occur, a security violation is triggered, initiating asynchronous remediation actions aligned with the relevant security policies. It's important to highlight that once the remediation execution engine assumes responsibility for these actions, it can autonomously inform the violation processor of the violation details, executed remediation actions, and their outcomes. This is a mere guideline for a good solution. You can have additional components or modify these core parts to the content detection engine.

Context Rule Matching

Possibilities for context rules can vary for each channel. Table 4-1 will give you an overall idea of context rule possibilities for every channel.

Table 4-1. Context Rules for Each Channel

Channel name	Possible context rule parameters
On-Premise Email/Cloud Email DIM	From, To, CC, BCC Recipient email addresses and domains, Subject, Is Attachment present, How many attachments are there, Attachment sizes
Network Share DAR	Creator, Collaborators, Operation type (Read, Write, Share, Delete, Copy, Move), If Copy or Move then Destination Folder attributes like creator, collaborators, Size of the file, Type of the file, Last Modified Date, Created Date
Network DIM	Network Traffic Details (Application, User, Protocols), Source Folder and its attributes, Destination Folder and its attributes

(continued)

CHAPTER 4 DATA SECURITY SOLUTION DESIGN

Table 4-1. (*continued*)

Channel name	Possible context rule parameters
Endpoint Channel DIM	Device Attributes (Logged-in user, OS type, OS version, etc), Network (On the VPN or Off the VPN, or In the Office), Type of Operation (Copy, read, write, move), Source path, destination path, Website URL, Upload/Download/impacted file attributes (name, type, size, last created, last modified), Application attributes if applicable (application name, Type, Corporate, Not corporate), USB, Print, etc.
Endpoint Channel DAR	Created on, Modified on, Device Attributes (Logged-in user, OS type, OS version, etc), file attributes (name, type, size, last created, last modified)
BYOD/Mobile Channel DIM	Similar to Endpoint DIM
BYOD/Mobile Channel DAR	Similar to Endpoint DAR
Cloud Network	Similar to Network DIM
Cloud Applications DIM	Similar to Network DIM
Cloud Applications DAR	Similar to Network DAR

Security policies can be authored by specifying context rules as straight rules, or exceptions. Again, any number of rules can be joined together using Boolean operators. This flexibility is essential to ensure policy administrators have more expressive language while authoring policies. Context rule exceptions are critical, as they can be of great value to most organizations, and often organizations have these exceptional circumstances where they would prefer an operation to be allowed.

With the matching of context rules or exceptions, context rule matching can promptly halt resource-intensive operations. For instance, let's consider a security policy stipulating that any alterations to files by

167

users belonging to a specific AD group, regardless of their content, must be prohibited. In such scenarios, security breaches can be identified, and the operation terminated upon satisfying the context rule. Context exceptions serve to cease any further processing of the message. For example, envision a security policy specifying that all messages from the CEO to employees are exempt from scrutiny. In this case, upon the context-matching sub-component, identifying the CEO as the sender, it can allow the message to proceed without additional checks and proceed to the next message.

Message Parsing and Standardization

Message parsing, as previously discussed, entails the extraction of message components and their conversion into a standardized format. Security vendors can purchase any of the message-parsing solutions available today. Licenses can be purchased on a one-time or subscription basis by security vendors. These solutions can be readily integrated into the product. Alternatively, the message parsing solutions can be developed in-house too. However, creating and maintaining an in-house parsing solution requires significant resources and time commitments. The in-house solution involves understanding and parsing numerous formats, with even a basic task like extracting embedded MS Office files, potentially requiring months of development. Further, dealing with different media types, such as images and videos, introduces further complexity. Specialized software for image text extraction and video transcript extraction is necessary, both of which can be costly and time-consuming processes. The time required for these extraction processes is often prohibitive, particularly in contexts where critical operations should execute within seconds.

CHAPTER 4   DATA SECURITY SOLUTION DESIGN

The processing of images and videos, as well as text extraction, can be integrated either as unified components within the detection engine or developed as distinct modules. Similarly, the entirety of the message parsing and extraction module can be shared among multiple content detection engine modules, given its stateless nature. Below, I outline how these message parsing and standardization components can be integrated with the content detection engine, offering both inline and shared options for consideration based on specific requirements.

It's important to note that the shared option may not be viable in every scenario. For instance, if your content detection engine operates on endpoint devices, sharing might not be feasible. Sharing could lead to significant network latency, as transmitting content and awaiting results back would impose considerable delays, potentially disrupting regular endpoint operations. Moreover, the bandwidth demands for each message scan would escalate significantly, posing a potential strain on the organization's network infrastructure or the network at the endpoint's location.

Figure 4-6 illustrates the process of content parsing and extraction for messages received by servers, whether cloud-based or on-premise, for content examination. As shown, a cluster of stateful server content detection engines is supported by a cluster of stateless extraction engines that handle various file formats. The detection engine must select the appropriate extraction engines based on file types. For example, if a text document contains embedded images, both the text and image extraction engines need to be invoked to extract the data.

CHAPTER 4 DATA SECURITY SOLUTION DESIGN

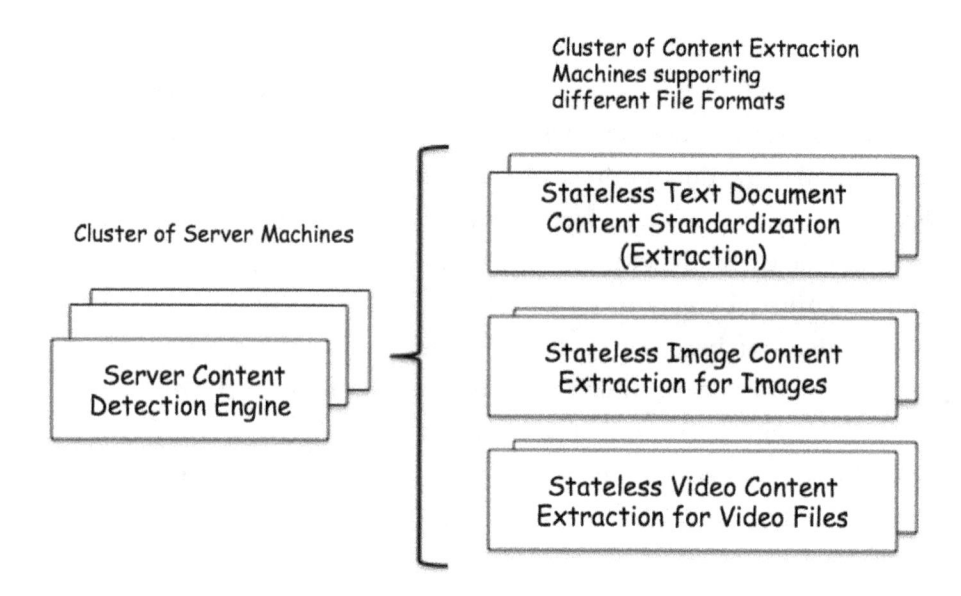

Figure 4-6. Content Standardization and Extraction on Servers

Figure 4-7 shows how agent-based content detection engines parse and standardize data for content examination. Given that these engines operate on laptops or BYOD devices, running image and video extraction can be challenging but not impossible. Therefore, it is definitely up to the security vendor to decide whether to support image and video extraction and detection for endpoints, including BYOD devices.

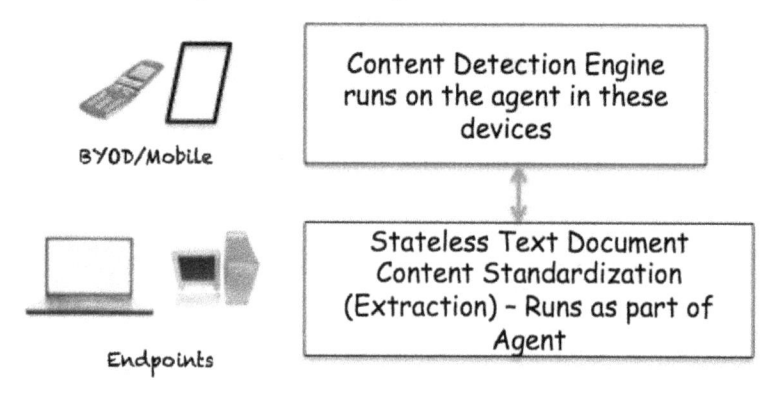

Figure 4-7. Content Standardization and Extraction on Endpoint Machines

170

Content Rule Matching

The efficacy of content rule matching hinges on two pivotal factors. Firstly, it relies on the presence of a broad range of data-matching choices. Secondly, its effectiveness is contingent upon the proper implementation of these solutions. By leveraging the diverse content-matching algorithms available in our solution, we can enhance the expressiveness of policy language. The following content explores potential and widely used data options that can be utilized effectively in our solution. For now, let's set aside considerations on how these rules are integrated into policies and focus instead on the matching process in the next section.

Keyword Matching

The simplest form of data matching involves using keywords, which are commonly employed across multiple policies and widely used as a data matching algorithm. Developing a top-tier keyword-matching algorithm is crucial. However, the intricacies of designing such an algorithm are beyond the scope of this book. Typically, security vendors opt to develop their keyword-matching algorithms rather than purchasing implementations from third-party sources. It's important to note that both options are available.

There are two approaches to keyword matching: either extracting keywords from each policy and matching them individually against the content, or aggregating all keywords into a single list and conducting a single match against the content. Consolidating all keywords into one list requires knowledge of which keywords belong to each policy, bearing in mind that the same set of keywords might apply to multiple policies.

Advanced options may be available based on the policy engine, such as matching only if a certain number of keywords from the set are present, requiring specific distances between keywords, or conducting case-sensitive matches, among others. The possibilities are extensive and

CHAPTER 4   DATA SECURITY SOLUTION DESIGN

depend on the level of sophistication in defining security policy keyword rules. Regardless of the chosen options, once the algorithm identifies matches between keywords and the content, these become additional filter rules applied atop the matches.

Figure 4-8 provides a clear picture of how keyword lists and keyword pairs are created and configured within a security policy.

Keyword Lists

Sensitive	Dental
Confidential	Agreement
Important	SSN
Classified	PatientPII
Financial	Address
Intellectual	Surgery

Configuration
Case Sensitive: True
Match At least: 2 words

Keyword Pairs

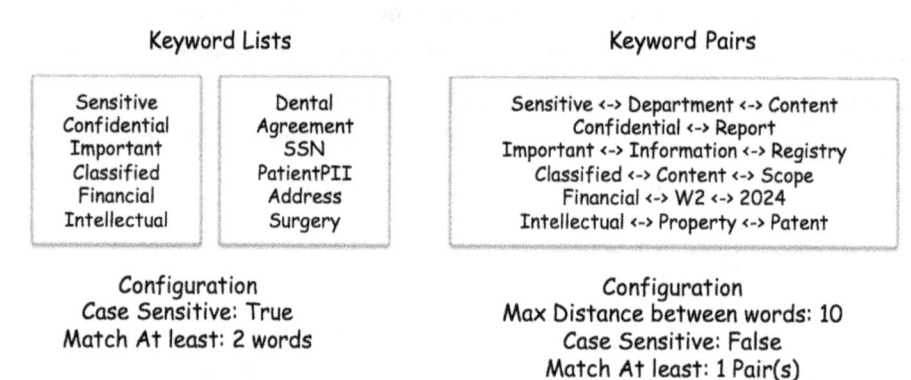

Sensitive <-> Department <-> Content
Confidential <-> Report
Important <-> Information <-> Registry
Classified <-> Content <-> Scope
Financial <-> W2 <-> 2024
Intellectual <-> Property <-> Patent

Configuration
Max Distance between words: 10
Case Sensitive: False
Match At least: 1 Pair(s)

Figure 4-8. *Keyword Lists and Keyword Pairs Configuration*

Regular Expression Pattern Matching

In addition to keywords, regular expressions are widely utilized in security policies. Regular expression matching applies to a broad spectrum of content, including instances where keywords are disguised as regular expressions, which the matching algorithm can identify. This raises the question: Do security vendors need to develop or adopt a separate keyword matching algorithm when regular expressions can serve dual purposes? The straightforward answer is: Yes, distinct algorithm implementations or third-party solutions are necessary for enhanced efficiency. Despite the negligible difference in matching speeds, which may be measured in nanoseconds, the cumulative effect could become significant, especially considering the potential volume of content processed daily, reaching hundreds of thousands if not millions.

CHAPTER 4　DATA SECURITY SOLUTION DESIGN

Similar to keywords, regular expressions from all policies can be consolidated into a unified list and utilized for content matching. It is essential to maintain clarity regarding which regular expressions correspond to each policy and to apply any relevant additional filters to the matches identified.

Figure 4-9 presents a straightforward list of regular expressions, along with a configuration indicating that at least two patterns from this list must match within the message (content to be examined) for it to be considered a violation.

RegEx Lists

```
\d{5}(-\d{4})?
1\d{10}
[2-9]|[12]\d|3[0-6]
((\d{3})(?:\.|-))
(\d{3})(?:\.|-)(\d{4})
```

Configuration
Match At least: 2 Patterns

Figure 4-9. *Regular Expression Lists and Configuration*

Over time, regular expression-matching algorithms have seen enhancements, and resources detailing their construction are available. However, most organizations opt not to develop regular expression matchers in-house. Instead, they prefer to utilize existing solutions, as fine-tuning in-house matchers to achieve optimal performance requires significant resources and expertise.

Popular Unique Identifiers Matching

The unique identifiers matching algorithm comprises two components: initially, the structure of the unique identifier's grammar, followed by supplementary validations aimed at mitigating false positives. Similar

CHAPTER 4   DATA SECURITY SOLUTION DESIGN

to the matching algorithms previously explored, matches are initially identified within the content, and subsequently, akin to filters, validations are applied to refine and potentially eliminate matches as necessary.

In security policies, both the grammar and validation predominantly rely on regular expressions, making this type of matching typically accomplished using regular expression matchers. However, some organizations may define proprietary identifiers with their grammar. Within the regular expression matcher, there is no distinction between general identifiers and custom ones.

Figure 4-10 shows the regular expression for the popular unique identifier matcher for US Social Security Number but then all numbers of the format which are XXX-XX-XXXX are not valid hence we need to have validations on top of it.

Popular Unique Identifier Matcher for US Social Security Number:	^\d{3}-?\d{2}-?\d{4}$
Validations for US Social Security Number:	^(?!(000|666|9))\d{3}-(?!00)\d{2}-(?!0000)\d{4}$

Figure 4-10. *Popular Unique Identifier Configuration*

Structured Content Matching

Structured content matching entails precisely matching the structured data content defined during the creation of the rule. Structured data typically takes the form of tabular content found in spreadsheets, databases, or any custom format delimited by predefined delimiters. Consider Table 4-2 as an example assuming it represents the source table provided during the creation of the security rule.

Table 4-2. PII Data Table

First name	Last name	DOB	Social security number
Alice	Campbell	01/01/1980	456-78-1234
Steven	White	04/09/2001	987-65-4321
Jim	Yang	03/12/1962	432-98-6543

Let's assume that your security rule says if the content matches 3 of the available four columns then it is a match or violation. Now consider the content in an email:

Alice Cambell 01/01/1990 456-78-1234

Ben White 04/12/2000 987-65-4321

Now, observing this content, you'll notice that the first row matches three out of the four available columns. Considering the breadth of possible matchers for such scenarios, the industry often refers to this type of matching as Exact Data Matching (EDM), as it entails precisely matching the input contents with those under examination. Here are three suggested approaches to guide this type of rule:

Firstly, you can employ a combination of keywords and regular expressions to represent the table, integrating appropriate validations. For instance, the "Date of Birth" column in the table could be represented using a widely recognized identifier with suitable validations. Subsequently, matches can be scrutinized by comparing them to the actual date of birth, treated as a keyword.

Secondly, you can utilize regular expressions to precisely capture the contents of each column, row by row, followed by matching and applying filters and aggregations as needed.

Thirdly, and my recommended approach, is to generate hashes of the content in each column and then precisely match these hashes. While hash collisions may occur, they can be easily addressed using established

CHAPTER 4 DATA SECURITY SOLUTION DESIGN

techniques such as employing a large hash table and robust hash functions. By leveraging hashing, content can be matched accurately and swiftly, as the hashing process is rapid and matches can be made against precomputed hashes. However, this method is notably memory-intensive, particularly when dealing with structured data spanning millions of rows. To facilitate matching, all source hashes must be loaded into memory and readily accessible. For instance, if there are ten tables, each requiring a significant hash table containing hashes of all source column data, all ten hash tables must be loaded into memory to ensure the content detection engine can perform matches efficiently.

Given that this form of matching necessitates a larger memory footprint due to the requirement of loading hashes into memory, it is impractical to execute this type of matching on devices where memory usage is critical, such as laptops, mobile devices, and similar platforms.

Unstructured Content Matching

As implied by its name, unstructured data matching involves comparing against unorganized data. This type of matching necessitates being conducted on a specified set of input source files. The input source files are provided to a process that generates a rolling window of hashes. These hashes are then fed into the policy engine, which subsequently get used in the content detection engine(s) to match the content, as illustrated in Figure 4-11. Unstructured data matching involves an exact match of the hashes, but the content is not expected to be organized as in structured data. Therefore, options may be specified as a percentage of the match. For instance, a security policy could be configured to block operations if the content matches 75% of the input source files, allowing for partial matching.

Unstructured data matching is often favored by organizations when they are aware that the contents within a set of documents are sensitive, yet they are uncertain how to incorporate these documents into the policy engine as input. Since the data is unstructured, it cannot be classified in any systematic way. In such scenarios, unstructured matching emerges as the preferred option.

Like structured data matching, unstructured data matching also requires loading hashes into memory. Therefore, conducting this type of matching may not be feasible on platforms where minimizing memory usage is essential.

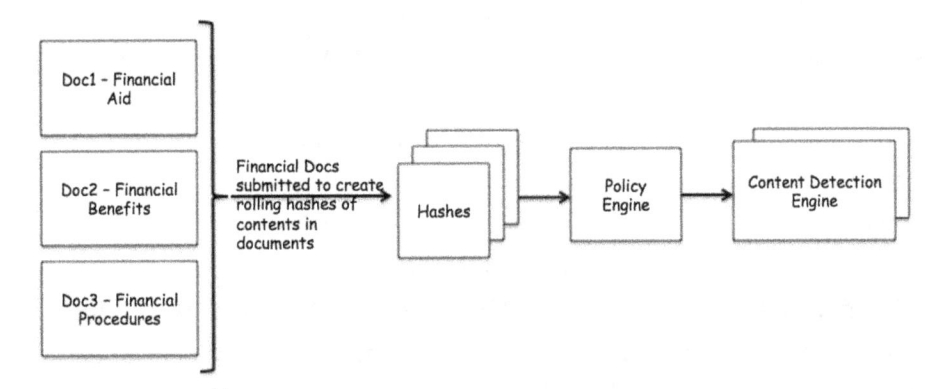

Figure 4-11. *Unstructured Content Matching Dataflow*

Identity-Based Matching

Identity-based matching relies solely on the identity of users and the groups to which they are affiliated. Identity providers can range from on-premise Active Directory (AD) to cloud-based services like Azure AD, Okta, Ping, and others. The key is to define policy rules that specify the criteria for matching, such as users belonging to C-Level Executives. When content is received, the users associated with that content (which could be senders, recipients, collaborators, creators, logged-in users, etc., depending on the channel and activity) are typically matched against the defined criteria.

Identity-based matching can be implemented as either a context rule or a content rule, but it's typically a content rule because it often involves querying the identity provider. As a general rule of thumb, any rule that can be executed quickly to expedite the content-matching process is implemented as a context rule, although rules involving running content-matching algorithms or querying external systems are implemented as content rules.

If the identity provider is not accessible to the content detection engine, the rule can be executed if the engine already has the relevant information from the identity provider synchronized and loaded in memory. The effectiveness of matching in such cases depends on the synchronization schedule and on how frequently organizational changes occur.

For endpoint or mobile platforms, executing rules based on the logged-in user is straightforward, as the user is typically logged in, and querying AD for user details is feasible if the device is registered with AD. However, certain rules, such as blocking emails based on recipients belonging to the HR group, may not be feasible on mobile platforms due to limitations in synchronizing AD information. Nevertheless, rules like blocking emails if the sender belongs to the HR group and the content contains the keyword "confidential" can still be executed.

For BYOD platforms and devices not registered with the identity provider, policies must be more restrictive and specific to accommodate the BYOD channel.

Figure 4-12 shows the data flow between the identity provider and our security product. The synchronizer can run on-demand or on a fixed schedule to update our product. The policy engine is responsible for distributing the updates to all content detection engines. While each content detection engine instance could gather the data directly, having the policy engine distribute policies and their dependencies ensures consistent and uniform content examination, which is a superior design.

CHAPTER 4 DATA SECURITY SOLUTION DESIGN

```
[Security Product Identity Synchronizer] ←— Synchronization based on fixed Schedule/on-Demand —— [Identity Provider]
         |
         | Identity Synchronizer updates Policy Engine with Updates
         ↓
[Policy Engine] —— Policy Engine Transmits policies to Content Detection Engine(s) along with Identity Data ——→ [Content Detection Engine]
```

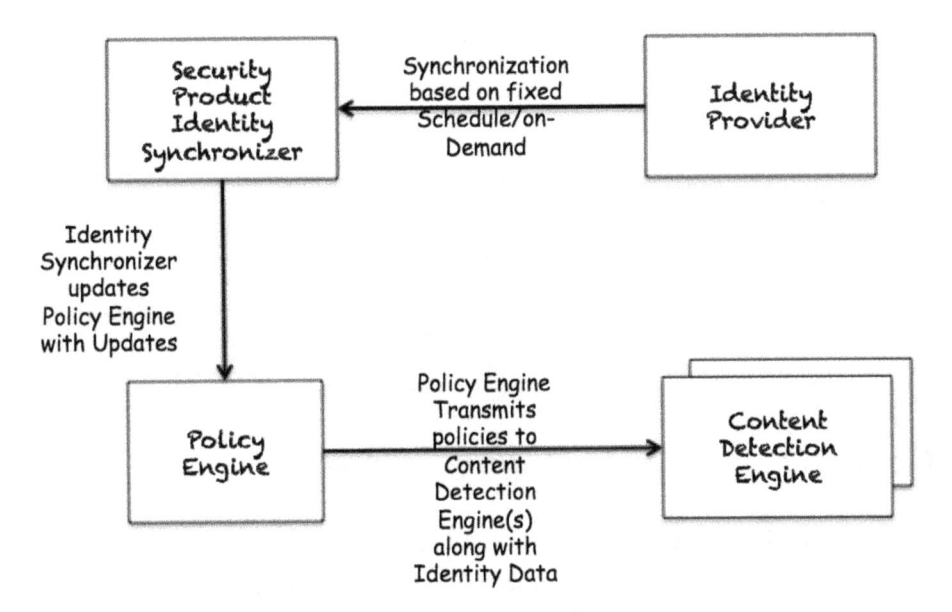

Figure 4-12. Identity Provider Integration and Dataflow

Classification Matching

This approach primarily revolves around the use of classification sensitivity labels or tags applied to documents. Titus classification and Microsoft sensitivity label classification are two prominent tagging services available. By integrating the product with these classification providers, the content detection engine can extract tags from documents and match them based on them. Ideally, classification label extraction occurs during content message parsing and standardization, followed by matching as part of context rule matching. Figure 4-13 showcases a typical dataflow for classification-based matching.

CHAPTER 4   DATA SECURITY SOLUTION DESIGN

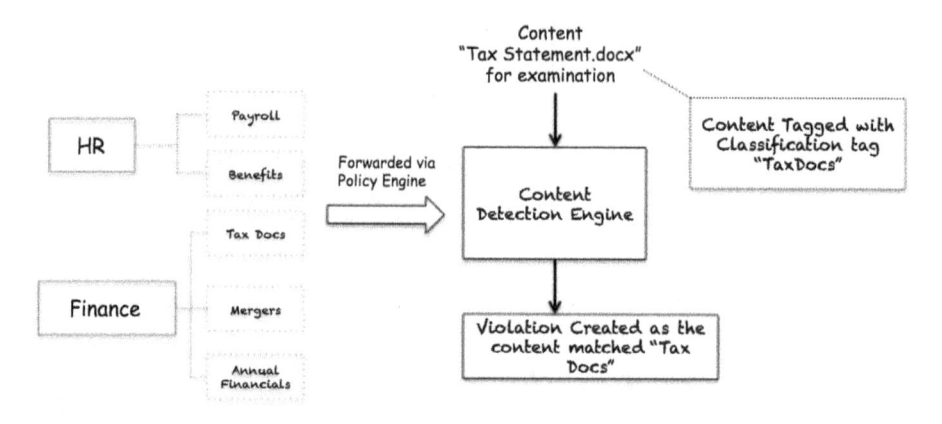

Figure 4-13. *Classification Matching Dataflow*

Classification solutions typically enable organizations to establish a hierarchy of labels, upon which content matching is based. This method is highly effective, as sensitivity labeling has already been applied, and the matching process focuses on discerning whether the content is sensitive. With continuous monitoring appropriately configured, documents can be classified in advance, so when content undergoes matching, the solution simply matches against the pre-classified content. This application of classification tags to a document is carried out as a remediation action in the system.

Suspicious Operation Matching

This represents a more sophisticated matching technique where our solution assesses whether the operation raises suspicions. The identification of suspicious intent constitutes a distinct module, which we'll delve into in subsequent sections. For now, let's set aside the details of how the suspicious engine identifies such behavior. Sending a query to the suspicious intent identification engine with the context and data should enable us to determine if the intent appears suspicious. If flagged as suspicious, appropriate content matching can then be conducted. Related to this, the user risk level can also be adjusted based on this matcher and given as feedback to the system.

Threats Matching

This form of matching relies on inputs from malware and threat prevention systems. To develop a matching technique based on threats, a security vendor must first ensure the presence of a prerequisite: a robust threat intelligence system. With such a system in place, content can be scrutinized for zero-day threats and virus signatures to facilitate content matching.

Threat intelligence systems are inherently forward-looking, often lacking specific policies tailored to individual threats. Nonetheless, a generic policy can be implemented stipulating that if a threat is detected, the content or operation should be blocked and the content quarantined. Such a policy is capable of matching against any type of threat.

Furthermore, threat intelligence systems can identify malicious applications, allowing content uploaded or downloaded from such applications to be considered a threat. However, these suggestions merely scratch the surface of possibilities, dear readers. I leave it to your imagination to explore further.

Machine Learning-Based Matching

Machine learning-based matching refers to a broad category encompassing matchers capable of analyzing content using learned patterns. Security solutions may employ a range of learning algorithms, including rule-based learning, supervised feedback-based learning, and unsupervised learning. While we'll delve deeper into this topic in the next chapter, for now, imagine that through machine learning, you could determine whether content is sensitive or not. Security policy rules may incorporate confidence thresholds, as machine learning algorithms typically output matches as a percentage.

CHAPTER 4　DATA SECURITY SOLUTION DESIGN

Custom Script Matching

The custom script provides policy administrators with the flexibility to develop their matching script for execution. However, it's important to restrict the language options to prevent the inclusion of custom runtime components. Once compiled on the policy engine, the script is transmitted to the content detection engine for execution. Within the content detection engine, the execution of custom scripts operates as a black box, generating a Boolean result for matching.

Compound Conditions and Exceptions

Usually, every policy correlates with a sophisticated array of context rule data matching conditions interconnected by Boolean operators, as detailed in Chapters 2 and 3. The essence lies in sequencing the matching algorithms to streamline the elimination of conditions. This concept can be elucidated with an example. Consider the following Boolean expression, where each alphabet denotes a condition. For the sake of simplicity in this illustration, the condition type is disregarded.

$$(A\ OR\ B)\ AND\ (C\ AND\ D)\ AND\ E$$

The guideline here is to convert this expression into a postfix or prefix expression to specify execution order precedence to the system. Now from the expression above, see for yourself what order the content detection engine must evaluate the conditions.

$$(A\ OR\ B)\ is\ AND'ed\ with\ (C\ AND\ D)\ which\ is\ again\ AND'ed\ with\ E$$

Here, condition E would be the ideal initial condition to assess, as its evaluation determines whether subsequent segments of this Boolean expression warrant evaluation. If condition E does not match upon evaluation, the engine can proceed to the next policy. However, if condition E is a match, the subsequent evaluation of condition C can expedite the matching process. Should condition C yield a true result, condition D is evaluated next, followed by conditions A and B. In an OR condition, both condition operands must undergo an evaluation for the matches to be shown in the security violation.

Priority of Matching

The sequencing of matching algorithms is pivotal for upholding business continuity within an organization. Each matching algorithm necessitates evaluation time, prompting solution developers to ascertain the best, average, and worst-case execution times for all matchers. Subsequently, the solution can be structured to prioritize the matching algorithms based on their execution times relative to a policy condition.

Please refer to Table 4-3, which outlines the average execution times of matching algorithms and other operations. It's important to note that this is a sample representation, and the exact times may vary depending on the implementation strategies of the algorithms themselves.

Table 4-3. Average Execution Times of Matching Algorithms

Matching algorithm	Average time taken
Contextual Match	<1 millisecond
Text Content Extraction	300 milliseconds
Decrypting the encrypted content	500 milliseconds
Text Content Extraction from Image File	10 seconds
Text Transcript from Video or Audio File	2 minutes
Keyword	10 milliseconds
Regular Expression	5 milliseconds
Structured Data Matching	600 milliseconds

(continued)

CHAPTER 4   DATA SECURITY SOLUTION DESIGN

Table 4-3. (*continued*)

Matching algorithm	Average time taken
Unstructured Data Matching	400 milliseconds
Machine Learning Matching	200 milliseconds
Identity-Based Matching	2 milliseconds
Classification-Based Matching	1 millisecond
Custom Script Matching	Unknown

Consider the scenario where the content detection engine possesses this information; it can then prioritize the execution of conditions within the Boolean expression. Once a matcher is executed, the design should ensure comprehensive evaluation across all policies. As discussed earlier in this section, invoking the same matcher multiple times should be avoided. This concept can be elucidated further with the example:

Policy 1: Keyword Condition A AND Regular Expression Condition B

Policy 2: Structured Data Condition C OR Regular Expression Condition D

Policy 3: Keyword Condition E. Exception: Identity-Based Condition $F => E\ AND\ (NOT\ F)$

When the engine needs to evaluate content (text only), it should employ a keyword-matching algorithm and regular expression matching once to assess policies 1, 2, and 3. The engine can make informed decisions as it knows the average execution times of various components and matchers. Considering the policies and assuming the Table 4-3 outlines the average case times, the execution order would be as shown:.

CHAPTER 4   DATA SECURITY SOLUTION DESIGN

Step 1: Text content extraction (300 milliseconds)

Step 2: Evaluate Identity-Based condition F (2 milliseconds)—a chance to eliminate policy 3

Step 3: Run the regular expression algorithm next as execution time is less when compared to the keyword algorithm (5 milliseconds)—an opportunity to eliminate Policy 1 and 3

Step 4: Keyword matching algorithm is the next (10 milliseconds)

Step 5: Structured data condition evaluation is the last (600 milliseconds)

Response Rule Triggers

After identifying a potential security breach and before actually generating the violation, the content detection engine's responsibility is to invoke the remediation execution engine with the specified remediation actions in the correct sequence. It's important to recognize that multiple remediation actions may exist, and their order is critical. Customers should be cautious about configuration errors; for example, a remediation rule ordering encryption followed by deletion may be nonsensical. Additionally, there may be channel-specific remediation rules, although a generic design is preferred, allowing for the creation of a channel-specific remediation engine for each channel.

The content detection engine does not need to concern itself with whether the remediation rules have been executed; its role is to proceed to the next phase of generating security violations. Since there may be multiple violations for the same content, multiple remediation rules specified by policies are possible. Therefore, it is imperative to aggregate all

CHAPTER 4   DATA SECURITY SOLUTION DESIGN

remediation rules in the remediation engine. Figure 4-14 below illustrates content violating multiple policies, each with its set of configured remediation actions.

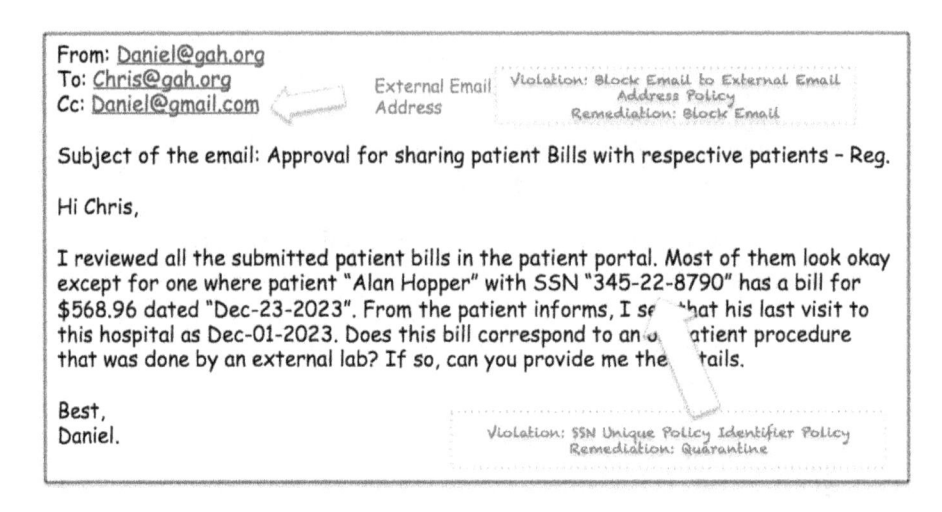

```
From: Daniel@gah.org
To: Chris@gah.org            External Email    Violation: Block Email to External Email
Cc: Daniel@gmail.com         Address                    Address Policy
                                               Remediation: Block Email

Subject of the email: Approval for sharing patient Bills with respective patients – Reg.

Hi Chris,

I reviewed all the submitted patient bills in the patient portal. Most of them look okay
except for one where patient "Alan Hopper" with SSN "345-22-8790" has a bill for
$568.96 dated "Dec-23-2023". From the patient informs, I se   that his last visit to
this hospital as Dec-01-2023. Does this bill correspond to an      atient procedure
that was done by an external lab? If so, can you provide me the     tails.

Best,
Daniel.                               Violation: SSN Unique Policy Identifier Policy
                                              Remediation: Quarantine
```

Figure 4-14. *Multiple Policy Violations with Remediation Actions*

Security Violation Reporting

This marks the concluding phase of the content detection engine's message processing. The occurrence of security violations in the detected content is less than 0.01%. Any increase in violations may suggest suboptimal tuning of policies or adherence to organizational procedures, as illustrated by the GAH example in Chapter 3, where organizations collected information on all print events related to prescription or drug usage procedures. This condition will be addressed in the next chapter. Out of all the previous steps, violation reporting is the simplest step where the engine needs to report all the matches it found in the violation.

CHAPTER 4   DATA SECURITY SOLUTION DESIGN

Policies may require the inclusion of the original content received for detection as part of the security violation. The original content might be large and it will translate to a large violation message. Violation processor design should be capable of handling large violations. In my experience, I have seen customers generating millions of violations every day because of poorly tuned policies. Millions of violations would test the scalability and robustness of our engine as a whole as well as violation processors.

It's important to emphasize that security violations must include comprehensive details about the matches, beginning with the violated policy, the violated condition, the exact text that triggered the matches, and other relevant information. You can find typical samples of security violations in the figure below, where the fields populated in the generated violation may vary depending on the channel.

Figures 4-15 and 4-16 illustrate typical violations for cloud email and endpoint channels, complete with all metadata fields. Please review these fields to ensure they make sense to you as some of the fields vary between cloud email and endpoint channel violation. Understanding these violations is crucial, as they are a key aspect of our security product. Violation information on the right side of the images contains details about the matches in the content (Number of matches, Matches highlighted, etc), including the offending text, if you will. You are free to design the structure of the violation, but I want to show you the level of detail you need to include in the violation through Figures 4-15 and 4-16.

CHAPTER 4   DATA SECURITY SOLUTION DESIGN

```
Id: 234                                              Violating Information: ..........
Policy Id: 23                                        ................................................................
Date Detected: 04/12/2024                            ................................................................
Channel: Cloud Email                                 ................................................................
User: Daniel Gains                                   ................................................................
User Risk Level: Medium
Source: Daniel@gah.org
Destination(s): Chris@gah.org, Daniel@gmail.com
Application Name: Gmail
Application Type: Email
Original Content: <<Attached eml file content>>
Content Size: 25KB
Remediation Action(s) Taken: Block
Remediation Action(s) Result: Successful

Status of Violation: Open
Triaging Options: <<Options Displayed>>
Manual Remediation Action: <<Options>>
Comments:
```

Figure 4-15. Sample Cloud Email Violation

```
Id: 235                                              Violating Information: ..........
Policy Id: 25                                        ................................................................
Date Detected: 04/15/2024                            ................................................................
Channel: Endpoint DIM                                ................................................................
User: Mark Damon                                     ................................................................
User Risk Level: Low
Violating Action: Copy
Source: C:/Mark/Imp/sensitive.txt
Destination: //SharedServer/public/sensitive.txt
Application Name: WINSCP
Application Type: SCP
Original Content: <<Attached text file content>>
Content Size: 1MB
Remediation Action(s) Taken: Quarantine
Remediation Action(s) Result: Successful

Status of Violation: Closed
Triaging Options: Closed <No options>>
Manual Remediation Action: <<Options>>
Comments: Closed on 04/17/2024
```

Figure 4-16. Sample Endpoint Violation

Special Cases in Content Detection

There are a few cases that need special handling when performing content detection. The process is essentially the same, but the system needs to accommodate special handling in terms of both external integrations and hardware resource requirements.

Large File Content

Typically, any design entails input limitations, and I strongly advise against developing solutions without such constraints in place. Let's consider a limitation of our content detection engine: it can only process files smaller than one gigabyte. With this constraint, we need to address how to handle files larger than one gigabyte, which can be approached in two ways.

Firstly, the engine can choose to ignore files exceeding one gigabyte in size. Alternatively, it can process only the first gigabyte of such files, effectively disregarding the bytes beyond this threshold. However, handling files larger than a gigabyte poses challenges for content extraction and standardization, as most solutions require loading the entire file into memory simultaneously. This raises scalability concerns, as loading multiple large files concurrently demands significant memory resources. You must think about all the systems through which the data flows when it comes to scalability. As a side note, handling large files is expensive in the cloud.

For instance, if the engine can concurrently process up to five files, each less than a gigabyte in size, the total memory requirement amounts to five gigabytes. Yet, when confronted with a 10 GB file, loading the entire file into memory becomes infeasible. One approach is to load a portion of the file or stream its contents, albeit limited to the first gigabyte. Designing solutions to accommodate such scenarios necessitates careful consideration.

While streaming or loading everything into memory are potential approaches, appropriate choices must align with hardware resource capabilities. While there's no one-size-fits-all solution, it's prudent to aim for optimal outcomes. In my experience, handling files up to a gigabyte adequately covers most use cases.

Moreover, envision how to transmit the entire gigabyte file alongside the security violation to the violation processor while retaining the original content. Picture multiple content detection engines concurrently sending such violations to the processor. Throughout this book, I aim to prompt you to contemplate diverse scenarios when designing security solutions. Each solution is unique and contingent on the implementation choices you make.

Managing extensive file content also entails considering the constraints of various components and processes. How can one effectively address the identification of large files in a cloud environment? What if the detection mechanism encounters difficulties in extracting the contents of a sizable file, leading to the necessity of skipping it? In such a scenario, how does one notify the system administrator of the inability to conduct detection, potentially resulting in a detection gap? It's impractical to design systems devoid of any detection gaps; situations like these are inevitable, where missed detections occur beyond control. The pivotal concern lies in promptly notifying and alerting stakeholders about the detection gap, as well as deciding on the course of action when operations involve large files. This decision-making process is critical and requires careful consideration.

Large Policy Set

If the policy set is substantial, surpassing the memory constraints of the content detection engine, it would impair the engine's functionality. Essentially, it cannot load such extensive policies into memory. Typically, the vast policy sets stem from sizable structured data hash files, often reaching tens of gigabytes in size. This considerable policy set would render the detection engines in mobile, BYOD, and endpoint platforms completely inoperative, while also posing challenges for servers to allocate sufficient free memory for loading policies.

The recommended approach to handle this issue is to decline to start the content detection engine when it faces such memory constraints. This proactive measure is particularly important in environments with high data loads, like server-based systems that handle Email (both cloud and on-premise), network traffic scanners, CASB, and on-premise network shares. By refusing to start the engine under these conditions, administrators are prompted to allocate resources more effectively. This ensures that when the engine does run, it can operate efficiently and without the risk of being overwhelmed, maintaining the integrity and effectiveness of the detection system.

Embedded Content

Any file subject to content detection may contain embedded content. A prime example of embedded content is a Word file containing an embedded Excel sheet. During text content extraction, the content extractor identifies embedded elements, such as the Excel sheet, and extracts them separately. Most modern content extractors automatically extract embedded content as individual files, providing extracted outputs for both the original file and its embedded files separately.

Now, the design decision lies in whether to conduct content detection separately on each file or concatenate all content and perform detection in a single operation. My recommendation is to handle them separately—not as entirely separate requests but as additional attachment files. When a file enters the detection engine, the input should accommodate the original file and any embedded files as attachments, similar to email attachments. The same principle applies to compressed files.

Compressed files may contain nested compressed files, potentially leading to a cascade of compressed files within other compressed files. All of these elements should be extracted and treated as auxiliary attachments to the input. Detection should be performed separately on each of these auxiliary attachments, and the violation results should be collated and reported together.

CHAPTER 4   DATA SECURITY SOLUTION DESIGN

Encrypted Content

The input file may be encrypted, requiring decryption to access its contents before performing contextual matching and subsequent text content extraction. To facilitate decryption, integrations must be configured to connect to a server capable of decrypting the content for the security solution or retrieving the decryption key using appropriate credentials. All of these arrangements must be pre-established to effectively handle encrypted content.

Another challenge in managing encrypted content is how to transmit this data as part of violation matches to the violation processor. It is essential to send the decrypted content, as the violation processor may lack the context or capability to decrypt the data on its own.

Remediation Action to Classify or Encrypt

There could be situations where the primary objective of supplying files to the content detection engine is for classification or encryption purposes. In such cases, if a match is identified, we would then know which classification labels to apply by invoking the relevant labeling services or encrypting the content using pre-configured encryption keys.

Given that the primary objective is classification or encryption, policy administrators and violation remediators wouldn't favor a security violation for each file. Therefore, it's necessary to suppress violations and instead provide lightweight reporting in batches to notify administrators about the actions taken. The critical aspect lies in the reporting mechanism. Reporting per file isn't scalable, so reporting per batch is preferred, but this requires setting batch or time limits. The process of processing and presenting this data to administrators must be carefully designed and implemented.

CHAPTER 4　DATA SECURITY SOLUTION DESIGN

Content Detection Engine Components Layout

After examining the inner workings of the content detection engine, let's delve into the layout of its components. By layout, I refer to the design of connecting various internal components, considering that some are stateless while others require state preservation. Ideally, all components should be stateless, but where state preservation is necessary, a stateful object like a session cookie must be circulated until the message traverses through all components. This is a design choice that you need to make.

Design for Single Tenant Servers

For single-tenant server environments, a design with all the components connected together like an assembly line processing unit would work. Figure 4-17 shows a linear sequence of components arranged one after the other, illustrating the data flow within a content detection engine. Now, since all the internal components are serving only the messages that come to that server, they don't have to preserve any additional state. The limitation would be on the number of files that it can handle in parallel, what is the largest policy set that it can load, and what is the content limit for handling large files.

Content Detection Engine

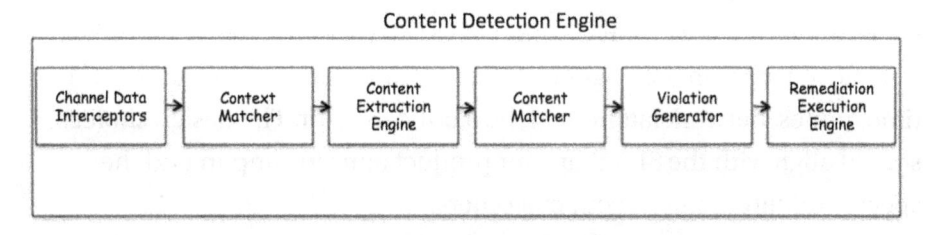

Channel Data Interceptors → Context Matcher → Content Extraction Engine → Content Matcher → Violation Generator → Remediation Execution Engine

Figure 4-17. Components of a Content Detection Engine

However, alternative designs are also possible. You can share components such as content extraction and data interceptors across different servers, as shown in Figure 4-18.

CHAPTER 4   DATA SECURITY SOLUTION DESIGN

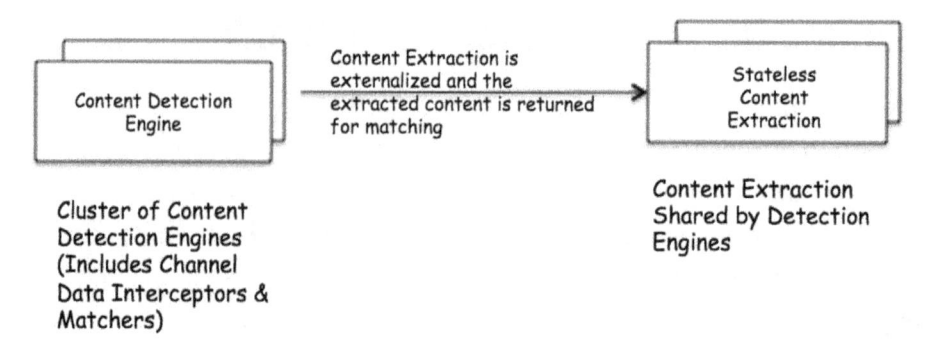

Figure 4-18. Sharing Content Extraction Across Cluster of Detection Engines

The focus on content extraction and data interceptors is because they are purely stateless, unlike core detection engine components, which possess statefulness due to varying sets of loaded policies and hardware limitations across different instances. However, this limitation can be mitigated if we have uniformity in policy sets, resource constraints, and limitations across all shared servers. In such cases, we can implement a group deployment strategy for servers and configure them as a cohesive unit, thereby facilitating the sharing of matchers.

These matchers can be deployed as microservices and shared among the servers as shown in Figure 4-19. It's essential to consider the network latency involved in communication between these microservices. Given that most detection messages need to be processed in sub-millisecond time frames, network latency can be a critical factor. The design choices should align with the SLA that your product aims to support and the specific requirements of your customers.

CHAPTER 4   DATA SECURITY SOLUTION DESIGN

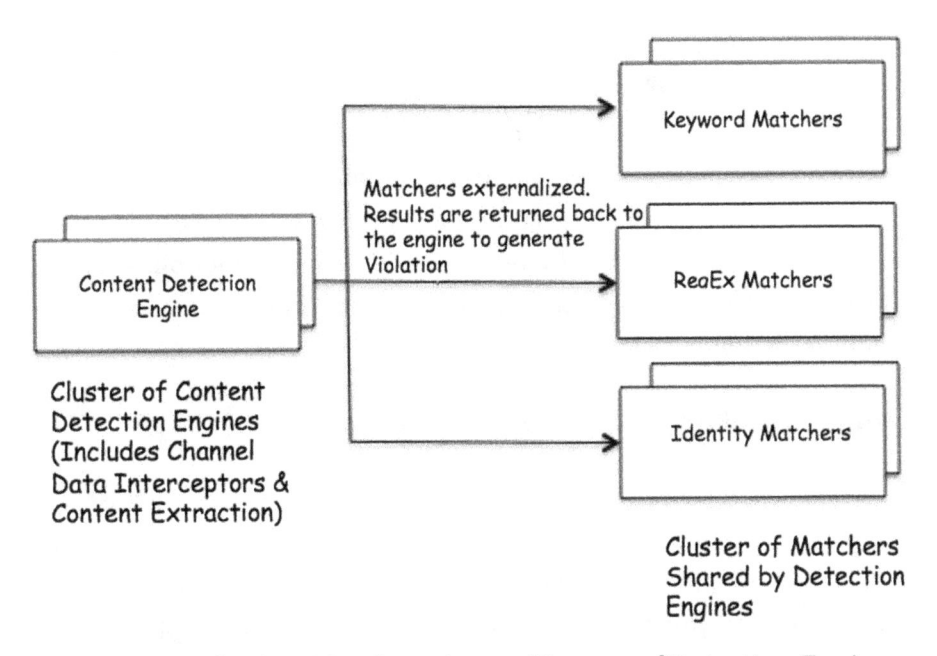

Figure 4-19. Sharing Matchers Across Clusters of Detection Engines

Design for Endpoints and Mobile Devices

As previously mentioned, endpoints and mobile devices face limitations in hardware resources. Therefore, the content detection engine must maintain a minimal set of components, resembling assembly line processing where each component is tightly interconnected in sequence.

Messages originating from endpoints or mobile devices cannot be feasibly transmitted to on-premise or cloud servers for detection in the case of DIM events. The resultant network latency would significantly disrupt business continuity and present scalability challenges. Moreover, the bandwidth load on the organization's network would become prohibitively large. Consequently, for DIM events, detection must occur directly on the devices. Conversely, for DAR events, there exists the option to transmit files to servers. However, network bandwidth remains a critical consideration.

A viable compromise entails conducting as much detection as possible on the endpoint or mobile device itself and only transferring files requiring server-side detection to the servers. For example, tasks such as video or image extraction may not be suitable for endpoints. Therefore, only files necessitating server-based detection, such as those containing images or videos, should be forwarded. In the case of DAR events, endpoints can transmit messages to servers hosted either in the cloud or on-premise for content detection.

Design for Multi-tenant Cloud Servers

Multi-tenant servers can be designed with components shared across multiple microservices, each hosting a service operating in a multi-tenant manner. For instance, data interceptors may be structured as individual microservices. As you know, the primary role of a data interceptor is to fetch content and relay it to the content detection core for analysis. However, it's essential to acknowledge the load limitations of the data interceptor microservice. Therefore, it must be scalable independently and should not handle more customers than a predetermined threshold. A practical guideline is to limit the number of customers per microservice to a low single-digit figure, facilitating easier debugging in case of errors. This rule also applies to all other components. Figure 4-20 shows how the services can be shared in a truly multi-tenant world.

CHAPTER 4 DATA SECURITY SOLUTION DESIGN

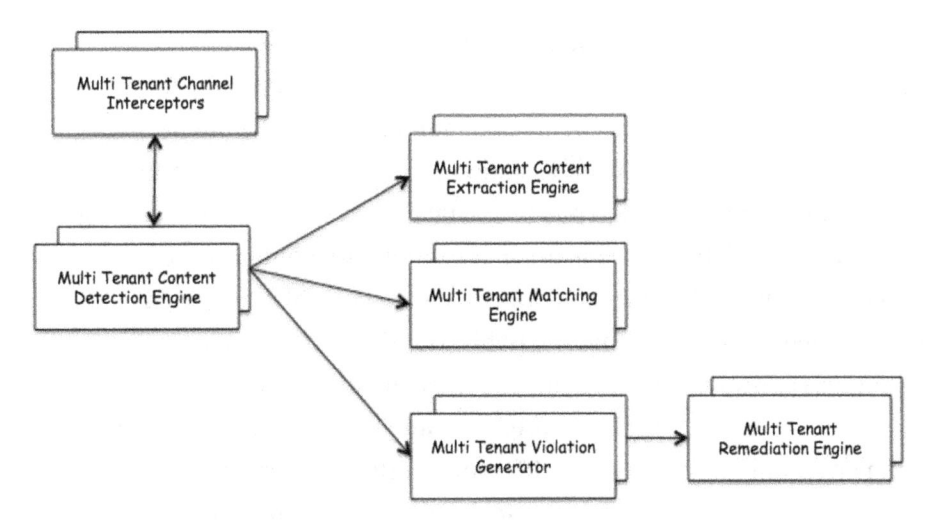

Figure 4-20. Multi-tenant Design With Shared Components

This isn't the sole design option available. There are alternative design choices to consider as well. For example, if you're a vendor catering to both on-premise and cloud environments and prefer maintaining consistency across designs, you could opt for mirroring the same design in both the cloud and on-premise settings.

Reviewing Design Against Requirements

A crucial aspect of component design often entails aligning with requirements and use cases. Keeping this principle in mind, let's proceed to evaluate how the requirements relate to the internal design of the content detection engine. We'll determine whether any specific improvements need to be integrated into our design.

Regarding our primary requirement of identifying and remediating confidential data, the discussed design elements seem comprehensive enough to address various scenarios. However, consistency is paramount. It's important to maintain consistency in our actions. Nevertheless, real-world scenarios may arise where the content detection engine cannot maintain consistency in its operations. Let's briefly explore.

CHAPTER 4   DATA SECURITY SOLUTION DESIGN

In this design, emphasizing the uniformity of the detection engine across all channels and deployment environments is paramount. Consistency in the engine's operations serves to mitigate the potential for discrepancies arising from variations among different channels and environments. Consistency is crucial to prevent confusion among violation remediators. For instance, if a repository containing 10,000 files consistently triggers ten violations against established policies, the content detection engine must reliably identify those same ten violations, regardless of how many times it's executed against the content.

However, as you may be aware, the same file subjected to detection in an endpoint DIM may yield different results compared to when it's processed on a server DIM due to technological capability differences. Sometimes, the content detection engine may encounter timeout or error conditions where complete detection is not feasible, resulting in further inconsistencies. All robust software designs do re-tries, and if there is a chance to re-try, then you must choose to retry. Organizations highly value consistency and the absence of detection gaps.

Continuing with our requirements, our focus remains on achieving comprehensive data coverage across all channel points and ensuring uninterrupted business continuity. In our design, we've successfully tackled these objectives. Moving forward with our solution configurability requirements, we'll delve into configurability, particularly concerning the policy engine, in the subsequent section. However, from the perspective of the content detection engine, our design boasts an extensive array of data matchers that are unmatched in their thoroughness.

After addressing configurability, our focus turns to feedback, learning, and continuous monitoring, which will be the primary focus of the next chapter. Lastly, scaling is a critical requirement, encompassing various deployment scenarios. Scaling the core detection engine hinges on finding the right balance between shared and exclusive components.

CHAPTER 4   DATA SECURITY SOLUTION DESIGN

Policy Engine

Contrary to popular belief, policy administrators do not frequently modify security policies as often as one might assume. Many organizations can attest to this. Typically, administrators establish policies and invest time in fine-tuning them, leaving them largely untouched unless there is a significant shift in the organization's threat landscape. While special circumstances such as acquisitions, mergers, or divestitures may necessitate policy overhauls, under normal circumstances, administrators rarely adjust policies once they are set up.

The policy engine should offer unparalleled flexibility, empowering policy administrators to craft policies tailored to their specific needs. The policy language must possess a high level of expressiveness. In Chapter 6, we will delve into how AI can enrich the expressiveness of the policy language. However, for the time being, it is crucial to acknowledge that the language should allow administrators to articulate conditions using a diverse range of Boolean expressions. In Chapter 3, we extensively covered various types of match rules, including test mode policies. All the insights gained from that discussion can be seamlessly integrated into our solution here. Given that the content detection engine supports a wide array of matchers, the same conditions can be made available for policy authors to define their conditions.

Pre-defined Policy Models

One of the important features of a security solution is to assist administrators in authoring policies. Policies can be broken down into the following types:

- Compliance and Regulations Policies
- Continuous Monitoring Policies
- Data Protection Policies

CHAPTER 4   DATA SECURITY SOLUTION DESIGN

- Threat Detection Policies
- Channel-Specific Policies
- Classification Policies
- Encryption Policies

The security solution's policy engine should offer predefined policy templates for each of the aforementioned types. When an author decides to create a policy, they simply need to select the desired type, and a pre-filled template will automatically appear. From there, they can customize the policy to suit their specific needs before publishing it to the content detection engine, which is strategically positioned at various coverage points to identify security breaches. This approach simplifies the process for policy authors, eliminating the need to start from scratch. Additionally, compliance-related policies can be pre-configured based on industry verticals and regulatory requirements. By leveraging pre-defined policy templates containing all the necessary conditions, policy administrators can seamlessly activate these policies to put them into service.

Policy Targeting and Detection Gaps

Policy targeting is a crucial feature that enables administrators to direct policies based on groups of servers associated with specific channels or geographical locations. This capability empowers policy administrators to apply a core set of policies to all servers, as commonly desired by most organizations, while also implementing specialized policies for each channel.

The implementation of policies must occur seamlessly, without any detection gaps. We previously encountered a scenario in the content detection section where structured conditions, such as input source file hashes, could be extensive, potentially exceeding the memory capacity of the content detection engine and leading to detection gaps. Therefore, the design should proactively assess whether policies and conditions are feasible to load onto the content detection engine. If not, appropriate warnings should be provided to administrators and policy authors to adequately provision the content detection engines.

Before loading a new set of policies, the content detection engine should examine the consistency and memory requirements of the new policy set. Any failures during these checks should prompt the content detection engine to operate with the previous policy set, ensuring that a consistently applied set of policies is always in effect for content detection.

Violation Processor

The Violation Processor stands as a cornerstone for organizations, serving as a critical means of identifying imminent threats. It acts as the central hub where all security breaches are reported, empowering administrators to initiate remedial actions either manually or through seamless business integrations.

Ensuring the scalability of this module is paramount, particularly in large organizations where it must contend with thousands of violations daily. Swiftly remediating these breaches is imperative for maintaining the integrity and effectiveness of the product.

Violation Processing

Figure 4-21 depicts the stages in violation processing once a violation reaches the violation processor. Upon the arrival of violations, the primary step involves deduplication, a process often overlooked by many systems, resulting in the proliferation of redundant violations. Deduplication holds equal significance for Gmail violations, given Gmail's tendency to fragment emails into separate messages grouped by email domain. For instance, an email sent to recipients with addresses ending in yahoo.com and rediff.com will be treated as two distinct messages. Consequently, if our security

CHAPTER 4 DATA SECURITY SOLUTION DESIGN

solution identifies a violation within the email body, it would detect violations in both messages. Deduplication relies on various factors such as unique message IDs, content hashes, and other criteria to streamline the identification and elimination of duplicate violations.

The subsequent phase in violation processing involves the violation validator, tasked with ensuring that all mandatory fields essential for violations are correctly populated. In distributed systems, where services of varying versions may be deployed, discrepancies in data formats can arise despite the services' forward and backward compatibility. Therefore, before persisting violations in a persistent store, any necessary data formatting adjustments must be made. Unfortunately, numerous security solutions frequently neglect validation, yet it remains a critical aspect for us to uphold.

Upon completion of validation, the subsequent stage involves persistence. It's crucial to note that these violations may encompass original content, potentially including sizable file attachments. Therefore, judicious decisions must be made regarding data storage to accommodate the original content. Typically, such files are stored in external NFS or SAN shares to prevent them from occupying valuable space within the solution's data store. Given that these original files are seldom inspected, and even when they are, they are rarely accessed repeatedly, storing them externally proves to be a more efficient approach.

CHAPTER 4   DATA SECURITY SOLUTION DESIGN

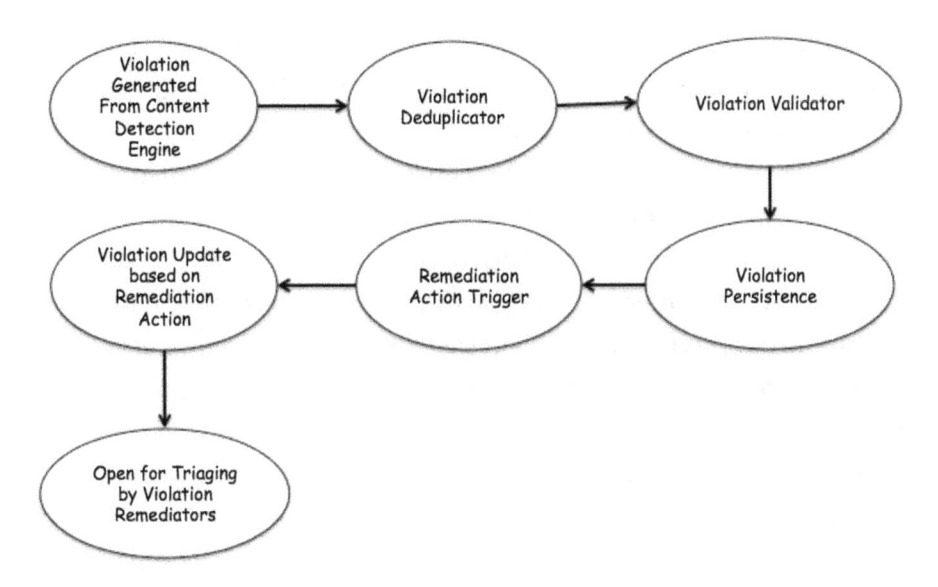

Figure 4-21. Violation Processing Stages

Remediation actions, anticipated to be initiated based on violation persistence, can be activated. These remediation actions commonly entail generic tasks such as notifying the administrator or the user's manager responsible for the violation. The triggers for remediation are asynchronous, meaning that the results are reported back to the violation processor at a later time. Importantly, the failure of remediation actions should not impede the processing of violations. Therefore, employing asynchronous execution and reporting mechanisms is highly logical.

As emphasized earlier, the scalability of the violation processor is paramount. It should possess the capacity to persist numerous violations per second, typically in the order of tens per second, if not hundreds.

Remediation Actions Integration

Results of remediation actions may originate from remediation execution engines positioned adjacent to the content detection engine, strategically placed near channel coverage points, or from execution engines situated alongside the violation processor. Asynchronous results are delivered here, facilitating the updating of violations. The specifics of the remediation engine's output will be explored in the subsequent section dedicated to the remediation execution engine. The outputs of the remediation engine serve as inputs for the violation processor, facilitating the update of violations based on the remediation action outcomes.

In cases where remediation actions fail, notifications are sent to the administrator. Typically, incident severity is automatically elevated if remediation actions fail to capture the attention of the violation remediator. Figure 4-22 shows how remediation actions are triggered by the content detection engine, then executed by the remediation engine, and finally, asynchronously update the already persisted violations in the violation processor.

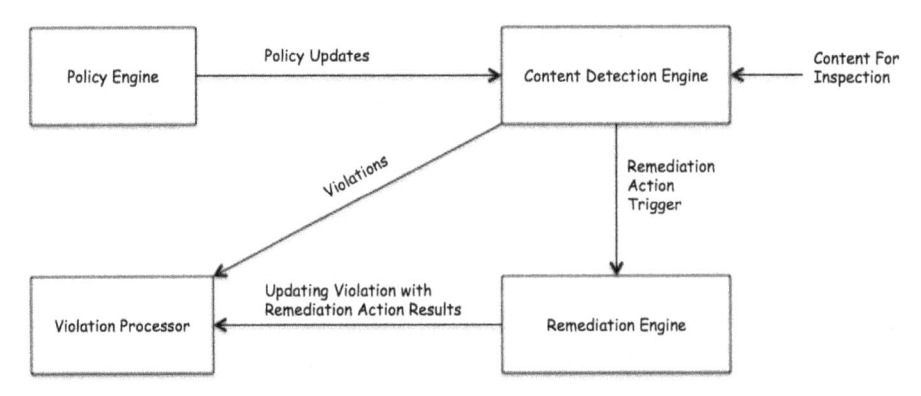

Figure 4-22. Block Diagram—Remediation Engine Updating Violations Asynchronously

Violation Retention Period

The duration for which violations are retained constitutes a significant setting that requires configuration by the violation remediator, super administrator, or compliance administrator. Typically, violations are retained for one year before being archived. Once archived, they are no longer visible in results or reports; however, they can be unarchived to become visible again. While I'm presenting these guidelines as the ideal functioning of the product, they should be regarded as recommendations for a robust solution. Violations may be permanently deleted after three years from the archive, a setting that can also be controlled. It's worth noting that some security-conscious customers may request a retention period of up to seven years.

In the upcoming chapter, we will delve further into harnessing the insights gained from processed violations and exploring strategies for enabling actionable feedback to enhance the overall security posture.

Remediation Execution Engine

The remediation execution engine will operate in two system areas: alongside content detection and close to the violation processor. It's essential because remediation actions may originate from both the content detection engine and violation processors. The content detection engine can trigger remediation actions based on violated policies. Violation remediators can then choose manual or automated actions as needed.

Remediation Engine Design

As previously mentioned, the content detection engine can initiate remediation actions when content breaches defined policies. However, remediation actions are tailored to specific channels and may not be relevant in other contexts. Unified policies could lead to remediation actions that are inappropriate for a particular channel. Therefore, the remediation engine must carefully determine which actions are appropriate and the sequence in which they should be executed.

Inputs and Outputs

The remediation engine inputs are tabulated in Table 4-4.

CHAPTER 4   DATA SECURITY SOLUTION DESIGN

Table 4-4. *Remediation Engine Input Fields*

Input field	Description
Channel	The channel in which the security violation occurred
DIM/DAR	Field specifying DIM or DAR
Message Identifier	Input message unique identifier so that the remediation action and results can be correlated later.
Violation Identifier	Violation identifier so that when remediation action results get reported back, violation processor can correlate.
Policies Violated	Name and Identifiers of the Policies Violated
Remediation Actions	Remediation actions include the remediation action in the order corresponding to each policy violation along with the policy identifier.
Object or Entity	The entity details on which the remediation action needs to be executed.

The outputs of the remediation actions can be found in Table 4-5.

Table 4-5. *Remediation Actions Output Fields*

Output field	Description
Message Identifier	The unique message identifier for which the remediation action was run.
Violation Identifier	The violation that was responsible for this remediation action execution.
Remediation Actions	Remediation actions results. Also includes failed and ignored remediation actions.
Object or Entity	The entity details on which the remediation action was executed.

CHAPTER 4   DATA SECURITY SOLUTION DESIGN

Remediation Actions Determiner

The determiner's role is to consolidate all remediation actions in a logical and executable order and provide them to the executor for implementation. Using the set of parameters explained next, the determiner assesses which actions are appropriate. The set of parameters includes the priority of remediation actions configured for the violating policies, the applicability of actions for the channel where the violation occurred (since we recommend unified policies, not all remediation actions may be applicable to all channels), and the success or failure of previously executed remediation actions. First, the determiner considers the channel where the violation occurred, along with whether it is a DIM or DAR event. Then, it prioritizes all remediation actions to create a unified list. Finally, it flags the remediation actions that need execution.

A sample scenario can exemplify this. Upon detection of a violation, imagine the content detection engine generates the following inputs as in Table 4-6 for the remediation engine.

Table 4-6. *Remediation Actions Input Fields*

Input field	Description
Channel	Network Share
DIM/DAR	DAR
Message Identifier	MessageUUID
Violation Identifier	ViolationUUID
Policies Violated	Policy 1: NetworkShareQuarantine
	Policy 2: EmailBlock
	Policy 3: EndpointDIMNotifyLoggedInUser
	Policy 4: NetworkShareEncrypt

(*continued*)

Table 4-6. (*continued*)

Input field	Description
Remediation Actions	P1:Quarantine, P2:Block, P3:Notify P4:Encrypt
Object or Entity	\\share\sensitive\securedata.txt Quarantine folder: \\share\quarantine Encryption Creds: Creds1

Now, based on these inputs, the determiner gathers the remediation actions that need execution in a list: {Quarantine, Block, Notify Logged In User, Encrypt}. However, since the "Block" and "Notify Logged In User" actions do not apply to a DAR scan. Hence, they are ignored.

Next, there are two actions: Quarantine and Encrypt, associated with different policies. Consequently, the order can vary across two distinct policies, but not within the same policy. The determiner evaluates Quarantine and Encrypt, determining that Encrypt should precede Quarantine. Therefore, the executor receives the order and entity details as input.

Remediation Action Executor

The executor's task is straightforward: it carries out the actions specified by the determiner in the designated order and records the outcomes. Subsequently, the results are conveyed to the violation processor if the remediation action engine is set to execute the actions asynchronously, or to the content detection engine (the caller) if synchronous execution is required. If the remediation action engine is linked to the violation processor, then asynchronous execution is exclusively supported. This is illustrated in Figure 4-23.

CHAPTER 4 DATA SECURITY SOLUTION DESIGN

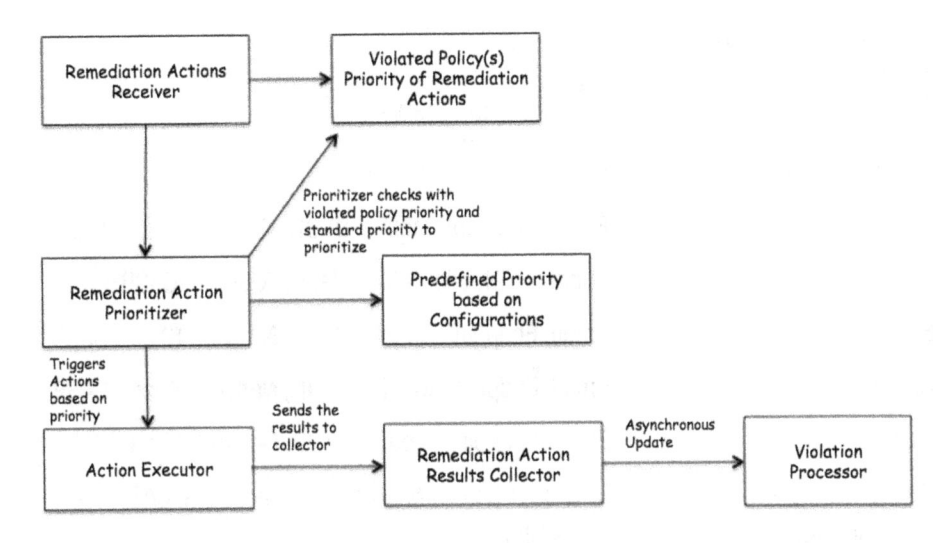

Figure 4-23. Remediation Executor Design

Remediation Action Types

While remediation actions are tailored to each channel, certain actions possess a generic nature. Table 4-7 outlines the potential remediation action types and indicates whether they are generic or specific.

Table 4-7. Applicability of Remediation Action by Channels

Remediation action	Channels applicable
Notify/Email Administrator	Generic
Notify/Email Manager	Generic (IDP integration necessary)
Increase Violation Severity	Generic
Decrease Violation Severity	Generic
Mark Violation as False Positive	Generic
Mark Violation auto-closed	Generic

(*continued*)

Table 4-7. (*continued*)

Remediation action	Channels applicable
Add Notes to Violation	Generic
Block	Email, Endpoint, Mobile, BYOD, Network Share, CASB
Delete	Endpoint, Mobile, BYOD, Network Share, CASB
Encrypt	Email, Endpoint, Mobile, BYOD, Network Share, CASB
Classify	Email, Endpoint, Mobile, BYOD, Network Share, CASB
Quarantine	Email, Endpoint, Mobile, BYOD, Network Share, CASB
Remove External Collaborators	Network Share DIM, Network Share DAR, CASB DAR, CASB DIM
Remove Share	Network Share, CASB, Endpoint, Mobile, BYOD
Notify Logged-In User	Endpoint, Mobile, BYOD
Request User Justification	Endpoint, Mobile, BYOD

Reporting Engine UI

Welcome to the reporting realm! In this section, we'll skim through the world of reporting. First up, let's dive into the heart of reporting—the reporting engine. Later we'll explore the diverse landscape of reporting types and options around it.

To kick things off, the reporting engine must support the following options. Readers should review these options thoroughly, as each one is crucial for organizations in terms of usability.

Report Criteria Specification

Every report must have specified reporting criteria, and these criteria should be savable for future use. Reporting criteria may encompass filters such as "last 90 days," "violations greater than 5," "high severity violations only," and similar options for a violation report. This report criteria should be stored under a name and capable of cloning (save as) to another name.

Report Distribution List

Having a pre-defined distribution list for each report type is a valuable feature to include in the product. Alternatively, we can introduce a role called "report reviewers," where any user assigned to this role automatically receives a copy of the report. Additionally, we can implement sub-levels of report reviewers for each report type within this role, allowing users to receive individual reports based on their specific requirements.

Apart from a predefined list, every generated report should be downloadable immediately. Downloadable formats, such as "pdf" and "csv," should be available as applicable. Furthermore, the UI design should include features enabling users to configure distribution lists as needed.

Reporting History

All reports generated within the system should be archived and accessible for download or distribution at any given moment. Nevertheless, we cannot retain reports indefinitely. Users should have access to appropriate report settings to specify the historical report retention period. A prudent recommendation is to retain reports for the past year by default.

CHAPTER 4   DATA SECURITY SOLUTION DESIGN

Reports On-Demand

This represents the fundamental requirement for a reporting engine. It should have the capability to generate reports instantly upon user request. On-demand reporting options should encompass report type selection and a range of filters to refine the report criteria.

The conventional approach of a reporting engine querying the backend for data and then applying filters won't suffice, particularly in cases involving millions of rows in security violation reports. Thus, we need to integrate filtering with the query itself, allowing the backend to handle the heavy lifting of both filtering and querying.

Report Scheduling

The reporting engine should provide unparalleled flexibility in scheduling options, as shown in Figure 4-24. Common scheduling choices include setting reports to run periodically, with calendar options for selecting weekly, monthly, quarterly, and yearly intervals, or specific dates. Users should be able to select distribution lists, and once the report is generated, it should be automatically sent via email. Additionally, users should have the option to download the same report from the UI.

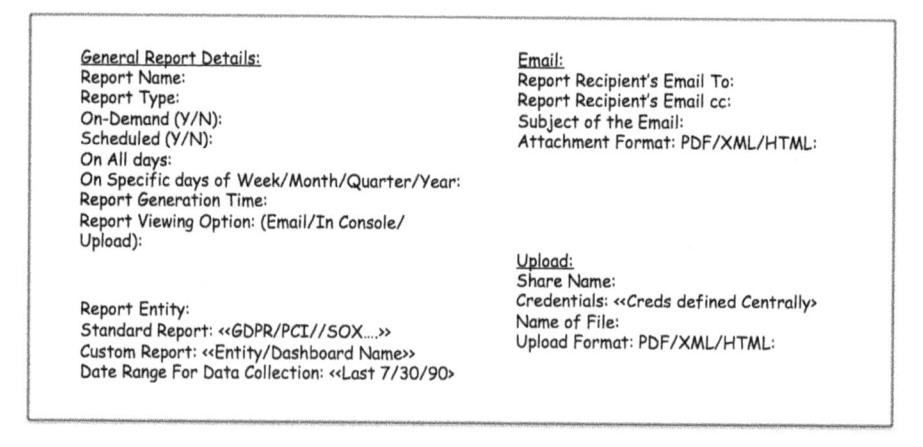

```
General Report Details:                              Email:
Report Name:                                         Report Recipient's Email To:
Report Type:                                         Report Recipient's Email cc:
On-Demand (Y/N):                                     Subject of the Email:
Scheduled (Y/N):                                     Attachment Format: PDF/XML/HTML:
On All days:
On Specific days of Week/Month/Quarter/Year:
Report Generation Time:
Report Viewing Option: (Email/In Console/
Upload):
                                                     Upload:
                                                     Share Name:
Report Entity:                                       Credentials: <<Creds defined Centrally>>
Standard Report: <<GDPR/PCI//SOX....>>               Name of File:
Custom Report: <<Entity/Dashboard Name>>             Upload Format: PDF/XML/HTML:
Date Range For Data Collection: <<Last 7/30/90>>
```

Figure 4-24. *Report Scheduler UI*

Reporting Engine Design

Reporting typically occurs as a backend process and should not impede any functionality of the security solution or disrupt the user experience when interacting with the solution. In my observation, many security vendors overlook the user experience aspect. Often, when a user triggers report generation, they restrict users from navigating or performing other tasks while the report is being generated. Both on-demand and scheduled reports should not interrupt user activities. Report generation should occur asynchronously in the background, with users receiving appropriate notifications.

Types of Reports

Here are some common types of reports that, as a security vendor, you can develop for the product.

UI-Centric Reports

Most on-demand reports in this category are straightforward UI reports, designed for users to view easily the exact content they are searching for within the user interface. For example, suppose a violation remediator seeks security breaches within the Email channel within a specified date range. In that case, they can export their findings as a report, falling under simple UI-based reports.

Dashboard Reports

Dashboard functionality is common in many applications, with some offering customizable options. It serves as the initial interface a security solution user encounters upon logging in. Dashboards typically present critical information in tables, charts, graphs, etc., which users may also want to export as reports. Supporting dashboard reporting is a valuable and frequently utilized feature.

CHAPTER 4   DATA SECURITY SOLUTION DESIGN

Pre-Defined Criteria Reports

Scheduled reports with pre-configured criteria are essential for administrators who require regular updates on security violations, scan results, monitoring data, and risky behaviors. These reports, generated weekly, monthly, or quarterly, offer executives insight into the organization's overall risk level, aiding in strategic planning and budgeting for enhanced protection.

Compliance Reports

Compliance reports are crucial for organizations to meet regulatory requirements, often generated quarterly or annually. They adhere to specific formats and cover compliance standards such as GDPR, HIPAA, PCI DSS, SOX, NIST, among others. These reports contain predefined content essential for compliance officers to review and ensure regulatory compliance. These are highly critical for an organization.

Audit Reports

These reports cater to both internal and external auditors responsible for auditing the utilization of the security solution. They require comprehensive audit trail reports covering a range of entities, including security policies, security violations, remediation statuses, and more.

User and Role Processor

The user and role processor plays a crucial role in the functionality of the security solution. This module functions similarly to user permissions in a Linux operating system. Not all users require access to every aspect of the security solution. Therefore, proper delineation based on roles is essential for the effective operation of the security solution. Role-based access

CHAPTER 4 DATA SECURITY SOLUTION DESIGN

control ensures compliance and facilitates adherence to audit regulations. For instance, a policy author does not need access to audit reports detailing changes in user permissions over the past month.

Role Hierarchy

A robust security solution should establish roles and empower super administrators to define role names along with the associated functionalities that users within each role can access, modify, and execute. Roles can be hierarchical, enabling permissions inheritance based on the role hierarchy. These roles are indispensable for the clear delineation of responsibilities and ensure the integrity of the security solution remains intact.

An illustration of role definition within a system is provided in Table 4-8.

Table 4-8. User Role Definitions

Role name	Parent role	Privileges
Super Admin	N/A	No Restrictions
Admin	N/A	Can't create user and roles
Policy Admin	N/A	Can author policies, view/create policy reports, violation reports
Policy Super Admin	Policy Admin	Can view violations
Violation Admin	N/A	Can view violations, execute remediation actions
Violation Super Admin	Violation Admin	Can view policy reports, violation reports
Compliance Admin	N/A	Can manage and run compliance reports
Auditor	Compliance Admin	Can manage and run audit reports

215

Alternatively, instead of explicitly defining roles, role definitions can be inherited from the identity provider. The super administrator can designate appropriate Active Directory (AD) groups to define roles and hierarchy. Consequently, users within the AD belonging to these roles will automatically inherit corresponding privileges.

User Functions and RBAC

Users can be assigned to roles, automatically inheriting the privileges associated with those roles. This Role-Based Access Control (RBAC) is essential for any security solution. Compliance and other data regulations often mandate that users are restricted to only the privileges they require, making RBAC crucial in ensuring adherence to these requirements.

RBAC grows with your organization, like a flexible framework that adjusts seamlessly to your expanding needs. Whether you're a startup or a corporate giant, RBAC scales effortlessly, effortlessly handling more users, roles, and permissions as your organization flourishes, all without missing a beat in performance.

Summary

This chapter has delved into the fundamental components that constitute a comprehensive security solution, ranging from the intricate workings of the content detection engine to the intricate processing capabilities of the user processor. Each of these systems plays a pivotal role in ensuring the optimal functioning of the security solution, working in tandem to uphold the integrity and security of the environment.

Throughout our discussion, we've underscored the critical importance of adherence to the core requirements outlined earlier. These requirements serve as the bedrock upon which the efficacy and reliability of the security solution are built, guiding the development and implementation of each component.

Armed with this knowledge, organizations are equipped with a solid understanding of the essential functionalities they should expect from a robust security solution. As we transition to the next chapter, we'll embark on a journey to further explore these foundational components, expanding upon our existing framework to create a more comprehensive understanding.

Central to our discussion will be the concept of unified policies and content detection engines, which form the backbone of a scalable, robust, and consistent product. Any deviation from these principles risks introducing inconsistencies and vulnerabilities across different access points, underscoring the necessity of maintaining a cohesive approach.

Looking ahead, the forthcoming chapter will delve into strategies for reducing reliance on security policies, exploring the role of feedback mechanisms and reasoning modules in achieving overarching security objectives. By harnessing these tools, organizations can chart a path toward greater resilience and adaptability in the face of evolving threats and challenges.

CHAPTER 5

Design Towards Autonomy

When does a security solution truly achieve autonomy? Is it when it can operate entirely without human intervention? Not quite! Even in self-driving vehicles, some level of input is necessary. For example, a car may learn your preferred interior temperature is 70°F, but it won't automatically adjust if you feel too cold (at 70°F) on a specific day. The point is that no system, including security solutions, can be fully automated. They require minimal guidance. The key to making security solutions autonomous lies in understanding the organization's and users' intent behind data breaches, whether malicious or negligent, to offer proactive protection. It's akin to defending against zero-day attacks by providing zero-day protection.

I'm not a proponent of cumbersome, one-size-fits-all policies that dictate specific actions based on the channel, as they often lead to maintenance headaches. Instead, I advocate for a blend of generic and channel-specific policies. Whether they're generic or channel-specific, I firmly believe in the power of reusable rules. Content detection rules can be standardized and applied across various policies, ensuring efficient and consistent detection.

But how effective are the policies we create? Are they performing as intended? What happens over the years? How do we keep them updated? These are some of the important questions that bring out the need for a

CHAPTER 5   DESIGN TOWARDS AUTONOMY

system to track their performance and make necessary adjustments. In this chapter, I will discuss with you how to monitor and measure policy efficacy. This tracking benefits administrators and our security system. With these learnings, our system can learn, automate routine tasks, and exceed expectations by auto-tuning the system.

In this chapter, we'll dive into the core components that pave the way to autonomy: the reasoning module, analytics engine, statistics engine, and feedback processor. Specifically, we will look into the functionality of each of these modules and how they interact. Additionally, we'll explore risk assessment and the process of developing holistic solutions, setting the stage for the next chapter on AI-driven data security.

Are you excited? I can't wait to share what I have learned with you. Let's get started!

Reasoning Module

What is a reasoning module? A reasoning module is the most sophisticated security component that analyzes partial matches and policies across various channels, considers violation remediation actions, and gets input data from the feedback processor.

Before we dive into designing the reasoning module, it's crucial to understand why this level of sophistication is necessary and how it supports autonomy. The previous chapter examined security products' challenges, such as detection and coverage gaps. These are significant issues that cannot be fully resolved by policy authors or security administrators alone. Each organization is unique in its practices for handling data. What is sensitive for one organization might not be for another. There's no one-size-fits-all solution. We need a system to learn an organization's practices, environment, and user behavior. By learning, we can determine what is sensitive, identify potential actions that could lead to a data breach, and provide proactive security.

I would call the module 'Reasoning' rather than 'Learning' because it draws conclusions or inferences based on the learnings. The reasoning could apply to a user action (DIM) or data residing in a cloud repository (DAR). It could draw inferences from successive user actions.

At this point, let's examine a couple of examples to understand the potential impact of the reasoning module on the system and its significance.

EXAMPLE USER ACTION

A user downloads a sensitive file from a Box folder. Let's assume that action is permitted as he can download it. Now, he uploads the sensitive file to his personal Google Drive. This is not approved, and let's assume there is no policy in the system to catch this operation. We must stop his upload to Google Drive as it is highly suspicious, even though no policy exists. Retrospectively, we can ask questions like 'There should have been a policy' and 'Why isn't there a policy as it looks pretty straightforward?' Trust me, most data breaches occur when users find simple gaps in the security system. Attackers or hackers don't try to strong-arm the system in the most complicated way. Returning to the example, the user account could have been compromised, and that is why we have the zero trust approach where we continuously monitor every action, even by approved users. Needless to say, continuous monitoring is one of our core security requirements.

So how does the reasoning module assist here? The Reasoning module, though there is no policy to protect the data, knows a couple of key facts: (1) It knows the file is sensitive. (2) It knows the user is trying to get the file out of the organization domain (to his personal space). Knowing the file is sensitive, it is a partial match. Then it knows sensitive files are blocked on email channels for external domains. Hence the reasoning module figures out it is a coverage gap and blocks the upload to the personal Google Drive folder. Additionally, a violation is created.

CHAPTER 5 DESIGN TOWARDS AUTONOMY

> **EXAMPLE EXECUTIVE EMAIL**
>
> An executive from the organization emails content classified as a merger to an external email address. Let us assume a violation was created, but the email was not blocked. The violation remediator then closed the breach as a false positive. The reasoning module knows and remembers this because the feedback processor fed the data into the reasoning module. Now, the same executive emails another message with content classified as a merger.
>
> The reasoning module allows the system to create the violation but automatically closes it as a false positive.

You can see that the reasoning module is designed to perform beyond the expectations of policy authors and violation remediators, offering autonomous, proactive protection. For instance, in the "Executive Email" example, the system could have intelligently prompted the user to create an automatic policy exception when the violation remediator marked it as a false positive. We'll explore this further in Chapter 6. One of the most significant flaws in a security system is its tendency to generate false positives. False positives can overwhelm system administrators. Therefore, we should design our system in every possible way to minimize false positives.

Primarily there are three facets through which the reasoning module can collect data and use it to provide proactive protection. This serves as a general guide, and there may be additional methods. I aim to present a foundational approach that can lead to consistent and promising results in the field. Let's examine them one by one in depth.

Policies Across Channels

Organizations create policies based on numerous parameters, all with the ultimate goal of preventing data breaches. Each policy is formulated with context rules, content rules, and potential exceptions, as we discussed in the previous chapter. Every rule has a specific reason behind its creation by the administrator. For a security system to be intelligent, it must understand the intent of the policy administrator in crafting these varied rules and exceptions—not just for a single policy but for the entire set.

To design an intelligent system, we first need to understand the critical parameters that policy administrators use when creating policies. Our system should identify what is considered sensitive content and what is not, with the help of these policies. This is the primary, and often the only, way to determine what an organization considers sensitive. The system should also account for exceptions when certain content is not deemed sensitive. Since data exfiltration can occur through different vectors for each channel, policies are usually more specific to individual channels. Let's start by examining one channel at a time. As we delve into each channel, we'll also explore how our reasoning module should be constructed to adapt and learn from the system.

Email Channel

Figure 5-1 illustrates the critical fields in an email that policy authors use to establish criteria for policies. Whether it's cloud-based or on-premise email, the critical fields remain consistent, and our approach to analysis is the same.

CHAPTER 5   DESIGN TOWARDS AUTONOMY

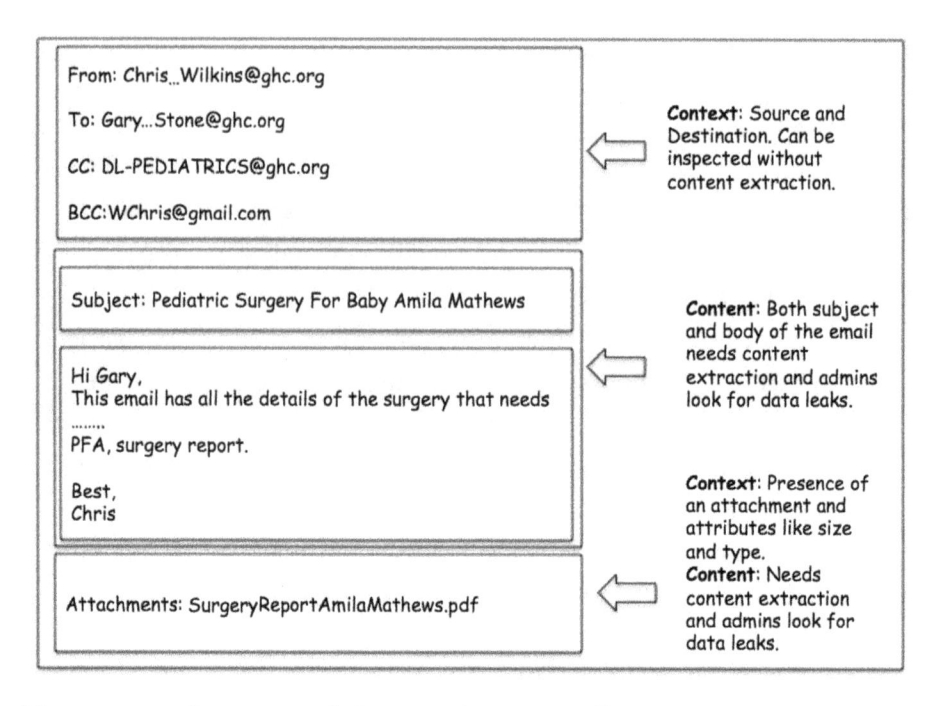

```
From: Chris...Wilkins@ghc.org
To: Gary...Stone@ghc.org
CC: DL-PEDIATRICS@ghc.org
BCC: WChris@gmail.com
```
⬅ **Context**: Source and Destination. Can be inspected without content extraction.

```
Subject: Pediatric Surgery For Baby Amila Mathews

Hi Gary,
This email has all the details of the surgery that needs
.........
PFA, surgery report.
Best,
Chris
```
⬅ **Content**: Both subject and body of the email needs content extraction and admins look for data leaks.

```
Attachments: SurgeryReportAmilaMathews.pdf
```
⬅ **Context**: Presence of an attachment and attributes like size and type.
Content: Needs content extraction and admins look for data leaks.

Figure 5-1. *Context and Content in an Email*

In the case of email, which is the most straightforward of all communication channels, context is key. This context includes details such as who the email is sent from, who it is sent to, and who is copied or blind copied. Refer to Figure 5-1. Typically, email policy context rules revolve around senders, sender domains, recipients, recipient domains, subject keywords, and whether or not there are attachments. If attachments are present, the file types also matter. Contextual exceptions are also like context rules and they are centered around the same set of parameters.

Policies can include exceptions, which might be individual email addresses or distribution lists (DLs). For example, in Figure 5-1, the DL "DL-Pediatrics@ghc.org" is being copied. When inspecting for security, we have two choices: match the DL name as is, or check if any members of the DL are on the prohibited list. The email can only proceed if all members are on the exception list; otherwise, our security system must take a conservative approach.

CHAPTER 5 DESIGN TOWARDS AUTONOMY

Advanced context considerations might include the classification tag of the whole email, sender identity groups, recipient identity groups, attachment classification tags, encrypted attachments, subject lines matching regular expression patterns, and the size of the email, among other factors.

Figure 5-2 presents a typical policy that restricts PII and HIPAA content to external domains. As you can see the policy also has an additional context rule of attachment size > 1MB (the policy named didn't get updated though the policy got updated).

```
Policy P1 - Restrict PII & HIPAA to External Domains in Email

Channel: Email

Context:
    Rules:
        R1: Has attachment of size greater than 1 MB
                    OR
        R2: External Domains in To, CC, BCC fields
    Exceptions:
        R3: Executive DL (DL-Executives@ghc.org) in To, CC, BCC fields

Content:
    Rules:
        R4: PII Data
            OR
        R5: HIPAA Data
    Exceptions:
        NONE
```

Figure 5-2. *Sample Email Channel Policy*

Next, when it comes to content rules, policies can be based on the subject, body, and attachments of an email, or any combination of these elements. Policy administrators search for sensitive content, which can vary widely. Typically, not all sensitive content is lumped into a single rule with numerous conditions. Instead, policies are built over time by policy authors to protect the organization's most critical information at any given moment.

CHAPTER 5   DESIGN TOWARDS AUTONOMY

For instance, if an organization is working on a confidential project, policies might focus on preventing leaks related to that project to protect intellectual property. As new projects emerge, new policies are created to safeguard the new information, while old policies are rarely deleted and remain in the system.

Attachments are critically important in an email as they are the main source of data breaches. Attachments can be of different file types. As discussed in the earlier chapter, our content detection technology needs to be advanced to detect any text, image, video, encrypted, compressed, or embedded file types.

Now, turning to the aspect of learning, the reasoning module should initially focus on identifying sensitive content. By learning the signatures of sensitive content, it can apply the same logic to partial matches across all channels, which would be highly advantageous for identifying coverage gaps. Next, the reasoning module should prioritize understanding the context: who has access and who doesn't. This learning process can be segmented based on users, user groups (if applicable), and domains. Additionally, all other relevant parameters should be considered, such as encrypted content, classified content, and any rules based on file properties like name, size, and type. This approach will assist the reasoning module in minimizing false positives.

Next, it is crucial for a reasoning module to prioritize learning the remediation actions associated with each policy. Does the policy author prefer solely monitoring or intervening in policy matches? In other words, it is the difference between Monitoring and Preventing, as we discussed in Chapter 2. Prevention may involve various actions such as blocking the email, quarantining it, encrypting attachments, or applying classification tags. Regardless of the action, the reasoning module needs to be comprehended. It's akin to deciphering the intentions of the policy authors.

CHAPTER 5   DESIGN TOWARDS AUTONOMY

Network Shares Channel

Let's explore what the reasoning module can learn from policies corresponding to the network shares channel. Figure 5-3 presents a typical DAR policy, while Figure 5-4 highlights the key elements in a network share file that is sent for content detection.

```
Policy P2 - Restrict PII & HIPAA in DAR

Channel: Network Shares

Context:
    Rules:
        R1:  Document is of size > 1MB
                          OR
        R2:  Shared to users from external domains
                          OR
        R3:  Download from non-corporate devices
    Exceptions:
        R3:  Document is of size > 1MB
                          AND
        R4:  Shared with users from Executive DL (DL-Executives@ghc.org)
Content:
    Rules:
        R4:  PII Data
              OR
        R5:  HIPAA Data
    Exceptions:
        NONE
```

***Figure 5-3.** Sample DAR Channel Policy*

CHAPTER 5   DESIGN TOWARDS AUTONOMY

```
Name: Surgery Report Amila Mathews

Size: 800 KB

Creator: Chris Wilkins  (Chris_Wilkins@ghc.org)

Created On: Jan-08 -2024

Last Modified on: Jan-09-2024

Collaborators: Gary Stone (Gary_Stone@ghc.org), DL-PEDIATRICS@ghc.org

Permissions: Edit Access to all shared collaborators

Classification: Not Classified

Encryption: Not Encrypted

Share Request : Wchris@gmail.com
```

Figure 5-4. *Sample DAR File for Content Detection*

This channel is all about DAR—Data At Rest. The files stored within it possess several critical attributes, as depicted in Figure 5-4. File Creator/ File Owner refers to the user who created the file, while File Collaborators includes those with whom the file is shared. File Permissions specify the read, write, and delete permissions granted for the file. Additionally, attributes such as File Created Date, Last Accessed Date, and Last Modified Date are vital timestamps associated with the file. Action in inspection should also be present in the request. Figure 5-4 shows the action as a "Share Request."

When policy authors create policies for this channel, they focus on contextual attributes like File Owner, Collaborators, and Last Modified Date, as well as file attributes such as name, type, and size. Advanced contextual considerations, similar to those in the email channel, might include encryption and classification. Content rules assess the sensitivity of the content, while remediation rules encompass actions like quarantine, deletion, and unsharing.

The reasoning module should grasp the sensitivity of files and understand which users have access to them and their respective locations. Through correlation, the reasoning module can identify the most critical locations or shares within an organization in contrast to less critical ones. Learning about user groups, and user domains, and specifically determining which external domains are safe to share content with is crucial for the reasoning module.

Cloud DAR Channel

The Cloud DAR channel focuses on data stored in cloud applications such as Google Drive, Dropbox, and similar platforms. This channel shares similarities with Network Shares. Alongside the contextual attributes and content rules observed in the network shares channel, the posture of cloud applications—whether they are approved corporate applications or non-approved ones—is crucial. In some organizations, multiple instances of the same application may run, each with separate administrators, login credentials, and other tenant controls. Our reasoning module needs to grasp these distinctions.

Remediation actions in the cloud may differ significantly from those in on-premise network share DAR channels. For instance, quarantine locations in the cloud may have specific sets of administrators with access to quarantined files. Encryption methods for cloud data may also differ from those used in on-premises. The reasoning module should strive to understand the specific intent of policy administrators when handling cloud data compared to on-premises data. Organizations often enforce stricter policies for cloud environments compared to on-premises ones. Cloud environments can vary between public and private clouds. While the reasoning module may not ascertain whether applications are hosted on a public or private cloud by examining policies and settings alone, posing this as a question could provide valuable insights. These learning points will be further explored in the next chapter.

CHAPTER 5   DESIGN TOWARDS AUTONOMY

Network Channel

Technically, the Network channel, encompassing both on-premise and cloud environments, also includes Email. However, due to the paramount importance of Email, we addressed it separately. Apart from Email, the on-premise or cloud network involves scanning all network traffic, including outgoing and incoming request responses. While the network allows us to identify applications in certain cases, in many instances, this may not be feasible. For instance, when a packet is addressed to a Google server, we can ascertain that it is intended for Google, but distinguishing between a Google search and other types of requests to Google servers may pose challenges. Network traffic may be encrypted due to end-to-end application encryption, rendering the traffic invisible. However, in this section, concerning the reasoning module, our focus is not on analyzing the traffic but rather on analyzing the policies. Whether it's a cloud network or an on-premise network (excluding Email), the constructs of policies remain similar. Cloud networks may have stricter rules akin to those in the Cloud DAR channel. Figure 5-5 depicts the critical pieces in network traffic. Think about how a security administrator should author policies to detect this type of content.

Key elements of network policies include contextual attributes such as source address, destination address, internal vs. external domain, payload size, encrypted traffic, application details like name, type, identifiable threat level, and content rule—content sensitivity. Remediation rules may involve blocking and monitoring, as these are two feasible actions.

The Reasoning module should learn about source and destination addresses and domains. This is the most critical piece of information. Now with these domains, we can correlate with the domains on the email channel or share DAR files to that domain.

CHAPTER 5   DESIGN TOWARDS AUTONOMY

Payload Size: 2000 bytes

Captured on: Jan-09-2024, 9 am EST

Source: 10.25.66.77 (IP Corresponds to user Chris Wilkins – Chris_Wikins@ghc.org)

Source Machine: Corporate Windows Laptop – Chris.wilkins.ghc.org

Destination: 142.225.220.0 (Gmail Server)

Application: GMAIL

Bytes: Encrypted Content

Figure 5-5. *Sample Network Traffic Capture for Content Detection*

Endpoint Channel

This channel represents the most intricate aspect of our security framework. The range of policies here is quite diverse, encompassing both Endpoint DIM and Endpoint DAR functionalities. Let's begin with Endpoint DIM. Within Endpoint DIM, we encounter various types of traffic, including email, application traffic, disk access traffic, network traffic between this endpoint and other locations, as well as peripheral traffic such as USBs, DVD/CD players, and memory cards.

Policy authors may establish specific policies for each type of traffic within Endpoint DIM. These policies could involve completely blocking all USB access, monitoring all print access, allowing certain applications while blocking others, and so forth. The role of the reasoning module is quite clear-cut in this scenario. One advantage is that the context of the sender is consistently the logged-in user, providing access to all user attributes. However, a potential complication arises in scenarios where it's a network-shared system with multiple users logging in. The reasoning module must continuously learn about the enforced policies and the corresponding remediation actions taken upon policy matches.

CHAPTER 5   DESIGN TOWARDS AUTONOMY

The primary content rule revolves around the sensitivity of the file, while contextual rules may encompass remote destinations and the type of activity, such as upload, download, encryption, access, etc. Figure 5-6 offers a detailed overview of the possibilities within the Endpoint DIM channel. As you can see, this figure shows both the available options and what configurations are typically enabled on a sample endpoint. For instance, Disk Drive Monitoring is available on the endpoint agent for all file-based operations and Figure 5-6 also shows available disk drives in a sample endpoint, namely, drives C, D, and E.

Disk Drive Monitoring: C, D, E

Network: Corporate Network

VPN: New York Gateway

Approved Applications: Notepad, Adobe,....

Restricted Apps: ABC, Dem,...

Monitoring: Remote Share Copy, Cloud Application Upload, Screen Capture

Features Available: Classification, Encryption, OCR

Browsers: FireFox, Chrome...

Remote Mounted Drive: O, G, H

Peripherals: USB, DVD/CD Writer

Figure 5-6. Available Features and Monitoring Options in Endpoint Channel

Endpoint DAR involves scanning the files stored on disk on the endpoint, which may also include peripherals like USBs. The remediation actions undertaken are of utmost importance, and the reasoning module must learn from them accordingly.

CHAPTER 5   DESIGN TOWARDS AUTONOMY

BYOD Channel

Managing this channel presents an immense challenge for security vendors due to the nature of non-corporate devices. Detection capabilities are limited, and policies within this channel tend to be highly restrictive. The prevailing context revolves around BYOD (Bring Your Own Device), which dictates the rules governing this domain. The reasoning module can segregate the context rules specific to BYOD from those of other channels. Similarly, content rules may also be notably stringent.

Attempting to correlate BYOD rules with those of other channels could distort the results and unnecessarily contaminate the learning process and application of policies and remediation actions across various channels. Thus, it is imperative to maintain a clear demarcation between the policy learnings of the BYOD channel and those of other channels.

Correlating Policy Learnings

Across all channels, key insights may encompass user-based rules, user groups and their exceptions, approved vs. non-approved domains, as well as encryption and classification rules. Particularly within the content rule, we would have established what constitutes sensitive information and what does not. Through this process, we would have identified generic policies applicable to all channels and those specific to each. By correlating channel-specific policies, as previously discussed, we can easily identify coverage gaps and propose new policies. Insights gleaned from policies can also aid administrators in fine-tuning existing policies, a topic we will delve into further in Chapter 6.

Security violation remediation is critical to forbid data breaches and curtail any impending threats. Learning about remediation rules is critical to close security violations which is highly beneficial to assess the threat level or the security posture of the organization. Also in audits, the open violations point to a major red flag. Our learning will not be complete without remedial rules. If encryption or classification is required, additional data needs to be gathered on other associated rules that go along with it. For instance, encrypt only the content in repositories 1 and 2, and ensure classification is always done for all documents in repository 3, and so on.

Another essential insight in Data at Rest (DAR) channels is the frequency of scans across various applications or repositories, whether cloud-based or on-premise. Organizations typically conduct these scans to maintain compliance and for security audits. Additionally, scans may be performed to provide high-level executives with crucial information. Therefore, it is important to understand which entities are involved in these scans and how often they occur.

Violation Remediations

The reasoning module should understand how violation remediators address violations. There are several violation remediation methods, with some of the most common categories outlined below. These serve as learning opportunities for the reasoning module. By assimilating this knowledge, the reasoning module can autonomously remediate violations, minimize false positives, and implement advanced remedial actions. Such insights form the foundation for maintaining continuous compliance within an organization.

Closing As False Positive

Violations can be closed as false positives by violation remediators in two scenarios:

Scenario 1: The remediators are aware that the issue has already been addressed.

Scenario 2: The remediators know that the action was intentional and not a threat.

The first scenario is risky because the remediation occurs outside the security organization, and the reasoning module cannot access this information unless the remediators provide details. The second scenario involves cases where the remediator wants to monitor the action without considering it a real threat. Monitoring violations, such as print monitoring, are intended to gather evidence of organizational activities rather than impose restrictions. For example, tracking print activities helps keep a record for future correlation if any issues arise.

For our reasoning module, both preventive and monitoring violations are crucial. Even if print monitoring violations are auto-closed, the reasoning module must be aware of them. At this stage, the reasoning module should not auto-close violations based on its learnings, as we are still in the learning phase.

Closed As a Known Threat

This situation is similar to false positives, but here the violation remediators provide a reason explaining why they believe the threat is known and not dangerous to the organization. While the reasoning module currently lacks the intelligence to parse and comprehend the language of these reasons, it should still learn from the actors involved and other variables, such as the channels and violated policies, that led the remediator to close the case as a known threat.

Closed After Initiating a Manual Quarantine

When a violation remediator initiates a manual quarantine, the reasoning module gains valuable insights into the context and specifics of the violation, including the quarantine details. However, it's crucial to understand that learning a remediation action from a single security violation doesn't immediately enable the reasoning module to apply the same step to thousands of similar violations. Learning is an ongoing process, and confidence builds with repeated actions for similar cases.

CHAPTER 5 DESIGN TOWARDS AUTONOMY

In the upcoming chapter, we will explore how to leverage this growing confidence to automatically create new policies and fine-tune existing ones.

Closed After Initiating a Manual Encrypt/Classification

Encryption and classification remedial actions are quite similar. Violation remediators may initiate manual encryption or classification actions. The reasoning module should understand the context and learn from these actions. In some cases, it can discern why automated remediation wasn't an option. Classification involves tagging content, and the reasoning module can further analyze which policy violations necessitated a tag, correlating this tag with the type of content. Accumulating such insights will lead to a knowledgeable system capable of automatically tagging sensitive content.

Closed After Removing Sharing or Removing the Collaborators

This remedial action is frequently observed in the DAR channel, typically arising when a user shares files with individuals who present a threat to the organization, or worse, with external domains. Remediators must meticulously examine these violations and address them by revoking access for risky parties. The reasoning module gains insights into internal users deemed risky and identifies external domains, as well as users attempting to gain unauthorized access or those granted access.

Closed As User Training

These instances highlight the need for specific user training. They represent classic cases of negligent users attempting shortcuts or performing actions without considering the potential risk to the organization. Training for these cases involves manually informing the users about their mistakes. The reasoning module can understand the circumstances under which the violation remediators initiated these actions.

Triaged to a Different User Indicating Investigation Needed

In this instance, the security violation remains open. The triaging process suggests that the violation is either unfamiliar to the violation remediator or that the specific remediator lacks the access or tools necessary to address it. The reasoning module needs to learn about the type of security violation that was delegated, along with the source and destination users involved in the delegation. The module will continue to gather information as the designated user logs in and takes action to address the violation.

Triggered a Workflow or Integrated with the Ticketing System

In certain organizations, violation remediation processes are integrated with external systems, enabling the delegation of remedial actions to other users. This approach, in my view, offers scalability. However, it complicates the functioning of the reasoning module, as it only receives information indicating that the violation has been converted into a ticket or that a workflow has been triggered in an external system. In all cases, the reasoning module lacks access or means to monitor the remediation process in the external system, rendering it a black box. Nonetheless, it is known that violations of this nature have been forwarded to an external system or a ticket has been raised.

CHAPTER 5   DESIGN TOWARDS AUTONOMY

Never Remediated

This is the most challenging and frequent scenario for the reasoning module. Most security violations remain unaddressed, which is particularly problematic for the reasoning module as it cannot learn from these unresolved cases. Often, organizations implement security products for compliance purposes but lack the resources to remediate violations. Consequently, the influx of violations far exceeds the rate at which they can be remediated.

With this environment-specific learning of remediation, our system can adapt to the customer organization and perform with much greater precision.

Storing Partial Matches

Partial matches form the basis for policy tuning in an organization. By partial matches, I mean whenever the content detection executes, some conditions in a policy might match and some won't. Storing all these partial matches would yield great results. This can be well explained through a concrete example.

Consider there are a couple of policies, P1 and P2 in the system. Policy P1 corresponds to the email channel with the following context and content rules

Policy P1:

If Sender is from Finance Group and Recipient is part of Non-Finance Group then

BLOCK all emails with content containing tax statements for the Yr 2024 except for Chris Watt.

Policy P2:

Block Sharing "TaxStatement2024" folder with members other than Non-Finance Group.

Take a moment to compare these two policies, noting the differences in how they address similar content across different channels.

Here, Policy P1 limits email access to non-finance group members, except for Chris Watt, when it comes to tax statements for the year 2024. On the other hand, Policy P2 restricts collaborators in the 'TaxStatement2024' folder to finance group members exclusively. The exception present in the email channel policy is absent in the policy for network shares.

Let's explore how partial matches can help in this scenario. Imagine several violations occur when a network folder share request, initiated by the finance admin and others from the Finance AD group, includes Chris Watt to view the 'TaxStatements2024' folder. Business-wise, Chris Watt is part of the Executives group and needs access to this shared folder. Due to a policy blocking the share request, Chris Watt cannot view the folder. To circumvent this, the Finance Admin sends emails containing the tax statements directly to Chris Watt, exploiting the exception in Policy P1, which prevents any policy violation from being triggered.

With partial matches, we would recognize that the email contained sensitive content, specifically the tax statements for 2024. This constitutes a partial match because the content rule was met, but the exception for Chris Watt prevented it from being flagged as a violation.

By identifying this partial match, we see that the email's content is equivalent to the content of the 'TaxStatements2024' folder. This leads to two potential actions: allowing future folder share requests for Chris Watt in Policy P2 or removing Chris Watt from the exception list in Policy P1.

From a security product perspective, the system identifies that Policy P1 (for the email channel) and Policy P2 (for the network shares DAR channel) are similar, except for the exception clause in P1. The system assumes that the exception clause might be a shortcut. Recognizing the business need, the proper course of action would be to add Chris Watt to the exception list in Policy P2, ensuring consistency across policies and channels. So the system also provides the option to add Chris Watt

CHAPTER 5 DESIGN TOWARDS AUTONOMY

to the exception list. Based on how the violations for share requests are remediated, the reasoning module can learn that Chris Watt needs to be added to the exception list.

Let's take this example further. Suppose there's an email from the finance admin to another executive team member, Damien Martin. Damien Martin and Chris Watt belong to the same "Executives AD Group" and are peers. Our security system would block the email because Damien Martin is not included in the exception list of Policy P1. Now, imagine the violation remediator closes this violation as a false positive. This indicates that Damien Martin should also be added to the exception list. These insights come from partial learnings and correlations. Since Damien Martin and Chris Watt are peers, instead of adding them individually, we could add the entire AD group to the exception lists of Policies P1 and P2. We will delve deeper into this in Chapter 6, but for now, it's all about learning.

The core idea behind storing partial matches is to capture all the partial matches for the content that either violates or doesn't violate policies. Storing these partial matches may require significant storage, but let's assume we have ample storage capacity for now. We will address the storage challenge in later chapters. Whenever a rule triggers based on content or context, we store the matches. These matches can be aggregated if they occur repeatedly. Once partial matches are stored, the system can, with the help of past violation remediations, determine the best course of action for drawing conclusions or inferences.

The reasoning module is thus responsible for analyzing policy matches across channels, processing violation remediation feedback, incorporating it to conclude, and storing partial matches to make intelligent decisions. Now, let's move on to the next core component, the analytics engine, whose primary purpose is data analysis.

Analytics Engine

Analytics engine has few primary functions in an autonomous system. They are as follows:

1. User behavior analysis
2. Data usage and trail
3. Continuous watch of all violations to calculate risk posture
4. Analytics on cloud applications security posture management

All these functions are necessary to satisfy the core requirement of continuous monitoring. With continuous monitoring, the analytics engine collects data and processes them drawing intelligent inferences. Let's look at the above functions in depth.

User Behavior Analysis

Popularly known by the acronym UEBA (User Entity Behavior Analysis), this function analyzes user behaviors to identify anomalies. Monitoring users continuously is crucial for detecting deviations from normal behavior. Anomalies or abnormalities signify deviations from typical behavior patterns. We can enhance basic anomaly detection by developing sophisticated systems that compare behaviors across peers, departments, and other metrics. Abnormalities in user behavior might suggest malicious intent or compromised credentials. This approach aligns with the zero-trust principle, where no one is implicitly trusted.

To illustrate abnormal behavior, let's consider an example involving Phil working for a financial organization. Every day for the past three months, Phil logs in from the New York office at around 9:30 AM EST,

CHAPTER 5   DESIGN TOWARDS AUTONOMY

clocks out at 5 PM EST, and mainly accesses financial folders on Google Drive without downloading them, using the edit online functionality instead.

Suddenly, Phil logs in from a European country at 10 PM EST. This is the first anomaly—why would he log in from a different location? It could mean he's on vacation or traveling for work. Phil's risk level increases as his behavior becomes suspicious. Next, he downloads a document from Google Drive, which he has never done before. This further raises his risk level, indicating he might be a threat to the company, especially since the financial documents are sensitive. Finally, he uploads the document from his corporate laptop to his personal Google Drive. This is the third strike.

At this point, we must question whether Phil is the real Phil or if his account has been hacked. When do we intervene?

User Data Collection

User data collection begins by determining if there are integrations with identity provider systems. Most security deployments include these integrations, allowing us to access a user's complete history, including department, location, manager, management chain, group memberships, and peers. This information is critical for associating user behavior with these attributes.

Next, it is essential to track every user in the system without exception. When encountering a user for the first time, we must gather all basic information across the channels we observe. Typically, if the user has a laptop, they will first be detected by the endpoint channel, or in some cases, via the BYOD (Bring Your Own Device) channel. We must correlate this user with their activities, monitoring everything they do from login to logoff.

For example, a user might upload data to the cloud, send emails via cloud email services, and access data from network shares. This specific user would then be interacting with multiple channels: Endpoint, Cloud DAR—Applications, Cloud Email, and On-Premise DAR—Network Shares.

CHAPTER 5   DESIGN TOWARDS AUTONOMY

Here is a sample list of attributes that you should typically track. Feel free to expand this list as needed.

- Login Time
- Login Device ID
- Login Location
- Logoff Time
- Logoff Location
- Device IP address
- VPN Connection Gateway Details
- Channel Accessibility
- User Identity Information (Manager, Peers, etc.)
- User Activities (uploads, downloads, emails, etc.)
- Application usage in organization device
- Usage of BYOD

The details for each of the aforementioned attributes should be collected every time the user is online. In certain situations, additional information might be required, such as when the user logs in from remote countries or frequently travels. Sometimes certain data might not be available for certain activity types. Any data should be acceptable. The Statistics engine, discussed later in this chapter, would perform activities like data cleanup and normalization to close the gaps.

The collected data can be aggregated together and sent off for analysis. We're talking about keeping tabs on everything everyone does, but there are certain things you could leave out. You're not necessarily holding onto every bit of data that's created, edited, or deleted. For instance, imagine a user chatting with a colleague—you don't need to save every single chat. Instead, you could note that the user utilized a chat application with a

243

specific person. However, even with this selective approach, the volume of data could still be massive. If managing all of it becomes impractical, you could limit data collection to instances where the user violates policies. In those cases, gather all the attributes mentioned earlier. But remember, we're not continuously monitoring at that stage.

After collecting the data, the data collectors can transmit the data to the centralized analytics engine for analysis. The frequency of this transmission largely hinges on the scalability of your solution. Typically, it's advised to send data once a day. Now, you might wonder how proactive protection is possible with daily data transmission. Excellent question! The answer lies ahead in correlation.

User Data Correlation and Analysis

Now, we arrive at the pivotal component of a user behavior analysis module: correlation. User data correlation involves many intricate elements. It includes tracking a user's activity across all channels, comparing the user's actions against their historical behavior to identify any anomalies, and then comparing these actions against their peers, groups, departments, and even across different countries. Analyzing this data is challenging, and as a security vendor, it's essential to dedicate ample time and resources to developing this process accurately. The analysis will provide valuable insights into user behavior and reveal how effectively administrators are managing risk.

Analysis of User Activity across Channels

Tracking user activity and understanding the context is vital. A user's actions are often interconnected. Typically, a user starts with the endpoint channel or BYOD channel and then moves on to performing various activities. It's essential to monitor these actions to understand their behavior. For instance, if a user downloads a document from the cloud and then attempts to upload it to a USB drive, we need to capture this sequence to provide a complete picture to the administrator. Simply stating that the upload to the USB was blocked doesn't offer much insight. Instead, we should detail the preceding and subsequent activities. For example, the user might have tried to upload to the USB, got blocked by our security software, and then attempted to print the document, which wasn't blocked. The user could have printed the document and taken it home. By providing this context, we enable security administrators to make informed decisions about what's happening.

Tracking high-risk users is crucial for preventing breaches. For this discussion, let's assume we already know who the high-risk users are in the organization. We'll cover how to calculate risk scores in the next section. High-risk users include repeat offenders and employees who have submitted their resignations. These individuals require close monitoring, as they are more likely to cause significant damage to the organization.

Stitching activities across all channels is complex, especially when data is incomplete. We often have to work with the information available. For example, imagine a malicious insider creating an application to exfiltrate sensitive data from the organization. Suppose this application is a batch program that runs nightly, using a generic admin account to send emails with sensitive content to external recipients. In this scenario, there isn't a specific user behind the action, but sensitive data is being emailed out. To address this, we need to identify that sensitive content is being read from an internal shared repository and attached to outgoing emails. We must detect that these emails are being sent through the email channel and recognize that the administrator's email account is orchestrating this data breach. Providing this context can save security administrators thousands of man-hours in forensic investigations.

CHAPTER 5   DESIGN TOWARDS AUTONOMY

User Self Analysis

Analyzing user behavior against their historical actions is the first indicator of a compromised account. Negligent users are particularly susceptible to phishing scams and ransomware attacks, as we discussed in Chapter 1. Identifying behavior changes provides valuable insights into potential issues and highlights security vulnerabilities within an organization.

For instance, consider a scenario where an external attacker compromises a user account and then

- Accesses an application that the legitimate user is not authorized to use
- Deletes all files from an internal repository containing sensitive content
- Logs into a cloud application without using MFA
- Changes the passwords for multiple accounts within a short period
- Opens internal folders for external domain access

What do these activities indicate? Take a moment to think about it.

Firstly, analyzing these actions together reveals definite abnormal behavior. It also highlights the organization's need to tighten its security posture regarding permissions. Here are the actions that could have prevented these data breach attempts:

- **Unauthorized application access**: Ensure appropriate permissions for all users accessing applications.
- **Mass deletion of sensitive files**: Implement permissions to prevent file deletions or prohibit mass deletions via security policy.

- **Logging into a cloud application without MFA:** Enable MFA for all cloud applications through single sign-on or by coordinating with the cloud provider.

- **Multiple password changes in a short time:** Establish a policy to block consecutive password changes by correlating subsequent actions (this can be challenging).

- **Mass sharing of internal folders externally:** Enforce a policy to block mass external sharing of folders.

Analysis can range from simple observations, such as a user who typically logs in with device A now using device B, to more complex patterns. While device B could be new, it might also signal a potential issue. On the more elaborate side, consider a user exfiltrating sensitive documents gradually over several days to avoid detection. Identifying such cases can be challenging, but by comparing the user's recent behavior with their historical patterns, we can spot these changes. Malicious actors often repeat suspicious activities at the same time each day. Using such heuristics in our analysis model can significantly enhance our detection capabilities.

Peer Analysis

Peer analysis involves comparing a user's behavior with that of their colleagues, such as those under the same manager or within the same department. This comparison helps identify deviations that may be abnormal. Some users may have higher privileges, so it's essential to first compare a user against their behavior before looking at peer comparisons. If a user's behavior changes, similar changes could be observed among their peers as well.

CHAPTER 5   DESIGN TOWARDS AUTONOMY

Peer analysis is critical, and a practical example can illustrate its impact. For instance, supposedly a user typically uploads an average of 15 documents in one day to Box and downloads about 20. Users' peers might average slightly higher numbers, such as 30 uploads and 40 downloads. Assume on a specific day, the user downloads 160 documents, significantly exceeding the daily average. Further supposedly all the users' peers on the very same day are still around their usual averages, this sudden spike of activities by the user in question is suspicious. There could be a legitimate business reason for this behavior, but it cannot be ignored. The key takeaway is that the user's behavior is flagged as suspicious, and a security administrator can review and provide feedback on whether this action is justified.

Figure 5-7 represents the data collected by a typical system and the comparison results. Results indicate that all are normal and no abnormality.

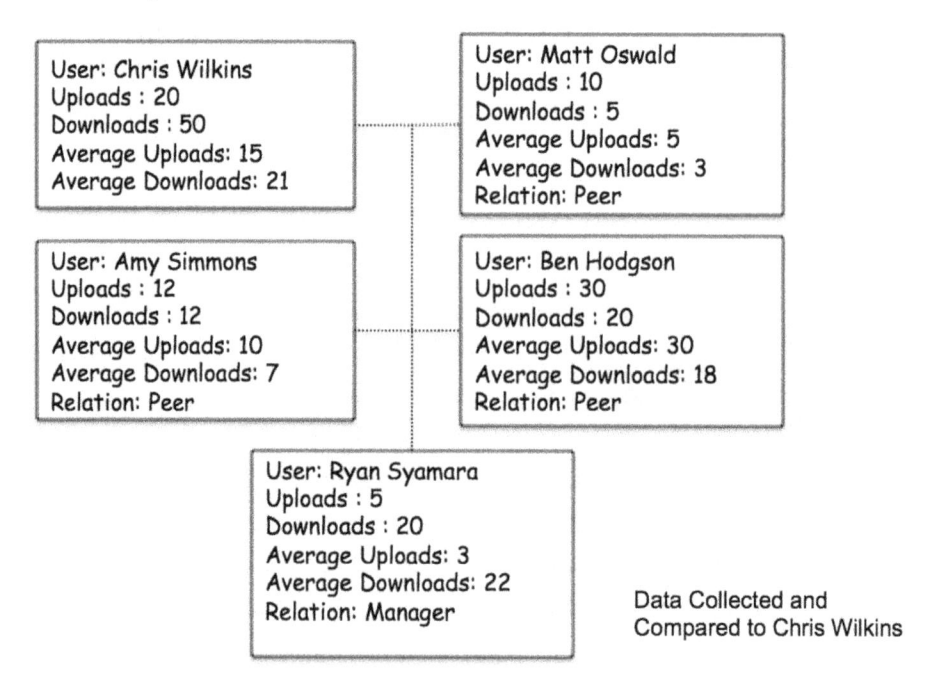

```
User: Chris Wilkins                    User: Matt Oswald
Uploads : 20                           Uploads : 10
Downloads : 50                         Downloads : 5
Average Uploads: 15                    Average Uploads: 5
Average Downloads: 21                  Average Downloads: 3
                                       Relation: Peer

User: Amy Simmons                      User: Ben Hodgson
Uploads : 12                           Uploads : 30
Downloads : 12                         Downloads : 20
Average Uploads: 10                    Average Uploads: 30
Average Downloads: 7                   Average Downloads: 18
Relation: Peer                         Relation: Peer

          User: Ryan Syamara
          Uploads : 5
          Downloads : 20
          Average Uploads: 3
          Average Downloads: 22      Data Collected and
          Relation: Manager           Compared to Chris Wilkins
```

Figure 5-7. *Data Collection and Comparison Against Peers*

CHAPTER 5   DESIGN TOWARDS AUTONOMY

Acting upon Abnormalities

Having analyzed and correlated the user data, we have to act on it. Actions can be multifold. Our sole motto is to provide administrators and enable our security system to spot these anomalous users easily and to track them effectively.

Providing Context

As discussed earlier, the initial step when identifying suspicious activity is to provide additional context. This context helps the organization understand why the activity is deemed suspicious. Such activities could indicate security vulnerabilities that need to be addressed or suggest that a user is abusing their assigned permissions. Typically, the context is organized chronologically to facilitate investigations. Refer to Figure 5-8 below, which illustrates sample suspicious activities and their associated context.

```
Suspicious User Context for Violation 123 - Data Exfiltration

Endpoint: Login: ABC logged into corporate device at 8.30 am

Cloud Applications: Corporate GDrive Access:   ABC accessed Gdrive at 8.35 am using SSO

Cloud Applications: Corporate GDrive Download: ABC download Records.pdf at 8.37 am

Network Shares : File Upload: Records.pdf uploaded at 8.40 am

Network Shares : Share Request: Records.pdf shared to Administrator at 8.40 am

Endpoint: Login: Administrator logged into Machine General at 8.45 am

Endpoint: Browser Email: GMAIL Login at 8.46 am

Endpoint: Browser File Upload: GMAIL File upload Records.pdf at 8.50 am
```

Figure 5-8. *Suspicious User Activity Context*

From Figure 5-8, the administrator gains a clear understanding of the context of events. This is made possible by correlating various activities. While it appears straightforward here, implementing such a solution in practice requires extensive data collection and continuous correlation of activities across multiple channels.

Risk Score Calculation

The analytics engine's primary function is to compute a risk score based on user activities, likened to points on a driving license for traffic offenses. This score helps identify both high-risk and low-risk users. A higher proportion of high-risk users increases the organization's overall risk score. Instead of using generic risk levels like high, medium, and low, I advocate for a numeric score derived from violations and suspicious activities, which offers more practical utility. Risk scores may decrease in the absence of anomalous user activities.

Let's look at an example of Computing User Risk Scores. The first step is data collection. The system collects data from various sources, including

- Suspicious Logins
- Suspicious access to sensitive files or systems
- Any other anomalous or suspicious activities
- Security violations combined across all channels

Once the data collection is complete, we can compute the scores based on risk factors and weightage to each factor as depicted here.

- Suspicious Logins—weightage: 10%
- Suspicious Sensitive File Access—weightage: 20%
- Anomalous Behavior—weightage: 20%
- Incident History: Single violation—weightage: 20%. Multiple violations—weightage 50%

CHAPTER 5 DESIGN TOWARDS AUTONOMY

Now based on the risk factor, we can compute the weighted risk score.

- Suspicious Logins—10 points × 10% weight = 1 point
- Sensitive File Access: 12 points × 20% weight = 2.4 points
- Anomalous Behavior: 12 points × 25% weight = 3 points
- Multiple Incidents: 5 points × 50% weight = 2.5 points
- Total Risk Score = 1 + 2.4 + 3 + 2.5 = 8.9

As I articulated earlier, let's assume the mapping for low, medium, and high risk scores are

- Low Risk: 0–3 points
- Medium Risk: 4–7 points
- High Risk: 8+ points

Hence the user with 8.9 points is of high risk.

Moreover, risk scores can be assigned to applications to highlight potential vulnerabilities. If a particular application is frequently exploited by employees, its high-risk score should trigger a comprehensive evaluation of its security posture.

Furthermore, we can empower security administrators to flag users for monitoring, significantly elevating their risk scores upon detecting suspicious activities. This user-specific approach enables proactive risk management. Additionally, we can implement policies that restrict user activities based on their risk scores, either manually or automatically.

Enhance Alarms

We can enhance alarms through the following measures:

- Escalating the severity of violations committed by high-risk users
- Maintaining a separate list of repeat offenders and closely monitoring them
- Automatically creating stricter policies for high-risk users to prevent data breaches
- Alerting the user's manager and security administrator specifically about high-risk users
- Prioritizing the remediation of security violations involving high-risk users
- Implementing the most stringent remedial actions for high-risk users

Strengthening Security Posture and Risk Assessment

Once high-risk users are identified, the security administrator understands the coverage gaps and vulnerabilities these users exploit. These vulnerabilities can include policy coverage gaps, content detection gaps, risky applications, access control weaknesses, dormant privileged accounts, and unused accounts. The security administrator is also aware of external threats that internal users might introduce, either negligently or maliciously.

Addressing these issues by tightening coverage and closing loopholes allows the organization to enhance its security posture and significantly reduce risks. This risk reduction can greatly benefit brand reputation, customer trust, and, most importantly, employee trust.

Data Trail

After monitoring users, the next crucial entity to focus on is the data itself. Monitoring data is essential since it is the ultimate asset we aim to protect. Data audit trails provide administrators with insights into how data moves within and, in some cases, outside the organization. Like user activity monitoring, data trails can also reveal organizational vulnerabilities.

A significant challenge is that data exists in various formats, making comprehensive protection complex. Malicious actors often embed sensitive data within non-sensitive data to exfiltrate it, similar to adulteration. Additionally, users may bring personal devices or manually copy and print data to remove it from the organization. Data trails provide vital clues and forensic evidence for investigations.

Let's explore how we can track data and highlight the essential steps for creating an effective data trail.

Following Data

What do I mean by following data? Which data needs to be tracked? Excellent questions! Let me answer the second question first. Only sensitive data, or data we deem sensitive, needs to be tracked. This sensitivity can be identified through partial or exact matches of sensitive content descriptions in policies. This is the data that needs to be followed.

Now, to the first question: By following data, I mean continuous monitoring. Continuous monitoring of data can yield significant results.

Imagine a scenario where a user logs into a shared device (used by many within the organization), logs in as an administrator, and downloads a file. This user then shares the file with a few others by placing it in a shared folder. Another user copies the file from the shared folder to their laptop. Later, they disconnect from the network and print the data using their home computer. At this point, the data has effectively left the organization's control.

Of course, monitoring only the final print activity could have protected the file, but we wouldn't have identified all the users involved in this exfiltration attempt. This process is similar to a forensic investigation where you follow the money trail to catch all the culprits. In this context, data is our currency. It's even more valuable than money.

Within an organization, vast amounts of data often remain untouched for years. This data, created by former employees, can exist in multiple repositories. It may be highly sensitive and in need of protection. Since it's forgotten or overlooked, no security policies are typically in place to safeguard it. Malicious actors seek out such low-profile sensitive data, making it a prime target for exploitation. Following such a data trail may lead to additional repositories where such data may be residing.

Data Transformations

The most common form of data exfiltration is through transformation. Renaming data file types, for example, can make it challenging for content detection software to inspect the data. Many security systems, if unable to inspect data within a few seconds, will fail to open to avoid disrupting business continuity. This compromises the organization's data security.

Other transformation methods include saving data as picture files, taking screenshots of content, recording videos of the content, embedding sensitive data within non-sensitive data, compressing or encrypting data using custom formats and encryption schemes, and moving data to remote locations where it can be further manipulated and transformed.

When dealing with data transformations, it's crucial to store the extracted data, as it may become unextractable after transformation. However, saving extracted data demands significant hardware resources, which may not be feasible. If data extraction is impossible, the entire file should be blocked as a precautionary measure to prevent potential data breaches. Practically speaking, even tracking file names and their locations can be a challenging task for security software. In large organizations, we are dealing with gigabytes, if not terabytes, of data. The extracted data or saved file names can pose a threat themselves, acting as honeypots that can be exfiltrated. Since we are tracking only the sensitive data, malicious actors might target the security software to steal the data by following its trail. We must be cautious while designing the software, additional layers of security need to be there for all this cached information.

Data Usage Suspicion

Data usage can raise suspicions, and here's a scenario to illustrate: imagine a user suddenly downloads a sensitive piece of content from a repository they've never accessed before. That's eyebrow-raising. It's crucial to closely monitor such data or keep tabs on it continuously to uncover any associated risks.

Once we have a good grasp of what's considered normal, we can start keeping an eye out for anything that seems out of place. Here are a few examples:

- Data being accessed or tampered with at odd times or from unusual locations

- Significant increases or decreases in the volume of data moving around, especially if it deviates from the usual patterns

- Attempts to access data that's supposed to be off-limits, particularly if it's sensitive or confidential

In summary, following and tracking sensitive data can lead to the following results:

> **Reducing Risks**: Keeping an eye on sensitive information helps us catch potential security issues early, so we can deal with them before they become big problems.

Keeping Things Safe: When we know where sensitive data is and who's using it, we can put extra protections in place to ensure it remains safe from hackers or other risks.

Playing by the Rules: Some rules and laws necessitate organizations to safeguard sensitive data by following a set of practices. By tracking it, we ensure that we're doing what we have to be doing and avoid getting into trouble.

Dealing with Problems: In the worst case, if a data breach happens or we are facing an impending threat from attackers, knowing where our sensitive data is can help us respond quickly and fix things.

Learning Useful Stuff: Watching how people use sensitive data can give us insights into how things work in our organization and help us make smarter decisions about security and risks.

Violation Monitoring

Monitoring violations is crucial for several reasons. First, it provides insights into the effectiveness of our security policies, highlighting areas where improvements may be needed. Second, it helps identify potential risks and vulnerabilities within the organization, allowing us to take proactive measures to address them. Additionally, monitoring violations allows us to understand how effectively our remedial processes are followed in response to security incidents. It also assists in assessing the overall risk profile of the organization, enabling us to prioritize and mitigate risks accordingly. Lastly, monitoring violations ensures that we maintain compliance with relevant regulations and standards for data protection and security.

Let's explore this in detail.

Security Policy Efficacy

Violations give us a clear picture of how well our security policies are working. They show us which policies are being broken and which ones are doing their job. By looking at violations, we can spot trends and figure out where we might need to make our security measures stronger. Sometimes, we might see that our policies are too strict (or lenient—depending on how you see it), causing harmless actions to be flagged as violations. Other times, we might find that certain rules are too loose, letting actual breaches slip through the cracks. This helps us fine-tune our rules to better fit our organization's needs and keep things secure.

Monitoring violations also helps administrators to see how effective the overall security setup is. It gives administrators insights into how well the security policies are being enforced and how quickly the violations are getting remediated per policy. With this data, administrators can make smart decisions about how to tweak the policies and other associated protocols to better protect against both internal and external threats. This ongoing process of keeping an eye on violations and tweaking the policies leads to a stronger, more adaptable security system that evolves with the changing risk. And in the next chapter, we'll dive deeper into how systems can learn and adjust based on this kind of analysis.

Risks and Vulnerabilities

Continuous monitoring of violations provides the analytics engine with valuable insights into the lurking risks and potential vulnerabilities within the organization. These insights are then summarized for administrators, along with recommended actions to address them. Such a comprehensive security solution would undoubtedly be well received. As executives reading this book, it's essential to demand this level of analytics capability from security vendors; settling for anything less could leave your organization exposed to unnecessary risks.

CHAPTER 5   DESIGN TOWARDS AUTONOMY

Identifying risks and vulnerabilities is a cornerstone feature of any effective security product, especially data protection software. By analyzing the types of violations across various channels, we can pinpoint which channels pose the greatest risks. Furthermore, categorizing and grouping violations by user enables us to create profiles of high-risk users within the organization. This approach allows us to identify common attributes and behavioral patterns among these risky users, empowering us to implement targeted protection measures and enhance overall security posture.

Monitoring external threats, ransomware attacks, and phishing scam violations yields valuable insights for strengthening the organization's infrastructure. Attackers continuously target outbound traffic-facing devices and appliances such as edge routers, switches, proxies, firewalls, and endpoint devices. Safeguarding these critical points against vulnerabilities is paramount, as emphasized throughout this book. Violations serve as tangible evidence, empowering administrators to advocate for enhanced security measures in vulnerable areas. This proactive approach ensures that the organization remains resilient against evolving threats, maintaining a robust defense posture in the face of adversarial activity.

Remediation Process

Analyzing the remediation process provides valuable insight into how effectively security vulnerabilities are being managed within the organization. This visibility is particularly beneficial for audits, offering a clear understanding of the organization's security posture and its responsiveness to threats. Different types of remediation enable security software to automate specific actions, reducing the need for manual intervention and streamlining the remediation workflow.

Compliance

Security violation analytics enable organizations to assess and manage compliance-related risks effectively. By identifying areas of non-compliance and prioritizing remediation efforts, organizations can mitigate the risk of regulatory penalties, fines, and reputational damage associated with compliance failures.

By continuously monitoring security violations, the analytics engine can identify instances where security policies and regulations are not being followed. This proactive approach leads to detailed compliance insights that can be shared with administrators. Using this, organizations can detect compliance breaches early and take corrective action to address them.

Now, let's dive into the fascinating realm of violation trends. These trends offer a captivating glimpse into the ever-evolving landscape of security breaches. By tracking and visualizing these trends, we keep administrators in the loop and empower our autonomous engine to glean valuable insights and take proactive measures, effectively providing automatic protection.

Violation Trends

Using violation trends allows us to foresee upcoming breaches and vulnerabilities, enabling proactive protection measures. Trend analysis proves especially valuable in autonomous systems. Here, the analytics engine can deduce insights from trends, determining whether the organization's risk profile is improving. Are violations on the decline? Is user coaching proving effective? Is remediation occurring automatically? These insights not only guide strategic decisions but also help fine-tune security measures to adapt effectively to evolving threats.

CHAPTER 5   DESIGN TOWARDS AUTONOMY

Figure 5-9 depicts a small violation trend in a fictitious organization. As you can see, visually capturing and representing trends across different channels helps both administrators and our security system.

Channel	Violations Past Week	Violations Yesterday	Violations Today	False Positives	Needs Investigation	Investigated	Suspicious Activity
Email	928	100	120	12	20	76	12
Endpoint	2000	28	229	18	33	164	14
Network Shares	878	67	22	10	4	1	7
BYOD	12	5	4	1	3	0	0
Cloud Apps	2899	567	876	80	122	662	12
Network	345	45	57	22	11	20	4
SSPM Drift	2	1	0	0	0	0	0

Figure 5-9. *Sample Violation Trends*

Cloud Applications Security Posture Management

In the realm of Cloud Application Posture Management, the analytics engine emerges as a pivotal force, delivering insightful revelations and wielding automation capabilities to fortify the security and compliance of cloud-based applications. The numerous benefits offered by these analytics are indeed profound.

Consider the intricate landscape of cloud applications, reliant upon precise configuration settings for their integrity. Any deviations from these configurations pose inherent risks, potentially exposing vulnerabilities. Enter the SaaS security posture management (SSPM) solution, a guardian ensuring the meticulous upkeep of configurations and swift remediation of any anomalies—a cornerstone of our comprehensive solution, as elaborated upon in Chapter 3.

CHAPTER 5   DESIGN TOWARDS AUTONOMY

However, now we are augmenting our SSPM solution with the prowess of analytics. No longer are we merely monitoring configurations; we are delving into the essence of the matter. We are discerning the individuals accountable for configuration drift, assessing the expediency of our responses, and evaluating our remediation strategies—whether aligned with product recommendations or organizational protocols. These analytics go beyond mere numerical data; they hold the essence of our autonomous system, guiding us toward automated refinement and optimization. It's like having a dedicated team of guards, always watching over our cloud applications, ready to take action whenever needed.

The next module that we are going to examine is the Statistics module.

Statistics Engine

You might ask why we need a statistics engine when we already have an analytics engine. Is the statistics engine the same as the analytics engine in terms of collecting, aggregating, normalizing data, and drawing inferences? They may appear similar in theory, but in reality, they are not. The statistics engine has unique features that the analytics engine does not address.

A statistics engine is primarily dedicated to processing and analyzing numerical data to derive descriptive statistics, including averages, frequencies, distributions, and correlations. Unlike an analytics engine, the statistics engine does not analyze various systems; instead, it processes the collected numerical data and computes statistics based on it. Its methodology revolves around classical statistical techniques such as hypothesis testing, regression analysis, variance analysis, and time series analysis, focusing on summarizing and interpreting data using established statistical methods. The statistics engine excels at generating descriptive statistics, identifying correlations, detecting outliers, and summarizing data distributions.

In our system design, I envision the Statistics Engine as an assistant to the analytics engine, specifically in processing numerical data and providing the necessary relevant statistics required by the analytics engine. In other words, while the analytics engine performs the overall workload, the statistics engine serves a supportive role in the background.

There are two important modules I'd like to discuss here: the data pre-processing module and the data visualization module within a statistics engine.

Data Pre-processing Module

Before we discuss visualizing data, we need to ensure it's in good shape. Pre-processing techniques like cleaning, filtering, and removing duplicates ensure our data is clean. Sometimes, data collector modules may fail to collect data because of varied reasons. This ensures that when we compute the numbers, our conclusions are based on accurate and reliable information. Missing data is like trying to complete a puzzle with some pieces missing. That's where pre-processing techniques like imputation or deletion come in. They help fill in the gaps or remove incomplete pieces, ensuring our dataset is complete and ready for analysis.

Lastly, we need to tweak our data to ensure it fits the bill for our statistical models. This could involve transformations like normalization, standardization, or even logging. These adjustments ensure our data behaves just right when we compute the numbers.

You might wonder why we encounter all these problems when all we're doing is following users, tracking data, and examining policies and violations. It's an excellent question! In the real world, there can be misses due to system failures, data loss, and other unforeseen circumstances.

By cleaning, normalizing, and transforming our data, we're laying the groundwork for accurate and meaningful insights. It's the first step on our journey to uncovering the secrets hidden within our data.

Data Visualization Module

In our security design, a statistics engine can facilitate data visualization in several ways: First, the statistics engine can generate visual dashboards that display key security metrics in a clear and concise format. These dashboards provide a high-level overview of security performance, including metrics such as threat rates, violation rates, violation response times, compliance adherence status, and so on. By analyzing historical data, the statistics engine can create visualizations that illustrate trends in security events and violations over time. Line charts, bar graphs, or heatmaps can be used to visualize trends in areas such as threat activity, vulnerability exposure, etc. This can aid administrators in better visualization.

For security violations with geographical relevance, the statistics engine can generate maps that visualize the geographic distribution of security violations. This can help security teams identify regional hotspots of malicious activity or areas with high concentrations of security vulnerabilities. The statistics engine can visualize network traffic patterns using flow diagrams or network topology maps. These visualizations can help identify abnormal traffic patterns, potential bottlenecks, and suspicious network activity. Visualizations can be used to depict patterns of user behavior, such as login activity, data access patterns, and privilege escalation events. Heatmaps, scatter plots, or timeline visualizations can highlight anomalous user behavior that may indicate insider threats or compromised accounts.

CHAPTER 5   DESIGN TOWARDS AUTONOMY

During violation response activities, the statistics engine can generate visualizations that track the progress of security incidents from detection to resolution. Gantt charts, timelines, or flowcharts can visualize the sequence of events, actions taken, and stakeholders involved in the incident response process.

The next question you may have after reading the above section is, how is this tied to autonomy? The analytics engine can draw insights, but the statistics engine seems like a background player. How would it contribute to autonomy? Let me explain.

The statistics engine plays a vital role in enabling autonomous decision-making and proactive risk management in data protection solutions. It aids in the overall tuning of the security system itself. Through statistical analysis of system performance metrics, the statistics engine identifies optimization opportunities to enhance the efficiency and effectiveness of data protection measures. It autonomously adjusts system configurations and resource allocations to optimize performance and maintain operational efficiency.

By leveraging statistical analysis techniques and insights, it enhances the autonomy, efficiency, and effectiveness of data protection measures, ultimately strengthening the security posture of organizations. It also feeds into the Analytics engine as well as AI modules that we are going to see in the next chapter. All of this will contribute toward a true autonomous protection solution.

Furthermore, a statistics engine can perform certain tasks: Utilizing statistical modeling and machine learning algorithms, the statistics engine performs anomaly detection to identify suspicious or unauthorized activities. It autonomously flags anomalous behavior, triggers alerts, and initiates response actions to mitigate security incidents.

In summary, while the analytics engine draws insights from data, the statistics engine provides vital support by enhancing the accuracy and efficiency of decision-making processes.

CHAPTER 5   DESIGN TOWARDS AUTONOMY

Feedback Processor

Next, let's discuss the design for the feedback processor. This is one of the essential components in our autonomous system that provides proactive protection. The main purpose of the feedback processor is to collect all the feedback from various systems, aggregate and do the first step of curation, and then forward the same to the reasoning module. This reasoning module in the next chapters will be explored further. The feedback processor is connected to all the components as depicted in Figure 5-10. The processor learns from each component and then passes the curated results to the reasoning modules which then take appropriate action to autonomously protect the data.

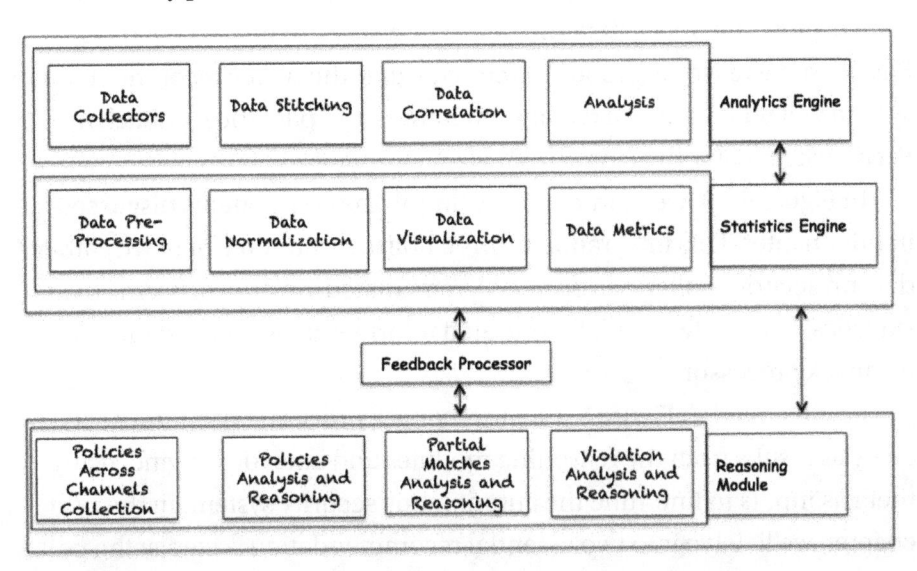

Figure 5-10. Tying Reasoning Module, Analytics and Statistics Engine, and Feedback Processor

As the feedback processor and the reasoning module are interconnected, sharing conclusions and insights is bidirectional. The feedback processor can store all the violation remediation feedback and relay it to the reasoning module. Additionally, it can store feedback on policy suggestions. With input from the Feedback Processor, the reasoning module can refine its conclusions and inferences. Let's examine a practical example to better understand this interaction.

For instance, assume our system recommended closing a coverage gap in the endpoint channel by blocking all uploads to a remote share folder. After the admin reviews this policy, they might provide feedback by accepting the policy but adding an exception for certain users from an AD group. The feedback processor then stores this input and passes it on to the reasoning module, which updates its learning to reflect that this policy recommendation was good but needed an exception clause. You might be wondering which system makes these policy recommendations. We'll explore the policy recommendation system in the next chapter. Based on the reasoning module's conclusions, the policy recommendation system will make suitable recommendations and pass the feedback to the Feedback Processor system.

In Figure 5-10, we're interconnecting all the components discussed in this chapter. This integration forms a holistic solution where we gather data on security policy performance, remediated violations, user activity statistics, and analytics. All this curated information is then fed into the feedback processor.

As illustrated in Figure 5-10, the feedback processor primarily receives analysis results from the reasoning modules and analytics engine, using them as inputs to fine-tune the autonomous security system. In the next chapter, we'll delve into two essential recommendation systems: the policy recommendation system and the violation remediation recommendation system. These recommendation systems rely on feedback processors' input to make intelligent recommendations. The majority of feedback processor activities are self-explanatory, and we'll depend on it to build a fully autonomous system.

CHAPTER 5   DESIGN TOWARDS AUTONOMY

A critical but often unspoken aspect of this system is its reliability and scalability. While it's fundamentally a security requirement, it's also essential for our application. All the modules feeding into the feedback processor must be resilient enough to recover from any failures. Although not covered in this book, organizations typically plan for High Availability and Disaster Recovery (HA/DR). As a security vendor, our solution should seamlessly integrate with organizational HA/DR plans. If you're on the cloud, you must design for HA/DR, and if you're on-premises, you must ensure provisions are in place for organizations to implement their HA/DR strategies. None of our design choices should hinder customers from achieving HA/DR.

Summary

In this chapter, we explored the pivotal components essential for elevating our foundational security design into a fully autonomous system. The reasoning module, analytics engine, statistics engine, and feedback processor emerged as the cornerstone elements shaping our future developments. These components set the stage for our next chapter, where we will advance the design further by integrating artificial intelligence to create automatic recommendation systems.

Among these modules, the reasoning module and feedback processor stood out for their ability to evaluate partial matches and generate insights beyond the scope of manual configuration. This module holds significant potential for further refinement, offering solution designers an avenue for enhancing its capabilities. For executives and organizational representatives, this chapter provides valuable insights into the journey toward autonomous security solutions and highlights critical features considered by security vendors.

CHAPTER 5　DESIGN TOWARDS AUTONOMY

Ultimately, the overarching goal remains the proactive reduction of risk and strict adherence to organizational protocols. We are moving toward a system capable of adaptation and learning, leveraging insights from user behaviors, violations, and remediations to become an intelligent administrator. This vision entails the creation of a virtual assistant, empowered to make informed decisions for the organization's security landscape.

Now, let your imagination soar. With all these components integrated into our security system, envision the possibilities for making intelligent recommendations. Once we achieve this, and administrators are confident enough to allow the system to operate on autopilot, we will have a truly holistic, autonomous, and proactive security system.

CHAPTER 6

Pro-Active Intelligent Data Security

In any security solution, the most critical aspects are policy authoring and the inspection and remediation of security violations. Can we make this easier? Isn't this a million-dollar question on the minds of everyone, from cybersecurity professionals and enthusiasts to executives seeking data protection? Can we entirely remove policy authoring and violation remediation from the hands of security administrators and fully automate these processes? Not possible. By now, I have emphasized many times in this book that every organization is different and every deployment scenario is unique. If we can't eliminate these tasks, can we at least reduce the manual and maintenance efforts? Now we're talking! I feel like we are getting somewhere. This chapter is about how to build intelligent capabilities into the security system so that it can go on autopilot for a variety of tasks, resulting in proactive, intelligent data security.

In literature, policy-less data security is often equated with zero trust security. Zero trust security embodies an approach wherein security measures consistently authenticate and authorize users and devices for various system activities, departing from reliance solely on conventional security policies. This methodology factors elements such as user devices, access locations, and activity types, regardless of any established trust within the network. Implementing policy-less data security involves deploying tools like identity and access management (IAM), multi-factor

CHAPTER 6   PRO-ACTIVE INTELLIGENT DATA SECURITY

authentication (MFA), encryption, and micro-segmentation, which enable flexible and responsive access regulation. Embracing a zero-trust mindset allows organizations to mitigate the risks posed by malicious insider threats, compromised credentials, and other internal or external attacks.

It's essential to recognize that zero trust represents just one step toward policy-less data security, not the entire solution. Without policies, no security system can effectively detect sensitive data within an organization. Organizations must classify and rank the sensitivity of documents to ensure appropriate protection. Security systems can learn from this classification and build on it. Similarly, administrators need to remediate violations so that the system can learn how they prioritize violations and what actions they take to manually remediate them.

When discussing intelligence and automation, I don't suggest completely overriding the security administrators (policy authors, violation remediators) to automatically deploy policies and remediate violations. While full automation is possible, the choice should always remain with the administrators. We can provide recommendations, but administrators must decide what actions can be automated. For example, administrators might approve categorizing certain types of violations as false positives and closing them automatically. In such cases, our system can proceed accordingly. However, any control decision should always be confirmed with the administrators.

In this chapter, I will introduce several recommendation systems designed to automate the security solution, proactively alerting and preventing threats and breaches. These recommendation systems will be built on the foundational components discussed in Chapters 4 and 5.

CHAPTER 6   PRO-ACTIVE INTELLIGENT DATA SECURITY

Policy Recommendation System (PRS)

Before we delve into recommendations, let's set the stage for how these suggestions, if implemented, will flow through the system. This is a proposed design outlining how a Policy Recommendation System could operate. Please refer to Figure 6-1. It all begins with the feedback processor.

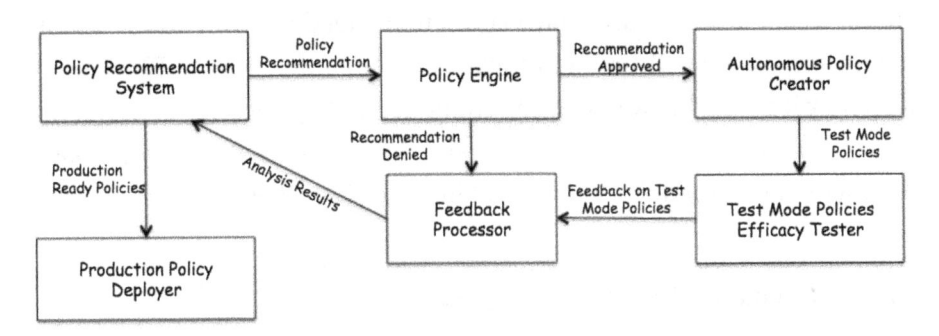

Figure 6-1. Policy Recommendation System Logical Flow

The feedback processor, based on all the analyses conducted, submits its results to the Policy Recommendation System (PRS). PRS then generates a policy recommendation and forwards it to the Policy Engine for approval from the Policy Author. The Policy Author has two options: to either proceed with the recommendation or disapprove it. If disapproved, the feedback is sent back to the feedback processor for further processing, and the analysis results are relayed to PRS again. Since the feedback was negative in this instance, PRS will refrain from suggesting the same recommendation to the Policy Author in the future. It is important to note that the feedback processor does not make any decisions. Instead, it processes the feedback and provides the analysis results to the PRS, which is responsible for making the final decision.

If the Policy Author approves the recommendation, the approval is sent to another module known as the Autonomous Policy Creator, which is responsible for creating policies. Initially, these policies are in test mode, meaning they are not widely implemented across the system.

CHAPTER 6   PRO-ACTIVE INTELLIGENT DATA SECURITY

Instead, test mode policies are selectively applied, and a subset of violations is analyzed to assess the policy's effectiveness before converting it into a fully operational production policy. This precaution ensures that the autonomous system does not inadvertently cause unintended consequences. Another module, the Test Mode Policies Efficacy Tester evaluates the efficacy of these test mode policies, as depicted in Figure 6-1. Once tested, the results are relayed back to the feedback processor, which then communicates with PRS to convey the outcomes. Finally, PRS deploys the policy into production using a Production Policy Deployer.

Let's examine the responsibilities and the operational methods of each of the associated modules introduced in the PRS workflow.

Autonomous Policy Creator

The autonomous policy creator module operates in two modes: test mode and production mode. Each policy, as discussed in previous chapters, includes context and content data rules, exceptions, and remediation rules. Based on input from the PRS, this module can create policies encompassing all necessary elements. Various types of remediation rules can be associated with autonomous policies depending on the channel or policy type, such as threat management, data protection, or posture management types of policies.

The autonomous policy creator can also generate compliance and regulation policies based on input from the PRS and compliance update templates. These templates, which security vendors need to update regularly, cover different types of data regulations such as PCI, DSS, PII, and compliance policies for SOX, NIST, etc. Since these policies govern various aspects of data protection, they are standardized and best managed through templates. When rules are updated, the security vendor can release new templates, which the autonomous policy creator can use to update organizational policies as needed.

CHAPTER 6   PRO-ACTIVE INTELLIGENT DATA SECURITY

Additionally, this module interacts with threat intelligence systems to stay updated on the latest threats and zero-day attacks, allowing it to create relevant policies. Later in this chapter, we'll discuss AI-based policies and how this module uses threat intelligence to develop these policies.

Test Mode Policies Efficacy Tester

We covered test mode policies in Chapter 3. As discussed, our security product should offer the option to create production and test mode policies. Policy authors should also have the ability to author test mode policies. These test mode policies can be selectively deployed, and the violations they produce are not considered real violations. No remediation rules can be executed on these test mode policies. As the name indicates, this is merely to test the system with the new policy. In large organizations with multiple coverage points, extensive infrastructure across countries, and hundreds of thousands of employees, deploying an erroneous policy could wreak havoc, disrupting business continuity or generating excessive violations if the policy isn't properly designed. For instance, erroneously deploying a policy that raises a violation whenever the CC field in an email is populated could create an overwhelming number of violations, which would then need to be painstakingly cleaned up.

Test mode policies allow the system to test the waters by creating sample test violations. These violations can then be analyzed to determine if the policy generates too many false positives or if it is too restrictive or loose. Once verified, the policy can be converted into a production one. The Test Mode Policies Efficacy Tester module is specifically designed to evaluate the effectiveness of autonomous policies. The system should be able to automatically analyze and confirm if the policies perform as intended. If the system cannot decide or reasonably predict performance due to changes in the environment or surrounding policies, it should send that feedback to the Feedback Processor, which in turn notifies the PRS to seek user input. In some cases, test mode policies need to be fine-tuned over multiple iterations based on user feedback. This process may take time before converting a policy from test to production mode. Deploying the correct security policy is crucial to prevent data breaches.

Production Policy Deployer

The Production Policy Deployer converts test mode policies into production mode by activating the remediation rules. While remediation rules remain inactive in test mode policies, they are essential and fully operational in production mode.

Now that we've examined all the associated modules, let's delve into PRS by itself and explore how it functions to generate these policy recommendations.

The PRS system, in addition to its recommendations, provides the context or reasons behind them to enable policy authors to make informed decisions. Let's look at an example first so that you can visualize as we dive deeper. A sample recommendation could be as follows.

EXAMPLE 1: POLICY WITH MISSING EXCEPTION RULE

Recommendation System Analysis:
The policies *Email External Domains Block Policy* and *DAR Channel External Domains Block Policy* are exactly similar except there is an exception rule that was added recently to the *Email External Domains Block Policy* and not to the *DAR Channel External Domains Block Policy*.

Reasons for this recommendation:
All context and content data rules of policies are the same.
All context exception rules are the same.
Email Channel Policy has an exception added on May 24, 2024, by Ross Wellington
Network Shares Channel Policy is missing the exception.

Recommendations for the policy author:
Option 1: Add the same Exception rule that exists in the *Email External Domains Block Policy* to the *DAR Channel External Domains Block Policy*.
Option 2: Don't make this modification.

As you can see, the policy author now has all the context and facts needed to make this decision. As mentioned earlier, PRS doesn't automatically enforce a policy. The recommendations have to go through the workflow and get deployed methodically.

Let's explore the design and functionality of the PRS. You might have noticed that the reasoning module discussed in Chapter 5 closely resembles or even constitutes a part of the PRS. The reasoning module can be enhanced into a full-fledged PRS, or better yet, serve as its core component. Before redesigning the reasoning module, let's review practical scenarios where a system like PRS would be beneficial. Using these real-world situations, we can develop heuristics for making effective recommendations.

Heuristics

The policy recommendation system is built on heuristics that I've observed to be effective over the years, and I'm excited to share this with you. Since recommendations must consider a wide range of parameters, the values of these parameters are correlated and analyzed over time, allowing the PRS to learn and develop these heuristics. These insights are then used to generate policy recommendations. Ultimately, the policy author has the final say on whether these recommendations are approved. Let's examine these heuristics one by one. Keep in mind that the techniques I provide are just a starting point. As a security vendor, you should build upon this foundation. Organizations can use these heuristics as a framework for managing their security solutions, offering valuable guidelines for policy authoring.

CHAPTER 6   PRO-ACTIVE INTELLIGENT DATA SECURITY

In Chapter 5, we discussed the analysis of policies across channels, the storage of partial results, and the use of these results to improve policies through correlation and learning. Now, we will pick up where we left off and build upon those concepts.

Policy DeDuplicator

Policy deduplication represents a straightforward yet powerful heuristic. Over time, organizations often encounter scenarios where policies are unintentionally duplicated within their security systems. As a security administrator, you may have experienced situations where you inadvertently recreated a policy without realizing it already existed. Many current security systems don't identify existing or similar policies. What constitutes similarity in this context? Typically, it involves examining exceptions within context or content rules or remediation action differences—a specialized heuristic used to identify security policies that are similar but not identical.

You might wonder, once a policy deduplicator has executed and recommended actions, what more needs to be done? Is this a one-time task? Certainly not! Policies are frequently created or modified, different policies may evolve to protect similar data. Therefore, a deduplicator is mandatory and should run whenever a policy is added or changed. For instance, consider the example of a "Policy with missing exception rule," where the distinction lies solely in a single exception rule. Such policies should be unified to achieve deduplication. Another example "Policies with missing remediation action" illustrated in Example 2 differs in remediation actions.

CHAPTER 6   PRO-ACTIVE INTELLIGENT DATA SECURITY

EXAMPLE 2: POLICIES WITH MISSING REMEDIATION ACTION

Recommendation System Analysis:
The policies P1 and P2 apply to the email channel and only differ by block remediation action.

Reasons for this recommendation:
All context and content data rules of policies are the same.
All context and content exception rules are the same.
The remediation rule to Policy P2 was added on June 2, 2024, by Ross Wellington.

Recommendations for the policy author:
Option 1: Unify the policies P1 and P2 by retaining only policy P1 and eliminating policy P2.
Option 2: Don't make this modification.

This deduplication heuristic can be further developed to identify additional similarities among policies. Currently, the proposed approach concentrates on discrepancies in exception rules and remediation actions.

To achieve this deduplication logic we must have a component in PRS that compares policies and identifies policy duplicates. This policy deduplication logic should be run whenever the policies are edited.

Coverage Gaps

The most important recommendation that the PRS system can make is to address the coverage gaps in policies. Channel-specific policies always result in coverage gaps. In Chapter 5, we discussed policy analysis by channel. As a security vendor if you offer a unified policy authoring solution across all channels such that if the same policy can apply to one or many channels then it would result in low coverage gaps.

EXAMPLE 3: POLICY SET WITH COVERAGE GAP

Policies:
Policy P1: Block all PII from the Endpoint DIM from being sent outside the organization.
Policy P2: Block all PII external sharing requests for Network Shares Channel DAR.

Channels Configured in the System:
Endpoint DIM, Network Shares DAR, Email DIM

You can see in Example 3, what I mean by a coverage gap. PII data needs to be protected and must not leak outside the organization. Endpoint, Network Shares, and Email are the three channels configured in the system. Currently, a couple of channels protect the data, but one does not. Take a moment to think about what the recommendation should be. It's straightforward, isn't it? Recommend a policy (P3) that blocks all PII data from being sent to external email domains via the email channel.

Can we improve this? How about consolidating all the policies and making that a recommendation too? Unify policies P1 and P2 and extend them to cover the email channel.

The final recommendations for the policy set in Example 3 are as follows.

RECOMMENDATIONS FOR THE POLICY SET IN EXAMPLE 3

Recommendation System Analysis:
Two policies P1 and P2 protect PII data from leaving the organization for channels Endpoint and Network Shares. The configured Email channel doesn't protect PII data.

Reasons for this recommendation:
All context and content data rules of policies are the same.
Email channel coverage is missing.

CHAPTER 6   PRO-ACTIVE INTELLIGENT DATA SECURITY

Recommendations for the policy author:
Option 1: Unify policies P1 and P2 to cover all configured channels, including the Email channel.
Option 2: Create a new policy to block all emails containing PII to external domains.
Option 3: Don't make this modification.

It's vital to note that policy deduplication and addressing coverage gaps may seem similar, but they are distinct processes. The proposed policy deduplication component doesn't deduplicate policies across channels. You might wonder: What if the policies aren't channel-specific from the start? Excellent question! If policies aren't targeted to a specific channel, then coverage gaps aren't an issue to start with.

How can we leverage the components within the PRS to achieve this? The reasoning module includes a dedicated component for cross-channel policy analysis. However, such comparisons can only be effective once the system comprehends the intent and significance of the current policies configured. Let's refer to that component as the Policy Analyzer, which understands the policy and breaks it down into different policy components so that the system can comprehend the policy author's intent.

Next, we require a policy comparator to compare policies across channels. Therefore, the Policies Across Channels Collection and Policy Analysis and Reasoning discussed in Chapter 5 transform into the Policy Analyzer and Policy Comparator.

We also need a component to interpret the results of the policy comparator to make actual recommendations. We will discuss this further as we explore other heuristics for PRS.

False Positives

False positives are identified through violation remediation. The feedback processor processes the results of violation remediation before they are integrated into the PRS. If there is a high number of false positives, it

CHAPTER 6 PRO-ACTIVE INTELLIGENT DATA SECURITY

indicates that the policy may not be suitable. In such cases, the PRS can recommend disabling the policy. But how many false positives are we talking about here? There has to be a substantial number of violations from that policy, or better yet, all violations from that policy are marked as false positives.

Sometimes, the organization wants to collect data and develop a policy to gather incidents for examination. Even though all incidents from that policy are marked as false positives, they need to be collected for potential future review. Let's review an example next to understand better.

Consider an organization that works with specific partners for digital marketing. The organization would have email correspondence and share materials with partners to market their products. It is prudent to have a policy to monitor all external sharing requests with a specific domain that the organization partners with. Incidents would be collected whenever emails are sent to the partner or when materials are shared through cloud storage. These incidents are merely monitoring incidents, intended to keep track just in case a data leak occurs.

So, as a security system, it cannot discern whether the organization has genuine false positives or if they are marking incidents as false positives for reasons similar to the example given earlier. All we can determine is that if a substantial number of violations are marked as false positives, the heuristic is to recommend disabling the policy.

To accomplish this, feedback from violation remediation is essential. Therefore, the PRS must closely interact with inputs from the violation remediation system. It's important to note that the false positives heuristic cannot be applied in cases where the violations are not remediated at all.

Incorrect and Outdated Policies

Understanding the policies within the system allows it to identify incorrect or outdated policies. For example: Let's assume a policy references an obsolete active directory group or members that no longer work for the

CHAPTER 6   PRO-ACTIVE INTELLIGENT DATA SECURITY

organization, that policy condition will never be met, making it a classic case of an outdated policy. As directory groups change or members leave the organization, it would be useful for the policy author to receive notifications. In such cases, the system should recommend updating the policy.

There could be other conditions where the policies can be outdated or incorrect and they are as listed below with examples:

> **Date-based rules**: Policy to match tax statements of the date 2023 when the year is 2024
>
> **Channel-based rules**: Policy to match emails when the email channel is no longer licensed
>
> **Incorrect remediation rules**: Policy having multiple contradicting remediation rules like having both delete and quarantine remediation action
>
> **Contradicting policies**: A policy to allow an external domain to be accessible and another policy restricting the same external domain for the same channel
>
> **Keywords/Regular Expressions Outdated**: A policy set that doesn't share keywords or regular expression rules gets updated for a policy and not updated for others
>
> **Wrong/expired credentials**: Having incorrect credentials for operations like encryption, and classification can render the policy useless

281

CHAPTER 6   PRO-ACTIVE INTELLIGENT DATA SECURITY

Loose Policies

Some policies can generate too many violations. We already discussed having a limit on the number of violations a policy can generate to circumvent the situations of policy administrators making a mistake while authoring a policy or genuinely the policy is too loose for the organization. Loose policies can hide real violations and negatively impact the system. Hence it is more important to disable the loose policies or tighten them. Loose policies can skew reports, all assessments, and automated learnings. Tightening loose policies involves policy administrators reviewing all the rules of the policy and making it more refined than being generic.

Let's assume the system has a violation limit of 25,000 violations per week on a policy. If the system hits the limit more often then we need to inspect the policies. Feedback from the violation processing system should be fed into PRS via the feedback processor to make recommendations. Example 4 here shows a typical recommendation of a loose policy.

EXAMPLE 4: LOOSE POLICY RECOMMENDATION

Recommendation System Analysis:
Policies P1 and P2 have constantly for the past 4 weeks reached the weekly violation limit of 25,000 violations. None of the violations raised by these policies have been remediated.

Reasons for this recommendation:
Weekly violation limit reached for 4 weeks.
No violation remediation for the violations.

Recommendations for the policy author:
Option 1: Disable policies P1 and P2.
Option 2: Disable policy P1 only.
Option 3: Disable policy P2 only.
Option 4: Don't make this modification.

Compliance and Regulations Adherence

Most organizations purchase security products to comply with various compliance standards and data regulations. With regulations frequently changing, it's advantageous for companies to rely on an automated security system that can notify them about their compliance status.

Compliance standards and regulations differ based on the business's location, industry, and the type of data they handle. Our security system can provide organizations with a simple questionnaire to determine which regulations apply to them. Based on their responses, the system can recommend security policies to ensure compliance. Of course, the policy author has the final say on whether to deploy the policy.

When regulations change, the system can notify the policy author and update the deployed policies accordingly. This reduces the workload for administrators and keeps the organization up-to-date and equipped to meet current regulations. In the case of mergers and acquisitions, organizations face a significant challenge in setting up a security system and ensuring all regulations are met. Having an automated system like this would be highly beneficial. Executives who are reading this book may appreciate the value of such a system more than anyone.

Additionally, the security software can utilize the reporting engine discussed in Chapter 4 to auto-generate compliance adherence reports for administrators and executives to review.

Zero-Day Threat Detection

With the explosion of AI in our lives, AI is now being used for everything—from automating mundane tasks to making complex decisions. Unfortunately, when AI falls into the wrong hands, it can lead to significant destruction. One such destructive activity is attacking the security infrastructure of an organization. Zero-day threat prevention is a crucial concern for executives in organizations, as they aim to ensure that their data remains uncompromised in any form.

CHAPTER 6   PRO-ACTIVE INTELLIGENT DATA SECURITY

The PRS module can play a pivotal role by integrating with threat intelligence software. The PRS module can receive up-to-the-minute reports on active and emerging threats. The threat intelligence platforms continuously monitor global cybersecurity threats. These platforms aggregate data from numerous sources, providing insights into the latest malware, phishing campaigns, and other cyber threats. By analyzing this data, the threat intelligence software can identify patterns and trends that indicate potential zero-day threats.

The cybersecurity landscape is constantly evolving. What is considered a zero-day threat today might be widely known tomorrow. The PRS module ensures that the organization's security policies are always up-to-date by continuously updating them based on the latest threat intelligence. This dynamic approach reduces the window of vulnerability, making it harder for attackers to exploit newly discovered weaknesses.

By leveraging AI, the PRS module can go beyond traditional security measures. It can employ machine learning algorithms to detect anomalies and unusual behaviors that might indicate a zero-day attack. User Risk is a separate heuristic that we will discuss in the next section but this is along the same lines.

For executives, the ability to prevent zero-day threats translates into peace of mind. They need to know that their organization's data, reputation, and operations are protected against the latest cyber threats. The automated creation and updating of security policies ensure that defenses are always aligned with the latest threat landscape, providing comprehensive protection against zero-day threats.

Classification

Some organizations prefer to classify all their data. Classification offers a crucial advantage by determining whether data is secure simply by checking its classification status. Without classification, extensive inspection is necessary. Beyond enhancing security, classification also yields benefits in terms of data management, operational efficiency, scalability, improved data quality, and cost management, among other advantages.

Implementing classification incurs costs. Initially, organizations must establish a classification hierarchy, which goes beyond a simple binary decision of 'secret' or 'not secret' to encompass a broader spectrum. Once the classification hierarchy is defined, it requires regular review to ensure it meets the organization's needs, as reclassifying all documents due to hierarchy changes demands significant resources and computing power.

After finalizing the hierarchy, the organization must identify all data repositories where documents may reside and proceed with classification. This includes cloud storage, email boxes, network shares, endpoint machines, and other storage locations. The security product initiates a classification scan as part of the remediation process for document classification. Emails and other correspondences can also be classified, with the option to reclassify, if necessary.

Once classification is complete, policies can verify the classification status rather than inspecting the data itself. The classification status remains secure unless malicious actors obtain credentials to the classification system.

Now coming back, what is the role of PRS in all this? The security system may come across documents and data that require classification because they were not classified previously. Additionally, new data may not conform to the rules of the established classification hierarchy, causing it to be overlooked.

The system can recommend policy changes to detect documents using classification tags, simplifying security policies. Remediation rules can also be suggested to ensure that documents are re-classified appropriately when their content changes.

CHAPTER 6   PRO-ACTIVE INTELLIGENT DATA SECURITY

There may be classification policies that lead to conflicts. The PRS system can efficiently identify these conflicts and present them to the policy administrator for refinement, aiming to resolve any issues. An example of such a conflict is illustrated in Example 5.

EXAMPLE 5: CLASSIFICATION POLICIES WITH CONFLICTS

Recommendation System Analysis:
Policies P1 and P2 conflict with each other because they specify similar content and context rules but have different remediation rules. This leads to content matching both policies, causing a classification conflict.

Reasons for this recommendation:
Similar content and context rules but not identical
No exceptions
Different classification remediation rules

Recommendations for the policy author:
Option 1: Suggestion to refine policies P1 and P2.
Option 2: Make remediation rules in policies P1 and P2 the same. Use remediation rule R1.
Option 3: Make remediation rules in policies P1 and P2 the same. Use remediation rule R2.
Option 4: Don't make this modification.

Encryption

Encryption is a critical method for safeguarding sensitive content. By encrypting data, even if it falls into the wrong hands, malicious actors face a formidable obstacle in accessing the raw information. However, implementing encryption involves trade-offs. The process of encrypting

CHAPTER 6   PRO-ACTIVE INTELLIGENT DATA SECURITY

and decrypting data can impose computational overhead and additional processing time, especially in environments where data access needs to be frequent and rapid.

Advancements in transparent data encryption have mitigated some of these challenges by integrating encryption processes seamlessly into existing systems and workflows. Transparent encryption mechanisms operate in the background, allowing authorized users to access and work with data as usual without the need for manual decryption steps. This approach helps maintain security while minimizing disruption to user workflows and operational efficiency.

PRS module can make recommendations in the following scenarios:

> **Scenario 1:** Use the classification tags we recommended and applied to documents in the previous section to our advantage. Alongside classification, we can recommend additional remediation rules to encrypt certain sensitive data.
>
> **Scenario 2:** Since our PRS module already integrates with threat intelligence systems to protect against zero-day threats, we can use these systems to identify the types of data targeted by malicious actors and recommend encrypting such data.
>
> **Scenario 3:** Recommend encryption policy templates based on industry standards and best practices to policy administrators. These recommendations can be made in addition to compliance and data regulation policies. There might be an intersection between data regulations and encryption policy templates, so it is beneficial to unify those recommendations.

CHAPTER 6   PRO-ACTIVE INTELLIGENT DATA SECURITY

Scenario 4: Suggest policies that consider the context in which data is used, ensuring appropriate encryption without disrupting workflows.

Scenario 5: Leverage AI to understand user behaviors and recommend encryption for data accessed by high-risk users or applications.

Scenario 6: Suggest appropriate encryption algorithms, such as AES-256, based on the sensitivity and type of data.

Let's look at Example 6 for a better understanding.

EXAMPLE 6: ENCRYPTION RECOMMENDATION FOR PII CUSTOMER DATA

Recommendation System Analysis:
Policy P1 classifies PII customer data with the tag PII-CD. Now encryption can be applied on top to secure the data.

Reasons for this recommendation:
No encryption was detected on classified sensitive content.

Recommendations for the policy author:
Option 1: Add additional remediation rule of encrypting the data matching policy P1.
Option 2: Don't make this modification.

User Risk

The analytics engine detailed in Chapter 5 discussed monitoring users and collecting their activities, including tasks such as data collection, stitching, correlation, and analysis. Following this analysis, the system presented suspicious user activities in context to the security administrator. Building on the capabilities of the analytics engine, the PRS can utilize these results to suggest policies to the policy administrator. These policies can help security administrators monitor users with the highest number of violations. Additionally, the list of suspicious users may include potential malicious actors, as the system tracks all user activities.

Based on user risk, a wide range of policy suggestions can be made. Sensitive data can be protected based on the user's role. Suggestions include implementing role-based access control policies, limiting privileges according to the principle of least privilege, and establishing time-based access control policies.

For users identified as high-risk, policy suggestions include requiring MFA every time they access sensitive data. Policies can also prompt high-risk users to provide a reason for access, especially on endpoint channels. Based on dynamic risk scores, policies can restrict access to sensitive files for high-risk users, as discussed in Chapter 5.

Policies can suggest setting up close monitoring alerts and tracking all activities of high-risk users. These policies ensure that high-risk users are closely watched and any suspicious activities are promptly addressed.

High-risk users can be required to use secure file transfer protocols to move sensitive data. Policies can mandate encryption of sensitive data both at rest and in transit. Additionally, data masking techniques can be applied to obscure sensitive information from users who do not need full access.

Now let's look at the watchlist. PRS can dynamically create a watchlist of users and monitor them closely. Policy administrators should be able to create or modify the watchlist and attach it to policies. The watchlist contains users that the system needs to monitor. The watchlist typically includes high-risk users and users with many suspicious activities. The watchlist needs to be dynamic. Static watchlists from policy administrators can soon get outdated and the PRS system with incorrect policies or outdated policies heuristic makes recommendations to remove such policies based on a static list. Example 7 explains how the PRS module makes recommendations based on a watchlist.

CHAPTER 6   PRO-ACTIVE INTELLIGENT DATA SECURITY

> **EXAMPLE 7: WATCHLIST ON USERS WHO ARE RESIGNING THIS WEEK**
>
> **Recommendation System Analysis:**
> Policy P1 is recommended to closely monitor users who are resigning from the organization this week. The policy recommendation suggests that the policy author create a distribution list (DL) or a user list, which should be updated weekly with the names of employees who are resigning.
>
> **Reasons for this recommendation:**
> No policies based on resigning employees exist in the system
>
> **Recommendations for the policy author:**
> Option 1: Add Policy P1 with a context rule matching the watchlist of employees resigning this week. The watchlist can be supported by a distribution list (DL) or an Active Directory (AD) query.
> Option 2: Don't make this modification.

By implementing these policy suggestions, the PRS can enhance the security measures for high-risk users, ensuring sensitive data is protected and potential threats are mitigated. This means that analytics engine output needs to flow to the PRS via the feedback processor to make user risk and watchlist-based recommendations.

Data Trail Discovery

Chapter 5 discussed monitoring users and data. Tracking users helps yield user risk scores while tracking data reveals how it is used, transformed, and stored. Discovering the data trail is vital in a security product; complete security isn't guaranteed without it. Monitoring users and data is a continuous process. The security product must never stop, as malicious actors continually find new ways to exfiltrate data that organizations have not imagined.

The first step is identifying where the data is stored. These repositories or shares might not have been included in the classification or encryption processes. It is essential to recommend policies to policy administrators for monitoring these locations, classifying, and encrypting any sensitive files discovered there.

Next, we need to monitor data transfer policies for these locations. Can users transfer sensitive data to these discovered locations? If not, data transfers should be blocked, and any sensitive data already present should be deleted. Continuous monitoring policy recommendations, which we will discuss in the next section, will address data deletion. Therefore, we should immediately classify and encrypt all existing data, allowing the policy administrator to decide whether data transfers to these locations should be permitted. Following this, we block access and delete any existing sensitive data. Security takes time, and comprehensive protection cannot be achieved in a single sweep.

Data manipulations like renaming the names or extensions can be stopped by making appropriate recommendations. Suspicious files can be binarily compared to see if the contents are identical. Such measures will increase the security level in any organization.

Managing the same data in multiple locations is challenging for organizations, as employees often create numerous copies. Imagine data created a decade ago that has since been replicated in 20 diverse locations, each under a different name. The contents remain the same, but the names have changed due to copying and renaming. This makes managing and deleting obsolete copies, particularly of sensitive data, very difficult. Addressing this issue requires specialized detection and tracking technology. We will discuss this in the next chapter.

CHAPTER 6   PRO-ACTIVE INTELLIGENT DATA SECURITY

Posture Management for Cloud

Cloud applications' security posture management is vital to ensure data doesn't get leaked due to poor application configuration. In other words, security administrators are responsible for configuring the cloud applications used in the organization, and any misconfigurations might risk the entire organization. Maintaining compliance for all cloud applications is mandatory, and all configuration changes should be reviewed in detail.

A sample change by a cloud administrator on a Box application configuration is shown below.

Cloud application: Box

User Password MFA Requirement: Old value True. New Value False

Configuration changed by: Alex Damian

Role: Cloud Administrator

Changed on: June 22, 2024.

Let's assume that compliance rules require all users to have Multi-Factor Authentication (MFA) enabled for accessing cloud storage. Now, imagine a change that violates this compliance rule. Should this change be permitted? Should a security system monitor such administrative setting changes to applications? These are excellent questions. The answer is that our security system should monitor these setting changes, report any non-compliance, and automatically remediate or block the changes as appropriate.

First, our security system needs to monitor settings changes in the cloud applications used within an organization, supported by appropriate policies. The PRS should recommend that customers have policies in place to monitor cloud applications if they have the cloud channel enabled.

CHAPTER 6   PRO-ACTIVE INTELLIGENT DATA SECURITY

Configuration is a detailed process, and as a security vendor, you have two options:

- Intercept all setting change requests and run them through the detection engine in our security system before they are deployed.

- Build a facade where customers log in to our security system to make changes. If the changes are compliant, the security system then calls the APIs of the cloud applications to implement these changes.

Both options require resources and time to develop. However, once built, they act as coverage points by intercepting all requests and allowing actions based on the configured posture policies.

With this system in place, the PRS can make appropriate recommendations. If no policies exist, it can suggest enabling policies to monitor these changes. If policies are already in place, it can recommend policies ensuring that auto-remediation or blocking remediation actions are triggered when noncompliant changes are attempted.

Defining what constitutes compliance is a question that needs to be addressed by the organization's security administrator. The security administrator has two options:

- Choose the setting value based on compliance and data regulations.

- Choose the setting value based on internal compliance directives from the organization.

For example, a compliance regulation might mandate a minimum password length of 12 characters, while the organization's internal policy could require passwords to be 15 characters long. Typically, organizations enforce stricter guidelines than those recommended by compliance and data regulation standards.

CHAPTER 6   PRO-ACTIVE INTELLIGENT DATA SECURITY

The security system configuration should allow administrators to choose between standard settings based on legal requirements (option #1) and custom compliance settings (option #2). Once a choice is made, the policies should automatically ensure that configurations are correctly set and proactively prevent misconfigurations.

The number of posture management policy violations can be reduced by training and coaching cloud administrators on proper cloud application configuration management.

Generating reports on cloud application posture management might be necessary to meet audit and regulatory compliance requirements. These reports should be produced based on the configurations set by the security administrator.

Statistical Trends

Statistics on various entities can reveal trends over time. For example, an increase in incidents related to a specific policy might indicate the need for administrators to closely examine that policy and understand the reasons behind the rising trend. This analysis can be automated, allowing the PRS system to provide recommendations by analyzing these trends.

Policy recommendations based on violation trends can significantly enhance an organization's security posture. Here are some recommendations that a PRS system might suggest:

First, if a specific policy shows a rising trend in violations, the system can recommend increasing monitoring and logging activities related to this policy to identify the root cause of the violations. This increased oversight can help pinpoint issues and address them promptly.

Second, the system can suggest refining or updating policies that have a high number of violations to better align with current organizational practices and compliance requirements. This ensures that policies remain relevant and effective.

Third, increasing violations might indicate a lack of understanding among users. The system can recommend targeted training programs for users on the policies they frequently violate, improving awareness and adherence.

Fourth, if violations are related to access controls, the system can recommend implementing stricter access control measures, such as role-based access control (RBAC) or multi-factor authentication (MFA).

Fifth, for policies with frequent violations, the system can suggest automated remediation actions to immediately address and rectify the violations, reducing the risk of data breaches.

Sixth, the system can recommend scheduling regular reviews of policies with high violation trends to ensure they remain relevant and effective. Regular reviews help maintain the integrity of security policies over time.

Seventh, for policies that are frequently violated, the system can suggest developing or updating incident response plans to address and mitigate the impact of these violations swiftly.

Eighth, if a policy's violation threshold is consistently exceeded, the system can recommend adjusting the thresholds to reflect the organization's current security landscape better. This adjustment ensures that policies are realistic and achievable.

Ninth, for policies involving sensitive data, the system can suggest network segmentation or isolation techniques to limit the potential impact of violations. Segmentation helps contain breaches and protects critical assets.

Finally, if unencrypted sensitive data yields violations, the system can recommend policies to enforce encryption for DIM and DAR use cases.

We need the PRS system integrated with the statistics engine through the feedback processor to recommend based on statistical trends.

CHAPTER 6   PRO-ACTIVE INTELLIGENT DATA SECURITY

BYOD Rules Enforcement

BYOD presence in an organization brings an entirely new dimension of threats that are challenging for security administrators to address and ensure compliance. Most customers don't know how to handle BYOD. So policy recommendations for BYOD become all that more important. There are many unknowns about BYOD starting from OS versions they run, and what type of devices—tablets vs. laptops vs. other handhelds. It is not easy for the security software to be installed on those devices and monitor all the activities for those devices. Hence security needs to be enforced externally on all the data that is being transferred from or to the devices.

Let's assume the handheld BYOD is trying to open a sensitive document or requesting access to a sensitive document then should we allow it? Of course, we should! As a security vendor, your job is to satisfy customer use cases. If an organization permits the use of BYOD then we should allow it and see how we can secure the data without being compromised.

Once the data is on the BYOD, the employee can do anything with the data once he takes it out of the network. Hence appropriate encryption should be in place so that even if the data gets exfiltrated, encryption acts as a strong barrier. Though encryption acts as a barrier, data can be still decrypted as malicious actors have unlimited time to decrypt. Hence a more sophisticated mechanism is necessary.

Tracking data through embedded URLs and scripts has been a prevalent practice in recent years, offering a heightened level of security. Documents can contain hidden URLs that, when accessed, communicate their location back to the server. Similarly, custom scripts can be created to embed in highly sensitive documents, enabling tracking through logging actions on the server. In scenarios where Internet access is unavailable, data can be locally logged on BYOD devices.

With PRS in place, the security system can suggest that only encrypted data should be transferred to any BYOD device. Additionally, the policy can enforce that data transfer is allowed only if embedded URLs or tracking through custom scripts are available. All data transfers to BYOD devices should be logged and properly maintained, which is another recommended practice.

Certain types of BYOD devices can be restricted entirely. For instance, if an organization decides to prevent mobile phones from accessing data, policies can be implemented to block access to these devices. To determine which devices should be blocked, the PRS system can generate a policy recommendation, presenting the customer with options as demonstrated in Example 8.

EXAMPLE 8: POLICY RECOMMENDATION ON ALLOWED BYOD

Recommendation System Analysis:
Policy P1 is recommended to block BYOD access.

Reasons for this recommendation:
No policies based on BYOD blocking access

Recommendations for the policy author:
Option 1: Add Policy P1 to block all BYOD.
Option 2: Add Policy P1 to block all BYOD mobile phones.
Option 3: Add Policy P1 to block all BYOD laptops.
Option 4: Add Policy P1 to block all BYOD tablets.
Option 5: Don't make this modification.

Based on the policy administrator's choice, the security system can learn the administrator's intent and what is important for the organization to guard against.

Custom Detection

Let's assume the organization is integrating with custom detection as a coverage point. This implies that the organization does not use a standard method for sending DIM and DAR requests to the policy detection engine. Instead, the organization needs to select a custom integration approach via APIs. The organization would develop a proprietary custom client, while the policy detection engine would expose APIs. The custom client would then send requests to the detection engine through these APIs and receive responses. Custom detection integration API invocations would be as shown in Figure 6-2.

Figure 6-2 describes two APIs, namely, an API to invoke the detection engine with a request and another API to report the results of the remediation actions. Let's call it the detection request API and remediation results API.

The Detection Request API's response may include a violation and remediation actions to be executed as applicable. Note that not all policies will have a remediation action. Since the security product is integrated with a custom application, it wouldn't be able to execute remediation actions as it lacks the necessary access and control of the custom application. The client needs to execute the remediation action and report back the results. If the client doesn't report back the results, the violation processor wouldn't know if the remediation actions were executed or not, leaving the violation in an unknown state regarding remediation actions. The violations generated based on these requests are sent to the violation processor without having to wait for the remediation execution results.

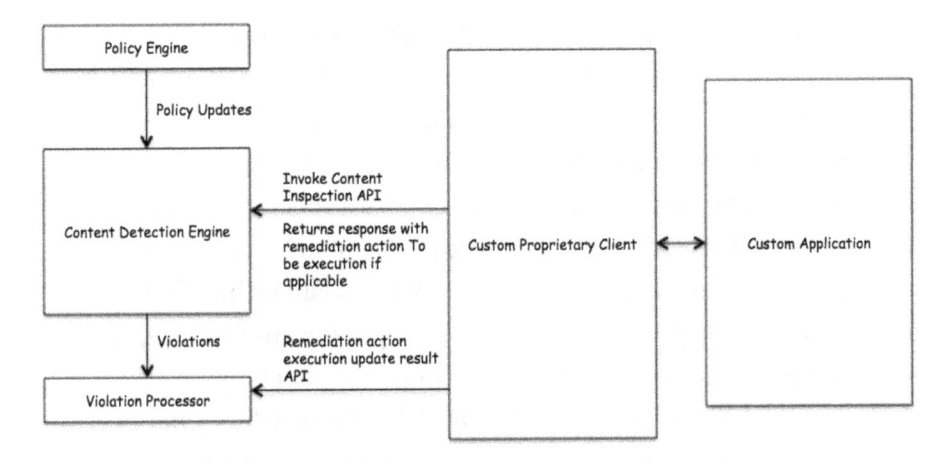

CHAPTER 6   PRO-ACTIVE INTELLIGENT DATA SECURITY

Figure 6-2. Custom Detection API Integration

The Remediation Results API is optional for clients to invoke, but if used, it will close the violations and inform the administrator whether the remediation actions were executed. It also provides the status of the remediation actions, whether they succeeded or failed. This API can be directly invoked on the violation processor, as it can update the violations.

Now, the PRS can offer tailored recommendations based on the types of incidents generated by these custom requests. It can also suggest how frequently the API should be invoked. If the detection engine struggles to keep up with the volume of requests, it can provide feedback to the statistics engine, prompting policies to rate-limit API invocations. Additionally, the PRS can recommend policy types based on the users responsible for generating violations, ensuring more effective and targeted security measures.

Partial Results

In Chapter 5, we explored the concept of storing partial matches and how these can provide valuable insights. To remind everyone, partial results are stored when only a part of the security policy condition is violated, and no

299

incident is generated. However, we didn't delve into the crucial aspect of storage. Adequate storage is essential for learning from partial matches, and my recommendation is to sample and store data selectively.

Many security developers overlook that not all policies need to be addressed simultaneously. The PRS can choose a specific policy, notify all detection nodes, and have them store partial matches for that policy. If additional storage is available, multiple policies can be handled concurrently. The key idea is to manage storage efficiently to maximize learning opportunities without overwhelming resources.

How should you prioritize policies and determine which channels the system should monitor? If this question crossed your mind, you're on the right track. PRS should begin by grouping policies by type. Here are some common categories:

- Compliance policies
- Monitoring-only policies by channel
- Identity provider-based policies
- Policies by remediation action by channel (e.g., quarantine, redact policies)
- Posture management policies
- Threat policies
- Access control policies
- Context rules-only policies
- User risk-based policies
- Application-only policies by type (e.g., cloud, corporate DIM applications)

This list is a guideline, and you can expand on it as needed.

Once the policies are categorized, PRS can manage them based on available storage. It can tackle one category at a time or divide policies from each category into sets, instructing detection nodes to handle each set sequentially. Data collection and aggregation should continue for a configurable time window, ideally at least a month, before drawing any conclusions. Repetitive data can be discarded, storing only the statistics. This function of data collection and redundancy removal can be refined further by categorizing partial results. If all results are repetitive, there's no need to extend the collection period beyond a certain point. This heuristic can be developed and improved iteratively.

The collected results are sent to PRS for analysis and recommendations. As PRS integrates with violation processor results, it can easily correlate data based on violation remediation. This process builds a security system that self-learns and adapts to its environment. We're not using pre-trained AI models; instead, the system starts learning and tuning from day one. Pre-trained models can be problematic as they might not fit all environments. By building a system that self-learns and proactively makes recommendations, we ensure a tailored, proactive security approach. This comprehensive enterprise protection plan is not achieved overnight, but through continuous learning and adaptation.

Now, let's delve a little deeper into the types of recommendations that can be derived from partial result analysis. I have curated a predefined set of recommendations for your reference:

- Question the validity of exception-based policies.
- Assess if certain context rules are causing partial matches.
- Evaluate the validity of date/time-sensitive policies.
- Recommend unifying policy rules if the system finds evidence of rules matching together.

- Suggest policy tuning based on violation remediations.

- Recommend including missing file attributes in policies based on content seen by detection.

- If large files are being ignored based on the file size, question the intent of those policies.

- Make recommendations to strengthen security around users who generate the most partial matches, unless they are explicitly excluded.

With these recommendations, policies can be fine-tuned to ensure optimal security. Organizational representatives reading this should consider evaluating their security policies using the strategies outlined above. Conducting an internal review of all policies every quarter is highly recommended to keep the system up-to-date and performing at its best.

Continuous Monitoring

Continuous monitoring is crucial, yet many organizations underestimate its importance. It's essential not only for maintaining compliance and meeting regulatory requirements, as discussed in earlier chapters, but also for ensuring the overall security of the organization. This is where PRS plays a pivotal role, offering policy suggestions that security administrators might not have considered, thereby enhancing proactive security measures.

PRS suggestions in the continuous monitoring realm are tailored based on the existing set of policies and coverage points. If there is already extensive coverage, continuous monitoring might seem redundant, but it is still vital to ensure no gaps exist. BYOD, endpoints, and network shares (both cloud and on-premise) all require comprehensive monitoring. Here are some top categories where PRS can make valuable recommendations:

CHAPTER 6   PRO-ACTIVE INTELLIGENT DATA SECURITY

- Policies to monitor all data transfer and storage activities across all coverage points
- Policies to monitor network traffic for suspicious activity
- Policy to monitor for threats
- Policies to conduct regular vulnerability assessments and penetration testing
- Policies to ensure regular patching and updating of all software

Another crucial factor to consider is the dynamic nature of security environments. Whenever security administrators update the security policies, it is imperative to re-evaluate all previously monitored and tagged content. This includes both sensitive and non-sensitive data.

Security policies evolve based on emerging threats, changes in compliance requirements, or updates in organizational procedures. When a policy update occurs, the criteria for what is considered sensitive or non-sensitive information might change. As a result, the previously tagged content may no longer align with the new security definitions or requirements.

To maintain an accurate and up-to-date security posture, continuous monitoring policies must include re-scanning protocols. This means that after every policy update, all content—whether it was previously identified as sensitive or not—must be scanned again to ensure it complies with the new standards.

I acknowledge that re-scanning everything can be time-consuming. Security systems should strategize by prioritizing the scanning of the most sensitive data first before moving on to non-sensitive data.

CHAPTER 6   PRO-ACTIVE INTELLIGENT DATA SECURITY

Design

Having explored all the heuristics, you now understand the capabilities of the Policy Recommendation System (PRS). Figure 6-3 provides a detailed view of the PRS components. As illustrated, the figure presents different layers of components. These layers form a framework upon which you can build further.

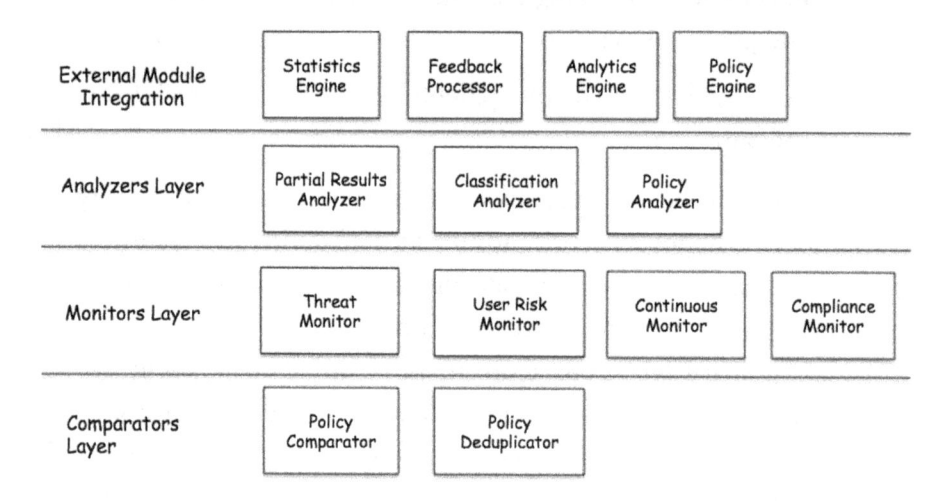

External Module Integration	Statistics Engine	Feedback Processor	Analytics Engine	Policy Engine
Analyzers Layer	Partial Results Analyzer	Classification Analyzer	Policy Analyzer	
Monitors Layer	Threat Monitor	User Risk Monitor	Continuous Monitor	Compliance Monitor
Comparators Layer	Policy Comparator	Policy Deduplicator		

Figure 6-3. *Components of a Policy Recommendation System*

The bottom layer in Figure 6-3 is the comparator layer, responsible for policy comparisons and deduplication. Above it, we have the monitoring layer and the analyzer layer, which constitute the brains of the PRS. As previously discussed, PRS integrates with external modules covered in earlier sections and shows the same in the top layer.

In the next section, we'll explore another recommendation system focused on violation remediations. This is arguably the most critical function of security software. Effective violation remediation closes the loop on vulnerabilities and assures that the threat has been neutralized. Previously, we discussed how the reasoning module can learn from ongoing violation remediations. Now, we will build on that foundation and expand into a comprehensive remediation recommendation system.

CHAPTER 6   PRO-ACTIVE INTELLIGENT DATA SECURITY

Remediation Recommendation System (RRS)

You might wonder, "Why not develop a fully automated remediation system? Why do we need remediation recommendations? Can't we auto-remediate?" These are excellent questions. The answer is yes, we plan to auto-remediate. However, before doing so, the security system must check with the violation remediator to confirm if it is acceptable to auto-remediate violations that meet certain criteria. Once the remediator approves, the security system can create auto-remediation rules, which will be triggered when the violation processor receives and processes violations from the content detection engine.

These auto-remediation rules should be available in the system so that administrators can review and disable any rule at any stage, if necessary. This ensures full transparency and visibility for all administrators. If the Remediation Recommendation System (RRS) performed remediation without visibility, administrators would have no way to review and provide feedback. Having auto-remediation rules documented in the system will also be beneficial for reporting and meeting compliance requirements.

Figure 6-4 illustrates the steps involved in suggesting a remediation rule to violation remediators and incorporating it into the system.

The Remediation Recommendation System (RRS) generates recommendations based on heuristics similar to those used by the Policy Recommendation System (PRS). These recommendations are then sent to the Violation Processor, where the violation remediators have two options:

- Approve the Recommendation: Allow the remediation rule to be created.

- Deny the Recommendation: Reject the suggestion.

CHAPTER 6   PRO-ACTIVE INTELLIGENT DATA SECURITY

If the remediator chooses to deny the recommendation, the feedback is processed by the feedback processor and sent back to the RRS, ensuring that the same recommendation is not made in the future. If the remediator approves the recommendation, it is forwarded to the Autonomous Remediation Rule Creator Component. This component either creates a new rule, if it doesn't already exist, or reuses an existing one. The remediation rule is then pushed to production via the production policy updater and deployer. The feedback processor integrates with the PRS, as discussed in the previous section, for continuous policy refinement.

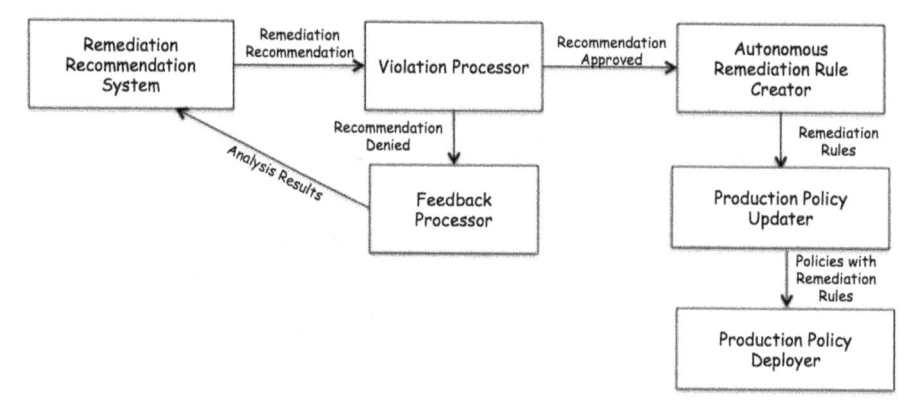

Figure 6-4. Components of a Policy Recommendation System

Let's look at some of the heuristics we can use in the RRS. These heuristics will provide a foundation for security solution developers to build upon as they develop the RRS further.

Heuristics

Similar to the heuristics in the Policy Recommendation System (PRS), the Remediation Recommendation System (RRS) is also built on field-tested heuristics. However, the violation remediator or the security administrator always has the final authority to enable a remediation rule. Once these rules are enabled, the system will experience significant improvements in addressing active vulnerabilities and achieving issue closure—a key factor that auditors scrutinize during product audits.

Automated systems eliminate the manual task of inspecting all violations, allowing violation remediators to focus on new threats and vulnerabilities rather than known issues. It's important to note that the violation rate should be around 0.01 to 0.1% of the files/messages scanned. Any rate higher than this indicates that the policies need refinement.

The heuristics used by the RRS can be categorized based on how an organization prefers to address violations. These categories are discussed in the subsequent sections.

Auto-Close

Violations that can be automatically closed fall into a specific category. Take a moment to think about all the types of violations that are auto-closeable.

All monitoring violations are collected for compliance and general monitoring purposes, making them candidates for automatic closure. But how does the RRS determine if they are truly auto-closeable and if organizations are comfortable with this approach? The RRS requires feedback from the violation processor, via the feedback processor, to make such decisions.

Consider a scenario where remediators consistently close print-monitoring violations upon receipt. The RRS system observes this pattern over time, recognizing which policy triggered the violation and noting the consistent workflow where remediators directly close these violations. Closing a violation does not mean deleting it from the system; closed violations are stored for forensic purposes.

Besides monitoring violations, what other types of violations can be auto-closed? Violations that are consistently closed by remediators without any manual remediation actions, such as those related to encryption and classification, can be considered. For instance, if the security system detects sensitive content and applies a classification label or encrypts the content, it may generate a violation based on the security administrator's configurations. If violations are generated for each encryption action and are consistently closed, the RRS can suggest auto-closing these based on observed patterns. It is important to note that an auto-close remediation action can leave a note in the violation record, indicating that it was auto-closed, which is useful for forensics.

At any time, if the violation remediator needs to suspend or delete this remediation rule, they can choose to do so.

False Positives

Based on how violation remediators triage incidents, false positives can be easily identified. The simplest way to determine if a violation is a false positive is when the remediator explicitly marks it as such. Another indicator is when the remediator closes the violation without taking any action, similar to an auto-close, but this applies to violations other than monitoring ones. Monitoring violations typically inspects a resource rather than the actual data. For example, a policy might generate a violation whenever a user sends an email outside the organization, focusing on context rules.

False positives are particularly noteworthy as they prompt a reassessment of whether a policy needs refinement or deactivation. Often, policies require tuning because organizations tend to adopt a conservative approach, attempting to match a broad set of rules. False negatives are detrimental to organizations, hence the conservative stance. Therefore, it's crucial to capture the match criteria accurately to identify which violations are marked as false positives for a specific policy.

Let's discuss a practical issue you might encounter in the field when implementing this. Consider the policies P1 and P2 defined in an organization, as illustrated here.

CHAPTER 6   PRO-ACTIVE INTELLIGENT DATA SECURITY

Policy P1:

If a BYOD user views corporate data containing credit card numbers then generate a violation

Policy P2:

Raise a violation if financial records are sent over an email to ABC law firm

Policy P1 may seem like a monitoring violation, but it's not—it includes a content rule defined as credit card numbers. Now, imagine that all violations resulting from Policy P1 are consistently marked as false positives by the remediator. In this case, the RRS can confidently recommend adding an auto-remediation rule to Policy P1, which automatically marks these violations as false positives. The key detail here is the context rule: "Any BYOD user." This means there's no distinction whether the CEO or a manager logs in from their BYOD device; if all violations are marked as false positives during the learning period, the RRS can safely make this recommendation.

Policy P2, on the other hand, lacks a specific context rule for the sender of the email. It simply states to raise a violation if any user emails the ABC law firm. In this scenario, suppose the remediator marks certain violations as false positives while leaving others open. The RRS must then analyze which violations are marked false positives and identify any patterns. If the RRS discovers that violations are consistently marked as false positives when the sender belongs to an executive group, it should add a condition to the false positive remediation rule specifying this context. For all other violations, the system should not auto-remediate as false positives.

By understanding and applying these nuances, the RRS can make precise recommendations, enhancing the efficiency and accuracy of the security system.

CHAPTER 6   PRO-ACTIVE INTELLIGENT DATA SECURITY

Manual Remediation Steps

Imagine a scenario where violations of a certain type from a specific policy consistently follow the same manual remediation steps. Over the learning period, the RRS can analyze this pattern and determine that the same steps have been repeatedly applied. By identifying the match criteria, the RRS can recommend converting these manual remediation steps into automated ones. This assumes that the violation processor is aware of all the manual remediation actions taken by the remediator. If the remediator handles some steps offline, the violation processor or RRS wouldn't have that information. Nevertheless, the RRS can still make the recommendation, as no changes go live in production without the remediator's approval.

Automating manual remediation steps significantly reduces the workload for remediators. It also allows the system to compare similar policies and recommend automated remediation steps for them as well.

However, some manual remediation steps can be complex, such as triggering a custom script as part of the remediation action. There might be permission issues and other complications. The RRS needs to be aware of these scenarios and handle them appropriately.

Violation Analysis

This is the most important heuristic, where a violation analyzer component will analyze all the existing violations and learn from them. The violation analyzer can diagnose a violation in the following categories:

- Channel
- Severity
- Policy violated
- Sender/Source

CHAPTER 6 PRO-ACTIVE INTELLIGENT DATA SECURITY

- Recipient/Destination
- Scanned File/Message attributes (type, size, name, etc.)
- Matching context rules other than those mentioned above
- Matching content rules
- Matching remediation actions
- Time of the violation
- Location of the violation
- Device details
- User risk
- Classification/Encryption status of the scanned data
- Application including cloud and on-prem
- Corporate network or not
- Posture management violation
- Remediation status

These categories lay the groundwork for the violation analyzer. The next component, the violation comparator, groups similar violations together and draws insights. These insights can drive policy refinements, adjustments in thresholds, exceptions, sensitive data rules, and context rules. Further insights could uncover the root causes of violations and methods for prevention. Financial analysis can estimate potential losses from data leaks. Patterns in user behavior and suspicious activities can inform new policies. Serious violations can prompt notifications to managers and administrators for critical actions. Process improvements, software upgrades, and training programs can all stem from violation analysis.

Another crucial component of violation analysis is the remediation analyzer, which studies how violation remediators address violations. By understanding which violations are critical to administrators and how they are remediated, the security system learns about administrator intentions. This insight can lead to intent-based violation remediation and prioritization. Intent-based detection and remediation is a significant area poised for a bright future. We will delve into this topic in the next chapter.

Tracking trends in generated violations reveals the organization's risk profile. The RRS can then recommend stricter remediation measures and provide feedback to the feedback processor. This enables the PRS to create more stringent policies based on the analysis.

Workflows

In Chapter 2, we explored how many organizations integrate their business workflows with security products. For instance, an organization might link its ServiceNow enterprise workflow automation engine with the security system. Administrators have the flexibility to design workflows tailored to specific violation types and attributes. These custom workflows are exemplified in Figure 6-5, showcasing their varied approaches that ultimately aim to resolve violations. Typically, workflows are constrained by time limits and cannot indefinitely wait for user input, whether from the violator or their manager. This integration ensures efficient and timely handling of security incidents across the organization.

CHAPTER 6   PRO-ACTIVE INTELLIGENT DATA SECURITY

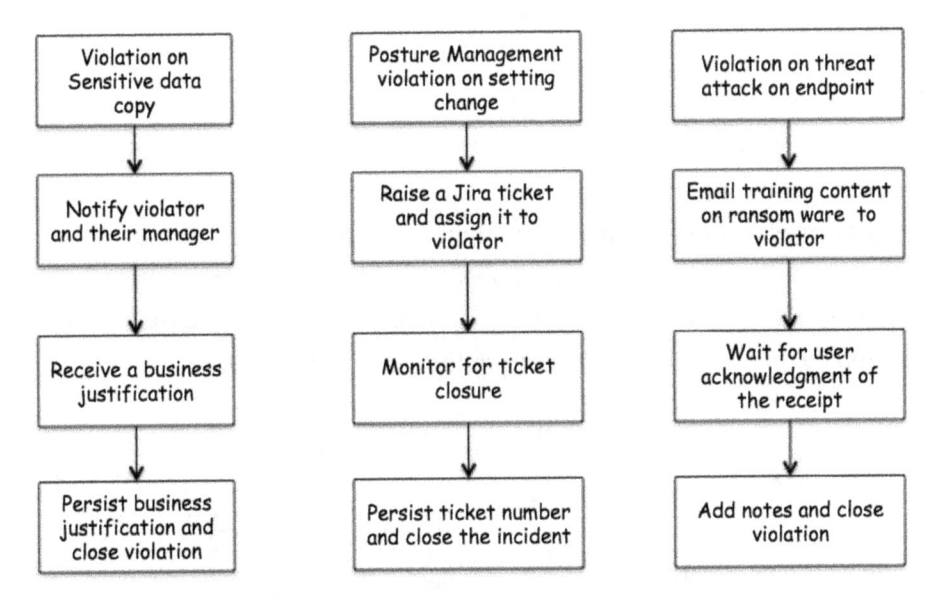

```
┌──────────────────┐    ┌──────────────────┐    ┌──────────────────┐
│  Violation on    │    │ Posture Management│    │ Violation on threat│
│  Sensitive data  │    │ violation on setting│  │ attack on endpoint│
│      copy        │    │     change        │    │                  │
└────────┬─────────┘    └────────┬─────────┘    └────────┬─────────┘
         ▼                       ▼                        ▼
┌──────────────────┐    ┌──────────────────┐    ┌──────────────────┐
│ Notify violator  │    │ Raise a Jira ticket│  │ Email training content│
│ and their manager│    │ and assign it to  │    │ on ransomware to │
│                  │    │     violator      │    │     violator     │
└────────┬─────────┘    └────────┬─────────┘    └────────┬─────────┘
         ▼                       ▼                        ▼
┌──────────────────┐    ┌──────────────────┐    ┌──────────────────┐
│ Receive a business│   │ Monitor for ticket│    │ Wait for user    │
│  justification   │    │     closure       │    │ acknowledgment of│
│                  │    │                   │    │   the receipt    │
└────────┬─────────┘    └────────┬─────────┘    └────────┬─────────┘
         ▼                       ▼                        ▼
┌──────────────────┐    ┌──────────────────┐    ┌──────────────────┐
│ Persist business │    │ Persist ticket number│ │ Add notes and close│
│ justification and│    │ and close the incident│ │    violation     │
│ close violation  │    │                   │    │                  │
└──────────────────┘    └──────────────────┘    └──────────────────┘
```

Figure 6-5. Sample Violation Remediation Workflows

RRS diligently monitors violation remediation workflows to ensure seamless flow without disruption, especially since organizations integrate workflow engines for automation. It's crucial that RRS does not interrupt this flow, maintaining business continuity.

Alternatively, when workflows aren't configured, RRS can suggest and recommend suitable workflows. These advanced workflows can dynamically adjust based on varying violation parameters. Organizations can implement these workflows using third-party applications or Security Orchestration, Automation, and Response (SOAR) tools. The automated outcomes from these workflows feed back into the violation processor, ultimately influencing RRS operations. The success or failure of these workflows plays a pivotal role in shaping their future within the organization.

CHAPTER 6   PRO-ACTIVE INTELLIGENT DATA SECURITY

Design

Figure 6-6 provides an overview of the components that make up a Remediation Recommendation System (RRS). Similar to PRS, RRS incorporates comparators, monitors, analyzers, and modules for integrating external systems. The violation comparator within RRS evaluates pairs of violations based on source/destination, channels, matches, and executed remediation actions. These comparisons are then utilized by the violation analyzer to refine policies as needed.

External Module Integration	Statistics Engine	Feedback Processor	Analytics Engine	Violation Processor
Analyzers Layer	Violation Analyzer	Remediation Analyzer	Workflow Analyzer and Composer	
Monitors Layer	False Positive Monitor	Auto Close Monitor	Workflow Monitor	
Comparators Layer	Violation Comparator	Remediation Rule Comparator		

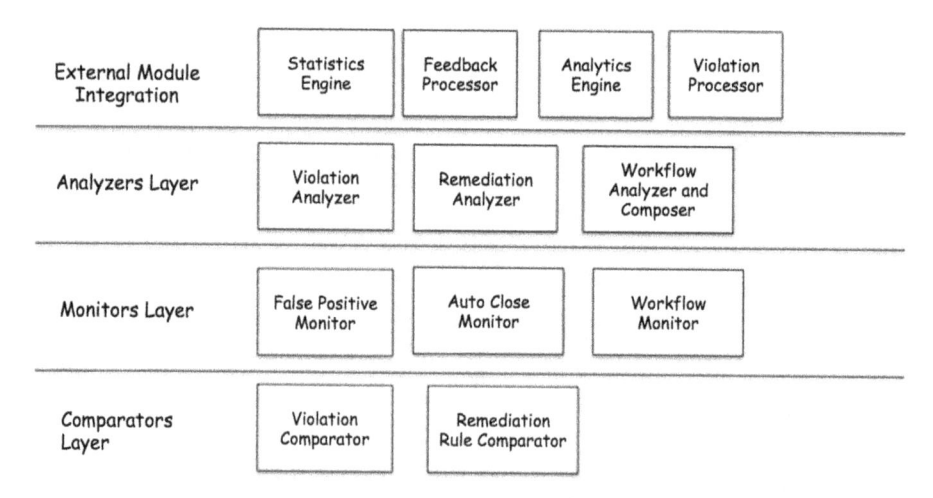

Figure 6-6. *Components of a Remediation Recommendation System*

By integrating the statistics and analytics engine, we can track the activation of automated remediation rules, along with the acceptance or denial of recommendations. Statistics and Analytics engines keep track of all activities happening in the security software and they can monitor which recommendations have been accepted by the user and which aren't. This engine forms the quantitative backbone of the remediation recommendation system, enabling decisions driven by data and ensuring ongoing monitoring. With this support, RRS can fulfill its role more effectively, continually adapting recommendations based on new data analysis to address evolving threats and dynamic environments.

Next, we'll delve into another recommendation system known as the settings recommendation system. Settings apply to a wide range of entities within a security product, presenting challenges in managing, maintaining, and optimizing the product to its fullest potential. Let's explore how the security product can enhance its usability, operability, and maintainability in the hands of security administrators.

Settings Recommendation System (SRS)

Every component within the security product, from the policy engine and violation processor to the recommendation systems, requires optimal configuration of settings. These settings provide administrators with the flexibility to tailor the product to their preferences.

Settings recommendations are often derived from monitoring the performance of the security product itself. Therefore, analytics and statistics engines play a crucial role in collecting, categorizing, analyzing, and drawing insights from this data.

Next, in the following section, let's explore the most frequently used settings that require tuning and recommendations from the SRS.

Coverage Points Settings

Coverage points within a security product signify the various facets of an organization's IT infrastructure that the product actively monitors, analyzes, and safeguards. Configuring these settings properly is vital to guarantee comprehensive security across the entire infrastructure.

In every security product, there are foundational settings that apply universally across all coverage points, ensuring a baseline level of protection. Additionally, there are settings specific to each channel or area of coverage, tailored to meet the unique requirements and risks associated with different parts of the infrastructure.

Let's briefly delve into these settings to understand their importance and impact.

General configurations include the following:

- Max message size of the content the channels should accept
- Channel Timeout for end-to-end detection and remediation rule execution of a message
- Continuous monitoring enabled
- File types to monitor
- File sizes to monitor
- Credentials, Certificates for the channel to be operational
- Memory allocation
- CPU
- Disk space
- If cloud—type of machine/pod
- Encrypted message scan support
- Content extraction technology support

Channel-specific settings include those that are specific to channels and are detailed below.

Network Share Channel Settings

Network share settings primarily involve configurations related to scans. Continuous monitoring settings are particularly relevant when requests involve Data at Rest (DAR).

CHAPTER 6 PRO-ACTIVE INTELLIGENT DATA SECURITY

SRS can recommend strategies such as parallelizing scanning processes and implementing remediation actions like classification and encryption. These recommendations are based on feedback gathered from the system through analytics and statistics engines. By analyzing data trends and performance metrics, SRS can optimize security measures effectively.

- Scan configurations
- Classification/Encryption configurations
- Bandwidth Throttling for ingesting files into the detection engine for scanning
- Number of parallel scans
- Cluster scan-specific configurations, if applicable

Endpoint Channel Settings

Configuring settings for the endpoint channel presents a significant challenge due to the sheer number of agents connecting to it within an organization's IT infrastructure. The endpoint channel encompasses both Data in Motion (DIM), referring to data actively moving across networks or between devices, and Data at Rest (DAR), which pertains to data stored on devices or servers. Each of these dimensions requires tailored configurations to effectively monitor, analyze, and protect data.

For Data in Motion, settings typically focus on real-time monitoring, threat detection, and response capabilities. On the other hand, Data at Rest settings concentrate on encryption, access controls, and regular scanning to safeguard sensitive data stored on endpoints. These settings are crucial for maintaining data integrity and confidentiality even when data is not actively being transmitted.

CHAPTER 6   PRO-ACTIVE INTELLIGENT DATA SECURITY

Given the dynamic nature of endpoint environments and the diverse range of devices and operating systems involved, optimizing these settings requires careful consideration of scalability, performance impact, and regulatory compliance. Effective configuration ensures comprehensive endpoint security while balancing operational efficiency and user productivity. Here are the settings most commonly used:

- Endpoint configurations that can connect and report back to the product
- Bandwidth supported for data transmission between agents and the server
- Number of agents that can connect in unison to the server
- Number of parallel scans on agent
- Rules that are applicable for data management on endpoint
- Endpoint channels that the application needs to monitor
- Encryption-related settings
- Classification-related settings

BYOD Channel Settings

BYOD settings closely resemble those for endpoints, yet the environment is notably more constrained than one might anticipate. These settings typically include policies for device authentication, data encryption, application management, and network access controls. Administrators must balance security requirements with user convenience, ensuring that personal devices comply with corporate security standards without hindering productivity. Effective BYOD settings aim to mitigate risks

CHAPTER 6   PRO-ACTIVE INTELLIGENT DATA SECURITY

associated with unauthorized access, data breaches, and malware threats, providing a secure environment for both corporate data and user privacy. Regular updates and monitoring are essential to adapt to evolving threats and maintain a robust BYOD security posture. Here are some of the common settings often used:

- Can BYOD connect to the network
- Registration information for BYOD
- Threat and malware prevention settings
- Number of parallel scans on BYOD
- Number of BOYDs a scan can manage
- Rules that are applicable for data management on BYOD
- BYOD channels which the application needs to monitor

Network Channel Settings

Network channel settings in a security product encompass various components crucial for monitoring and securing network activities. These channels typically include email, web, and packet sniffer functionalities, each serving distinct roles in maintaining network security.

Email channels are pivotal for handling communication security, operating in reflect (monitoring) and forward (active filtering and control) modes, as previously discussed. Reflect mode allows for passive monitoring of email traffic, identifying potential threats such as phishing attempts or malicious attachments. In contrast, forward mode enables proactive filtering and blocking of suspicious emails based on predefined policies, ensuring immediate threat mitigation.

Web channels focus on managing and securing Internet browsing activities within the organization. Settings here involve URL filtering, content inspection, and malware detection to prevent access to malicious websites and enforce compliance with acceptable use policies. This helps safeguard against malware infections, data exfiltration, and unauthorized access originating from web traffic.

Packet sniffer channels play a critical role in network monitoring by capturing and analyzing data packets traversing the network. Settings for packet sniffers include protocol analysis, anomaly detection, and traffic profiling to detect and respond to suspicious network behavior promptly. This proactive approach aids in identifying potential security incidents, facilitating quick incident response, and minimizing the impact of network threats.

Overall, configuring network channel settings ensures comprehensive network security, protecting against a wide range of threats and vulnerabilities while promoting secure and efficient network operations. Here are the settings frequently encountered:

- Network protocols to monitor
- Network port to monitor
- Email/Web/Packet Traffic
- Port number of Emails to listen on
- Downstream MTA
- Reflect Mode/Forward Mode
- Minimum packet size for inspection
- Blocked Web URLs

CHAPTER 6   PRO-ACTIVE INTELLIGENT DATA SECURITY

Cloud Application Settings

Cloud application settings within a security product are essential for managing both Data in Motion (DIM) and Data at Rest (DAR) within cloud-hosted environments. Continuous monitoring and secure data transfer are paramount considerations when deploying applications in the cloud. DIM settings focus on real-time monitoring of data movements across cloud networks, ensuring that all data transfers are secure and compliant with organizational policies. This involves implementing encryption protocols, access controls, and anomaly detection mechanisms to protect data integrity and confidentiality during transmission.

DAR settings, on the other hand, address the security of data stored within cloud applications. This includes encryption at rest, access management, and regular audits to verify compliance with data protection regulations and internal security policies. Managing these settings effectively ensures that sensitive information stored in the cloud remains secure from unauthorized access or data breaches.

Furthermore, configuring cloud application settings involves optimizing performance while minimizing latency and operational disruptions. It requires collaboration between security administrators and cloud service providers to implement robust security measures without compromising user experience or business agility. Regular updates and audits of cloud application settings are essential to adapt to evolving threats and maintain a resilient security posture in cloud environments. Here are the settings frequently encountered:

- Cloud onboarding of application configurations starting from credentials
- Bandwidth to monitor/Throttle on file scans
- Application level settings on which application to monitor and filters associated with it

CHAPTER 6   PRO-ACTIVE INTELLIGENT DATA SECURITY

- Cloud scan configurations
- Continuous monitoring settings

Once these settings are applied across different channels, SRS must recommend adjustments based on their actual utilization. Monitoring the volume and types of incoming messages per channel becomes critical. The workload on each channel directly affects the effectiveness of remedial actions. Therefore, the remediation engine's settings need to harmonize with those of the channels, enabling smooth coordination among all system components. This alignment ensures that remediation efforts are optimized to handle varying loads and types of data, enhancing overall system efficiency and responsiveness to security incidents.

Specifically, SRS should do the following:

Track the volume of incoming messages for each channel to identify patterns and potential overloads. High message volume might indicate a need for additional resources or more stringent security measures.

Evaluate the types of messages each channel receives to determine the appropriate security responses. For example, channels receiving sensitive information might require more robust encryption and monitoring.

Configure the policy engine, violation processor, and remediation engine to adapt its actions based on channel load. During high-traffic periods, the system should prioritize critical threats and delay less urgent tasks to maintain performance. Hence corresponding setting recommendations should be dynamically made. Ensure that the remediation engine works in tandem with channel settings. This integration allows for automatic adjustments based on real-time data, optimizing security responses without manual intervention.

By coordinating the channel settings with other system settings, organizations can enhance their security posture, ensuring that all components work together effectively to manage threats and maintain smooth operations.

CHAPTER 6   PRO-ACTIVE INTELLIGENT DATA SECURITY

Policy Engine Settings

Policy engine settings in a security product are foundational to its operation, governing how security policies are defined, enforced, and updated across the organization's IT infrastructure. These settings encompass a wide array of configurations, from specifying access controls and encryption protocols to defining permissible user activities and network behaviors. Administrators can fine-tune these settings to align with specific security needs and operational workflows, balancing between stringent security measures and operational efficiency. With SRS in the picture, this fine-tuning can be automated. Effective policy engine settings streamline security operations by automating routine tasks, monitoring compliance, and swiftly responding to security incidents. Hence SRS could end up playing a critical role in safeguarding sensitive data, protecting against cyber threats, and maintaining a resilient security posture across the organization's digital landscape.

- Number of policies that can be active in the system at any moment
- Continuous monitoring policies enabled
- Policy max size to be deployed
- Profiles max file size to be deployed

Content Detection Engine Settings

Detection engine settings are the most important in the system as they regulate how sensitive files/anomalous activities are detected. These settings need explicit testing as they can wreak havoc on the whole security system if set wrongly.

- Content extraction limit
- Embedded file detection

CHAPTER 6   PRO-ACTIVE INTELLIGENT DATA SECURITY

- Encryption, classification-related settings
- Max violations for a policy in a time frame
- Content detection engine internal settings
- Matcher settings

Violation Processor Settings

The violation processor in a security product handles critical tasks related to identifying, analyzing, and responding to security violations across the organization's IT infrastructure. It operates based on a set of configurable settings that govern its functionality and effectiveness in mitigating risks and maintaining compliance.

Firstly, violation categorization settings allow the violation processor to classify violations based on severity levels, impact on operations, and regulatory implications. These settings enable prioritization of remediation efforts, ensuring that critical security incidents receive immediate attention while less severe violations are addressed under their relative importance.

Secondly, automated remediation settings define how the violation processor automatically responds to certain types of security violations. This includes actions such as quarantining infected files, blocking suspicious network traffic, or resetting compromised user accounts. Configurable parameters within these settings determine the conditions under which automated remediation actions are initiated, ensuring they align with organizational policies and compliance requirements.

Thirdly, integration settings enable the violation processor to interact seamlessly with other components within the security ecosystem, such as threat intelligence feeds, incident response platforms, and security information and event management (SIEM) systems. These settings facilitate

CHAPTER 6   PRO-ACTIVE INTELLIGENT DATA SECURITY

real-time data sharing, correlation of security events, and streamlined incident response workflows, enhancing the overall effectiveness of the security infrastructure.

Fourthly, notification and reporting settings dictate how the violation processor communicates security incidents and remediation actions to stakeholders. Administrators can configure alerts, notifications, and reports to provide timely updates on security posture, compliance status, and incident trends. Customizable reporting capabilities ensure that relevant information is conveyed to executive management, auditors, and regulatory bodies as required.

Lastly, performance optimization settings allow administrators to fine-tune the violation processor's resource utilization, ensuring optimal performance without compromising system stability. These settings include parameters for data processing speed, memory allocation, and workload distribution across distributed environments, enabling scalability and responsiveness to fluctuating operational demands.

In conclusion, the violation processor settings are pivotal in shaping the security posture of an organization, enabling proactive threat detection, efficient incident response, and continuous compliance with industry standards and regulatory requirements.

After exploring the various categories of settings employed by the violation processor, it's evident that SRS holds significant potential for organizations by providing valuable recommendations. This capability allows administrators to enhance product configurations effectively. Across all the settings categories mentioned earlier, SRS plays a crucial role in advising on critical adjustments tailored to organizational needs, informed by administrator intent.

CHAPTER 6   PRO-ACTIVE INTELLIGENT DATA SECURITY

Summary

In this chapter, we marched ahead toward creating a truly autonomous and intelligent security system. Our goal is to ensure proactive security through innovative heuristics that enable our security product to self-adapt and self-tune. We explored three essential recommendation systems, namely, the Policy Recommendation System (PRS), Remediation Recommendation System (RRS), and Settings Recommendation System (SRS) designed to put our security product in autopilot mode when necessary. All these recommendations must be easily accessible via the security product's user interface, empowering administrators to modify and enable it anytime.

For the recommendations to be effective, emphasis should be placed on presenting statistical data to administrators, showcasing the performance of these recommendations. As more recommendations transition into production policies and automated remediation tackles common violation types, organizations will experience the full value of an autonomous security solution.

Repeatedly discussed in this chapter are the foundational principles and design elements that serve as building blocks for security developers. These elements are integral to the evolution and refinement of our security system's capabilities.

Organizational executives reading this chapter should view these automated remediations as an opportunity for brainstorming on optimal security product configurations. They are encouraged to assess their current security product installations and configurations critically, making necessary adjustments to align with best practices and organizational security goals. This proactive approach ensures that their security infrastructure is finely tuned and equipped to handle evolving threats effectively.

CHAPTER 6   PRO-ACTIVE INTELLIGENT DATA SECURITY

In our final chapter, we'll explore the future of security products, addressing the profound impact of AI and how we can leverage technological advancements to confront emerging challenges effectively. AI is now both a potent tool and a potential threat in today's cybersecurity landscape, with adversaries increasingly utilizing AI-driven tactics. We'll equip you with strategies to harness AI's potential for bolstering security defenses and staying ahead of evolving cyber threats. Additionally, we'll delve into compelling topics such as intent-based detection, cultivating expertise in advanced policy configuration, innovative remediation techniques, and more.

CHAPTER 7

Future Ready Data Security

In this chapter, I delve into key areas essential for future planning—a dynamic and multifaceted endeavor. The landscape, shaped by technological advancements and evolving security regulations, is both intriguing and complex. As I write, recent strides in artificial intelligence ensure its pervasive role in our lives. Every sector feels its profound impact, with forecasts suggesting AI could surpass human capabilities by 2030. However, there's another factor growing even more rapidly than AI: data. Data management and privacy will become top concerns for organizations worldwide in the coming years, presenting challenges we haven't fully prepared for. While often discussed in fragments, the impact of data will be far more significant than imagined, and with it comes the ever-present need for data security.

Security vendors will be tasked with automatically understanding organizational intent and safeguarding sensitive data. Organizations will expect security solutions to collect data, recommend necessary configurations, and implement measures to address all types of risks and vulnerabilities. These security products must operate with a high level of automation and independence. Scalability and business continuity will remain crucial to meet user demands. This highlights the enduring importance of the core requirements discussed in Chapter 1.

CHAPTER 7   FUTURE READY DATA SECURITY

As always, I invite you, dear readers, to imagine beyond the present and, as outlined in Chapter 3, to think beyond conventional norms. In this chapter, I'll take you into a world of data where the most important requirement would be managing data growth while ensuring security and privacy. We'll explore how to make our security products interactive enough to learn the intent of security administrators, understand business objectives, and guarantee proactive data protection. This chapter is about crafting a detailed enterprise plan for the future and leveraging AI to solve critical security challenges.

Imagine a future where your security system is not just a tool, but an intelligent ally. This isn't science fiction; it's the next step in our journey toward a secure, data-driven world. This is about preparing for the future and turning challenges into opportunities with the help of cutting-edge technology.

In the last two chapters, we've thought through from all angles and designed a robust security product to meet the needs of most organizations. It covers everything from comprehensive protection and clear policy language to incident remediation and, most importantly, ensuring business continuity for large-scale enterprises. Let's set the product aside for a few moments and shift our focus to data and data management.

Data Management

Data is growing astonishingly, with most of the resources we once handled physically now digitized. Everything from emails to documents has gone electronic. With the advent of tablets, phones, and laptops, we have become more mobile, accessing everything at our fingertips anytime, anywhere. This shift to digital has created an immense demand for storage servers. Managing data at this scale is a monumental challenge. Large organizations deal with petabytes of data spread across their infrastructure.

CHAPTER 7   FUTURE READY DATA SECURITY

IT administrators are responsible for data management and storage, while security administrators focus on protecting that data. In many organizations, these roles overlap. One of the biggest challenges administrators face today is duplicate data. The same data may exist in multiple places under different file names, or even worse, the same file name. Employees frequently lose track of where they have stored their data, which leads to numerous obsolete locations filled with redundant files. These forgotten storage spots accumulate duplicate data, creating inefficiencies and complicating data management efforts. The task of tracking and deleting these forgotten files falls to the IT administrators. Recent surveys reveal that more than 50% of data in organizations is classified as "Dark Data"—data that is collected, processed, and stored but never used.

First and foremost, an IT administrator's job is to track all the locations where employees store data. This isn't a one-time task; it requires continuous monitoring, as employees often create and use new storage locations. With the advent of cloud computing, employees frequently use specific applications to store data. While organizations don't have complete control over these cloud applications, they can at least consolidate data tracking in one place. Can a security product track these locations, across on-premise and cloud, while providing security? The simple answer is yes. In most cases, it becomes the security products' job to track all data locations to ensure comprehensive protection.

In Chapter 5, we talked about the importance of following the data. For security products to effectively track locations, they must follow the data wherever it goes. Data that isn't sensitive today could become sensitive later as users edit and update it. Therefore, it's crucial to monitor all potential storage locations for data.

CHAPTER 7   FUTURE READY DATA SECURITY

Tracking Data

I envision that data tracking will become incredibly important in the coming years, and we will develop innovative methods to achieve this. In earlier chapters, we discussed tracking URLs to monitor data transferred outside the organization, particularly in a BYOD context. As data can reside both in the cloud and on-premises, we must consider multi-tenancy and prevent data from getting mixed with other organizations' data.

This will probably lead to a new hierarchy of identifiers for each organization's data. At a minimum, there would be two identifiers: one indicating the organization to which the data belongs, and another unique to that specific data within the organization. Each piece of data would have an uneditable unique identifier, akin to Social Security Numbers in the US. Advanced technology will ensure that even if data is copied or renamed, the original data ID remains intact, with markers indicating any changes. This approach will simplify tracking data updates and transformations, ensuring comprehensive monitoring and security. Figure 7-1 illustrates this concept visually. Though the "DocId D123" is assigned to both files, Products.pptx and SaleReport.xls in the figure, these documents belong to different organizations.

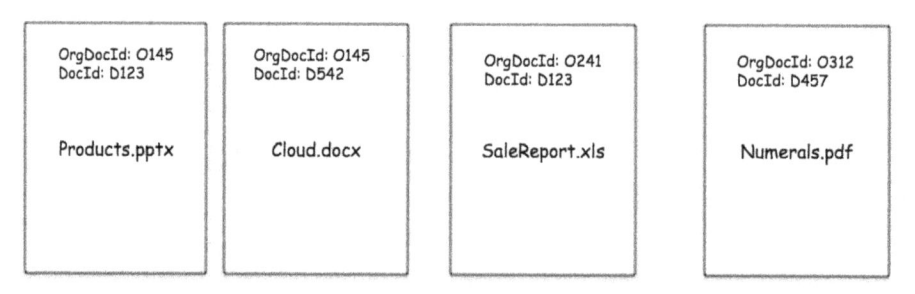

OrgDocId: O145 DocId: D123 Products.pptx	OrgDocId: O145 DocId: D542 Cloud.docx	OrgDocId: O241 DocId: D123 SaleReport.xls	OrgDocId: O312 DocId: D457 Numerals.pdf

OrgDocId O145 belongs to Organization A, O241 belongs to Organization B, and O312 belongs to Organization C

Figure 7-1. Document Identifiers for Tracking

CHAPTER 7   FUTURE READY DATA SECURITY

Using these identifiers or a similar mechanism, organizations and security products can track the data trail, enabling our security product to uncover hidden locations.

At this point, you might have two questions:

1. Does this method only apply to newly created data or data that has already been tagged and moved?

2. What happens to other files in these hidden locations that aren't tagged?

Great questions! You're right; this is not an easy problem to solve. For the first question, the answer is yes! This method applies only to new data or tagged data that is moved. The goal here is to discover hidden locations, not to tag all existing data files. For the second question, the untagged files will at least be tracked going forward. How to tag those files is beyond the scope of our security product's charter. However, we could consider mechanisms such as storing the hash and name of untagged files and matching them with tagged files when encountered.

Discovering all data locations is an ongoing process. In large organizations, it's unlikely we'll identify every single location. However, if a location is never accessed or data is never moved from it through the organizational network, we can at least be assured that no data loss occurred from that spot. Before we move on to enhancements for our security products, I want to stress that these locations can be updated at any time. Conducting monthly or quarterly surveys for continuous monitoring will help ensure our security product stays current with these locations.

For example, if an IT administrator decommissions a storage server, all data in that location is effectively destroyed. How would our security product know this location no longer exists? As I mentioned, we'd only know during the next scan when we discover that the location is no longer accessible. While it's impossible to keep every detail perfectly up-to-date, we can strive to be as current as possible.

333

CHAPTER 7   FUTURE READY DATA SECURITY

Security Product Enhancements

Our security product can be enhanced, if not already done, to store all these locations, which we'll refer to as content enumerations. With these content enumerations, continuous monitoring and Data at Rest (DAR) scans can be automatically configured to assess data sensitivity and apply remediation actions, such as classification and encryption, as needed. Once data falls under the purview of our security product, it should never leave our control without being thoroughly scanned by the product.

Analytics and statistics engines could play a crucial role in this process. By collecting and reporting on content enumerations and tracking locations, the security product could excel at assessing and reporting the risk of these locations. This assessment would be based on the number of sensitive files stored, user accessibility, and the risk levels associated with those users.

Is that all we need to do? Not quite. We haven't yet addressed the biggest challenge. Can you guess what it is? We've discussed scanning for the sensitivity of data discovered in hidden locations, but how can we ensure that the existing security policies are robust enough to accurately classify a file as sensitive? Don't worry! We have already built a strong foundation layer that could help us with this challenge.

We've stored partial matches and user risk scores, and the Policy Recommendation System (PRS) is well-equipped to use this data to make appropriate recommendations. Additionally, we have User and Entity Behavior Analytics (UEBA) and mechanisms to track suspicious activities. With these tools in play, we can enhance our policies and track data sensitivity as effectively as possible.

You might ask, can we be sure? It's a collaborative effort between the recommendation systems and the administrators who choose to accept those recommendations. If administrators don't make the right choices, we could misclassify data. However, most would agree that false positives are better than false negatives. To err on the side of caution, our security

CHAPTER 7   FUTURE READY DATA SECURITY

product could take stringent actions like blocking and quarantining suspected data leaks. Concerned users would then contact administrators if they truly need the data, drawing the administrator's attention to potential issues.

Are we disrupting business continuity by being conservative? To some extent, yes, but it's all part of building a proactive enterprise protection plan. Certain disruptions may be necessary to catch the eye of security administrators. Ultimately, it's up to you, the developers, to decide, as this can be a debatable topic.

Autonomous remediation actions created via the suggestions from the Remediation Recommendation System (RRS) would be of great assistance to the violation remediators to handle the large influx of violations as new locations are discovered. RRS would track the violations and might suggest new remedial actions.

Having discussed data management, let's get on to the next interesting topic of data privacy.

Data Privacy

Data privacy is all about making sure that data is collected, processed, and stored in ways that protect an individual's privacy rights. It focuses on safeguarding personal and sensitive information. While data management and data privacy are distinct concepts, they are closely intertwined and often overlap.

I foresee that data privacy will become an even hotter topic as we grapple with vast amounts of data. The uncertainty surrounding how our data is utilized is a significant concern. Organizations are increasingly wary of data sharing and storage in the cloud due to privacy issues. For businesses, data privacy is crucial for safeguarding their trade secrets. They must protect future plans, proprietary data, and the methods used to develop products to maintain their competitive edge.

CHAPTER 7 FUTURE READY DATA SECURITY

At its core, data privacy revolves around four essential pillars: compliance, consent, anonymization, and transparency.

Regulations like HIPAA and CCPA are critical as they ensure data is handled securely, reassuring customers that their information is safe in the hands of large organizations. Robust security policies are essential to ensure compliance with these regulations, alleviating the burden on security administrators from managing this manually. If our security product effectively manages compliance, it can address the majority of organizational use cases.

Consent involves obtaining permission from individuals or organizations to use their data. Types of consent include informed consent, voluntary consent, revocable consent, and partial consent for specific data uses. By respecting data consent, organizations foster trust with their customers.

In today's era, with the proliferation of AI chatbots like ChatGPT, people can easily share their data without realizing it. Organizations must rigorously ensure what data can legally be shared and what cannot. Therefore, safeguarding individuals from unintentionally leaking organizational data is crucial. In most cases, data leaks are unintentional and not malicious on the part of the users.

Anonymization involves removing personally identifiable information from data before it is shared. Implementing effective anonymization techniques is crucial for maintaining compliance, building trust, and reducing risks related to handling personal data. Our security product can assist in anonymizing data effectively. Leveraging its knowledge of sensitive content matches, our product is well-positioned to ensure robust anonymization processes. Anonymization is mandated by compliance laws to ensure that data cannot be used for specific purposes without proper anonymization.

Transparency is the final pillar of data privacy, requiring organizations and entities to disclose how shared data is being utilized. While this isn't directly related to our security product, it's essential to mention it for a comprehensive understanding.

Our next topic of discussion is intent-based security, where the security product can discern the organization's intent autonomously and respond accordingly.

Intent-Based Security

Looking ahead, organizations will demand highly intelligent security products capable of safeguarding data without extensive manual configuration. Currently, setting up and maintaining security products can be a significant burden, even a nightmare for many customers. While security companies often streamline management with unified dashboards and improved visibility, the overall complexity remains daunting for organizations.

Future advancements will focus on understanding the intent of security administrators and automating configuration and maintenance tasks. The goal is to deliver maximum security effectiveness with minimal manual intervention, ensuring robust protection against evolving threats.

Let's dissect this requirement. The initial step is to outline the configuration process for organizations, detailing what they need to acquire to secure their operations. Many organizations begin with modest security measures and gradually expand their infrastructure over the years. However, some still feel dissatisfied, lacking confidence in their comprehensive protection. Our goal as security vendors is to instill this confidence by ensuring organizations feel assured that their data is secure and all points of access are fortified and safeguarded.

Next, we move on to configuring policies and addressing violations. After carefully assessing coverage points, the next step involves customizing policies based on the organization's data protection practices. Scalability becomes critical as operations expand, requiring a content engine that can process large volumes at lightning speed. Effective violation remediations and decisive actions are essential to ensure a comprehensive security approach, as we explored in the previous chapter.

Now, let's delve into the details.

CHAPTER 7   FUTURE READY DATA SECURITY

Configurations

Setting up the security product is the first critical task for organizations. Can the security product configure itself? Yes, with minimal guidance from administrators. What input is needed? Let's start by identifying coverage points. The product needs to recognize all existing coverage points within the organization. How can we accomplish this? Take a moment to think about it broadly.

An organization might be spread around in different regions and may use cloud or not. We'll engage the administrator interactively to understand their setup. Here in Table 7-1 are some simple questions related to cloud applications:

Table 7-1. *Questions Regarding Cloud Applications*

- Does your organization utilize cloud applications?
- If yes, please specify which corporate cloud applications you use. (List all popular applications to choose from.)
- For each corporate-approved cloud application, what administrator credentials are utilized? (go one by one to onboard)
- How many cloud users are in the organization (ballpark number)?
- Enter the names of administrators who have rights to configure the cloud applications (for posture management of those cloud applications).
- Do you already have ICAP servers or gateways that intercept traffic between users and cloud applications? If yes, please provide details.
- Provide detailed steps for administrators to route their cloud ICAP traffic into the security product.
- Do you use a cloud-based Active Directory like Microsoft Azure AD?

Based on these questions, a security solution should be equipped to integrate and begin monitoring various cloud applications. This includes setting up CASB, Cloud Email, Cloud ICAP, and Cloud Application Posture Management for routing and monitoring tasks using straightforward

CHAPTER 7   FUTURE READY DATA SECURITY

inquiries. Of course, you can refine and expand these questions to improve them and incorporate any additional details necessary. I'm offering a foundation upon which to build and customize your approach.

On a similar note, Table 7-2 presents the administrator with a series of questions inquiring about their on-premise infrastructure.

Table 7-2. *Questions Regarding On-Premise Infrastructure*

Specify usage locations by country.
What kinds of devices are employees in the organization approved to use? (Provide the list—laptops, desktop computers, cell phones, tablets, BYOD)
Approximately how many employees are there in the organization?
Do employees work remotely? If yes, specify all the VPN servers they might use.
Which identity provider do you use? (Provide the list)
Do you use an on-premise Active Directory? If yes, please specify the details (there could be more than one server).
How do endpoint machines register? (Provide options for how users sign in—AD-based login or something else)
What are the approved peripherals for an endpoint, as applicable? (Provide the list—USB, CD/DVD/Blue-ray players, etc.)

- Specify the printer server addresses or import the list of network printers for each location.
- Specify all the network shares and their credentials known within the organization by location.
- Specify any on-premise email servers and MTA details (both upstream and downstream) used in the organization.
- Specify the proxy servers and firewalls used in the organization by location or traffic management sites.
- Do you approve of the use of AI software such as chatbots? (Provide a list to choose from.)

CHAPTER 7   FUTURE READY DATA SECURITY

Based on these questions, you should now have an understanding of how the security product can handle on-premise configurations. However, we still need insights into the organization's data volume, flow, and usage patterns. The security product can gradually uncover these answers as it begins monitoring operations.

Imagine this scenario: a security administrator overlooks some network shares. When the product detects a new share during monitoring, it automatically prompts the administrator for credentials to begin monitoring. This proactive approach eliminates the need for manual intervention, exemplifying the future direction I foresee for security products.

Now armed with these questions, our product can advise security administrators on the necessary infrastructure to secure their organization. If agents are required on endpoint machines, the product will indicate the need to deploy these agents. It will then proceed to inquire about distributing the agent installation packages to these endpoints and automatically configure them as needed.

While I'm painting an optimistic picture, reality may not always align perfectly. For instance, if an administrator specifies a cloud application that our security product doesn't currently support, we acknowledge this limitation. In such cases, the product can provide feedback to the vendor, urging them to develop support for the application, as it's crucial for the organization's needs.

Over time, this automated setup and configuration recommendation process will evolve into a self-learning assistant for security administrators. It's important to note that while we enhance automation, administrators still retain the option to manually configure the product. This additional support is particularly valuable for organizations that may have limited resources dedicated to security product installation and maintenance.

With the Settings Recommendation System (SRS) implemented, settings for various servers and deployment scenarios can be automatically recommended, simplifying the tasks for security administrators.

Policies

Next, how can we automate policy configuration? Once policies and remediation actions are in place, addressing violations becomes seamless. Before we start setting up policies, we'll begin with an interactive approach to gather the necessary details.

From the security product's perspective, we'll start by identifying the organization's name and the industry vertical it operates. Once the vertical is established, we'll prioritize enabling standard compliance and regulatory policies. Then, we'll focus on posture management policies for the cloud and other specific policies tailored to sensitive information. Threat-based policies and zero-day attack policies are easier to create and should be in place by default for any organization to mitigate threats.

While compliance policies cover known sensitive areas, identifying proprietary content owned by the organization requires additional steps. One approach involves querying administrators based on partial document matches to determine sensitivity. Alternatively, sampling documents can prompt administrators to define content sensitivity directly. Most organizations can easily classify documents and specify sensitive information, which allows our system to recommend effective policies through the Policy Recommendation System (PRS). This collaboration ensures that policies align closely with organizational goals.

Initially, our policies tend to be cautious but can evolve automatically over time. However, handling exceptions presents a tougher challenge than establishing general rules and content guidelines. Policy administrators must provide clear guidance for configuring exceptions, as the security system may not inherently understand these nuances.

For example, blocking all emails from Group A if they include external addresses is straightforward to implement. However, exceptions such as allowing all members of Group A except for Member B require specific administrator input and guidance. This ensures that our security measures align precisely with the organization's operational needs.

ML-based policies, generated from observed data, can simplify the process for administrators seeking more guidance. These policies can be further refined based on violation remediation outcomes.

Violation Remediations

Violation remediation remains the primary indicator of an organization's intent and priorities regarding security. When we observe how an organization handles security breaches and policy violations, it reveals a great deal about its commitment to maintaining a secure environment. If violations are not being addressed by the designated remediators, it reveals significant insights about the organization. It may indicate that the organization is more focused on detection rather than remediation, suggesting either a lack of resources, insufficient commitment, or perhaps a strategic decision to de-prioritize manual remediation efforts. This scenario poses considerable risks, as unaddressed violations can lead to security breaches, data loss, and potential damage to the organization's reputation.

In such cases, automated remediation becomes essential. Automated solutions can bridge the gap where human resources fall short, ensuring that security breaches are handled promptly and consistently. By implementing automated remediation, organizations can maintain a robust security posture even with limited resources. This approach not only enhances the efficiency and effectiveness of security operations but also alleviates the burden on human resources, allowing them to focus on more strategic tasks rather than routine violation handling.

Imagine an organization that promptly addresses violations as they arise. In this ideal scenario, policies can be fine-tuned based on the remediation process, leading to a dynamic and responsive security environment. When violations are dealt with efficiently, the feedback obtained from these incidents provides invaluable insights into the organization's vulnerabilities. This feedback loop highlights specific security gaps, identifies high-risk vectors, and pinpoints critical access points that need additional protection. By leveraging this information, the security product can concentrate on fortifying defenses in these areas, ensuring a more robust and resilient security posture.

Continuous monitoring and feedback are crucial for the ongoing refinement of automated remediation processes. As the security landscape evolves, new threats emerge, and the organization's operational environment changes. The automated remediation rules need to be updated accordingly. This requires a feedback loop where the outcomes of remediation actions are analyzed to determine their effectiveness. If certain actions are not yielding the desired results, adjustments must be made to improve their efficacy. This iterative process ensures that the automated remediation system remains effective over time, adapting to new challenges and threats.

However, it is important to recognize that automated remediation is not a one-size-fits-all solution. Different organizations have unique security needs and operational constraints. Therefore, the implementation of automated remediation must be tailored to the specific context of each organization. This customization involves understanding the organization's security landscape, identifying critical assets and vulnerabilities, and designing remediation strategies that align with its risk management framework. Collaboration between security professionals and other stakeholders is essential to ensure that the automated remediation system is aligned with organizational goals and objectives.

Furthermore, while automated remediation significantly enhances security operations, it should be complemented by robust incident response and threat intelligence capabilities. Automated systems can handle routine violations and breaches effectively, but sophisticated attacks and zero-day threats may require human intervention and expertise. Therefore, a comprehensive security strategy should include a blend of automated and manual processes, ensuring that all types of threats are addressed appropriately.

In conclusion, the ability to remediate violations effectively is a critical indicator of an organization's commitment to security. If violations are not addressed, it reveals potential weaknesses in the organization's security posture. Automated remediation provides a solution to this challenge, ensuring timely and consistent handling of security breaches.

AI-Based Detection

In today's rapidly evolving technological landscape, the use of artificial intelligence (AI) in cybersecurity is both a significant advantage and a point of contention. While AI enhances security measures, some organizations are hesitant to adopt these technologies due to perceived risks and a lack of understanding. As a result, these AI-skeptical organizations completely ban the use of AI, fearing the potential threats and prioritizing the risk of data loss over the benefits AI might offer.

Some organizations permit the use of AI but with strict guidelines. They allow pre-trained models for detection, but these models must be developed in-house by their security vendor or created on-site within the organization. This ensures that they are not relying on pre-existing models from the market, thereby maintaining greater control and security over their AI applications.

Let's look at how we can leverage AI to our advantage in content detection.

As cybersecurity threats become more complex, the need for advanced detection methods becomes increasingly important. A promising solution is using large language models (LLMs) like GPT-4 in security products. These models, renowned for their natural language processing (NLP) abilities, offer unique benefits in spotting and addressing security threats by understanding and analyzing large volumes of text data.

Understanding LLM-Based Detection

Commercially available large language models (LLMs) are pre-trained on extensive and varied datasets, which allow them to understand and generate human-like text across different domains and languages. In the realm of security, LLMs can be highly beneficial due to their capability to analyze and interpret various forms of digital communication and logs. They can be further enhanced to analyze sensitive data traffic and interpret suspicious user behaviors more effectively than ever, thereby providing proactive protection.

Let's explore some of the features that can emerge from these LLM-based detections.

Security vendors can leverage LLMs to analyze and interpret various types of digital communication, including emails, chat messages, and social media posts. These models excel at identifying suspicious language patterns indicative of phishing attempts, social engineering tactics, and other cyber threats. Additionally, by scrutinizing system logs that document IT infrastructure activities, LLMs can detect anomalies and unauthorized access attempts. They are adept at recognizing unusual patterns in log entries that may signal malware installations, brute-force attacks, or other potential security breaches. Integrating LLM-based analysis into security protocols can enhance threat detection capabilities and bolster overall cybersecurity measures effectively.

Large Language Models (LLMs) are increasingly being recognized for their potential to detect insider threats within organizations. Traditional methods of detecting insider threats often rely on monitoring access logs and behavioral patterns, but LLMs offer a more nuanced and sophisticated approach by analyzing language and communication patterns. One of the primary strengths of LLMs in detecting insider threats lies in their ability to process and understand vast amounts of data in a short time. By analyzing these communications, LLMs can identify anomalies or deviations from normal patterns that may indicate potential insider threats. For example, sudden changes in an employee's communication style, such as an increase in the use of technical jargon or frequent references to confidential information, could raise flags.

Furthermore, LLMs can interpret the context and sentiment behind communications, which allows them to distinguish between legitimate activities and suspicious behavior. They can detect subtle cues that human analysts might overlook, such as unusual requests for access permissions, inappropriate sharing of sensitive information, or discussions about unauthorized activities.

Using LLMs for insider threat detection offers several advantages. They excel in analyzing temporal communication patterns, detecting changes in frequency or timing that may indicate suspicious behaviors occurring outside typical work hours or during periods of heightened organizational sensitivity, such as before major announcements or financial disclosures. Moreover, LLMs can integrate seamlessly with other security tools and systems to create a comprehensive insider threat detection strategy. By analyzing access logs alongside linguistic patterns, they provide a holistic view of potential threats, enabling security teams to prioritize alerts and focus investigations on high-risk individuals or activities.

LLMs possess the capability to process and comprehend security reports, threat intelligence feeds, and cybersecurity research papers. They can effectively summarize and interpret this information, offering valuable insights into emerging threats, new malware variants, and vulnerabilities critical for organizational awareness.

Additionally, LLMs can provide actionable recommendations based on their analyses. For example, they can propose remedial actions for security breaches or suggest preventive measures based on historical patterns and current threat intelligence. This proactive approach enhances security readiness and helps organizations stay ahead of evolving cybersecurity challenges.

Further, LLMs can be continuously trained on new data, enabling them to adapt to emerging threats and changing attack vectors. This ensures that the detection mechanisms remain effective over time.

Incorporating LLM-Based Detection

The standard pre-trained LLM cannot be implemented directly within an organization by a security vendor. It must undergo customization and training using specific organizational data to ensure it comprehensively understands the organization's unique priorities and requirements.

Data Gathering

As emphasized in this chapter, data management forms the foundation of defense. Therefore, security vendors should inform organizations and begin by meticulously collecting diverse datasets tailored to their unique security needs, spanning emails, sensitive documents, non-sensitive documents, logs, and threat intelligence. Before this data can be utilized, it must undergo preparation—similar to our statistics engine—all data needs to go through crucial preprocessing to ensure cleanliness and optimization for training Large Language Models (LLMs). These models are pivotal in transforming security practices.

Training LLM

After collecting and preprocessing the data, the next step is to proceed with training the LLM. Security vendors can utilize existing libraries and functions provided by LLM vendors, to train the model, incorporating the existing model and collected data as parameters. This training process entails fine-tuning for adaptation and specialization. Over iterative training cycles, the model progresses, incorporating new data to proactively address emerging external threats and attempts at insider data exfiltration.

Training and running LLMs require substantial computational resources. Security vendors and organizations must invest in adequate hardware and infrastructure to support these models.

LLMs can generate complex and nuanced insights, which may be difficult for security teams to interpret. LLMs need regular updates and retraining to remain effective. This requires ongoing access to new data and dedicated resources for model maintenance.

If the LLM was developed in-house by a security vendor, it requires the appropriate skill set in resourcing to train the LLMs effectively.

LLMs in Multi-tenant Environment

Security vendors have the opportunity to deploy their own custom-developed and custom-trained Large Language Models (LLMs) in the cloud, even within a multi-tenant setting. However, training LLMs in such an environment presents several challenges and requires careful consideration. One of the foremost concerns is data privacy and security. Each tenant's data must be isolated to prevent data leakage. Techniques such as data encryption, access controls, and secure multi-party computation are essential in achieving this goal. Additionally, vendors must adhere to strict privacy regulations, such as GDPR, CCPA, and HIPAA, by implementing rigorous data handling policies.

Resource management is another critical aspect. The system needs to scale resources dynamically to accommodate varying workloads from different tenants. Efficient resource allocation, including CPU, memory, and storage, is necessary to balance the needs of multiple tenants without degrading performance. Model customization is also vital in a multi-tenant environment. Tenants should be able to customize and fine-tune the LLM for their specific requirements, which may involve training on proprietary data or adjusting model parameters. Supporting different versions of the model for various tenants is also important, as this enables them to use versions that best suit their specific use cases.

Performance and latency are crucial considerations. Load balancing mechanisms should be implemented to distribute computational loads evenly across servers, ensuring optimal performance for all tenants. Caching strategies can also be employed to speed up response times for frequently requested operations or queries. Cost management involves tracking and billing usage accurately, enabling tenants to understand their resource consumption and costs. Vendors can explore techniques to reduce costs, such as using spot instances or optimizing resource allocation.

Tenant-specific features are essential for providing a tailored experience. Vendors should offer custom APIs and interfaces that allow tenants to interact with the LLMs in ways that meet their specific needs. Tenant isolation is critical to ensure that each tenant's configurations and operations are separate, preventing interference from other tenants and ensuring a personalized experience. By addressing these challenges, security vendors can successfully offer scalable, customizable, and efficient LLM services in a multi-tenant cloud environment.

By using containerization tools like Docker and Kubernetes, LLM instances can be encapsulated, facilitating seamless deployment and management across multiple tenants. Federated learning offers another layer of sophistication, enabling tenants to collaboratively train models while ensuring their data remains decentralized and private. Balancing efficiency with customization is achieved by combining shared resources for common tasks with dedicated resources for tenant-specific operations, which caters to the unique needs of each tenant. Centralized orchestration tools streamline these processes, overseeing model training, deployment, and scaling across tenants. Finally, supporting multiple models within the same environment gives tenants the flexibility to choose or switch between models that best suit their needs, providing a tailored and efficient experience in managing LLMs. This approach not only optimizes resource utilization but also enhances the adaptability and functionality of the system, making it an attractive solution for readers interested in cutting-edge technology implementations.

CHAPTER 7   FUTURE READY DATA SECURITY

Using LLM in Content Detection

Our content detection engine can be enhanced to incorporate LLM. LLM would function as another matcher through which all content for detection would pass. Similar to other content matchers, LLM-based detection would provide results identifying suspicious users, threats, sensitive data, and more. Real-time analysis is crucial, enabling LLM to promptly identify and respond to emerging threats. The integration extends beyond technical considerations; it focuses on strategy, ensuring that the organization's defenses collaborate seamlessly, strengthened by the insights and capabilities of AI.

PRS and RRS Integrations

LLMs can also integrate into PRS to provide effective recommendations. They can analyze existing security policies, assess violations, and make informed recommendation decisions. This doesn't necessarily mean they're better than humans; rather, they can operate faster and analyze large datasets to propose resolutions and suggestions swiftly. Integrating LLMs into RRS can recommend remediation actions.

Before integrating it for recommendations, it's crucial to first integrate with the content detection engine. This ensures that LLMs are trained on organization-specific data, enabling them to make informed policy and remediation decisions effectively.

Policy Authoring

LLMs can effectively guide policy authoring. Policy authors can receive useful suggestions from trained models because they understand existing policies and violations within the organization. In other words, LLMs possess knowledge of both the strengths and weaknesses of the organization's security landscape, enabling them to effectively guide authors in creating policies. Channel-specific policies can be crafted to address particular vulnerabilities, with LLMs serving as experts in identifying and addressing specific security gaps within the organization.

LLM Performance

Once deployed, the LLM's performance needs to be monitored and subjected to continuous scrutiny. Its effectiveness in detecting threats, minimizing false positives, and adapting to novel attack vectors should be evaluated and appropriately tuned. Improperly trained LLMs could lead to an increase in false positives and, in the worst cases, even false negatives. Therefore, training the LLM correctly is the most crucial step.

So, LLM-based detection is a big step forward in cybersecurity. It uses the language skills of large models to help organizations find and stop tricky threats. Setting it up takes careful planning and resources, but the payoff—better threat spotting, understanding what's going on, and learning from it all—makes LLM-based detection a smart choice for any security setup. As time goes on, I foresee more security vendors leveraging LLMs to enhance their detection and protection capabilities.

Defend Against AI Threats

AI is both a tool and a potential threat. Many organizations are concerned about the risks of mishandling or exposing sensitive data. AI systems, especially those using cloud services or external vendors, could heighten the chances of data breaches or unauthorized access. Decision-makers and stakeholders often don't fully grasp AI technologies. The complexity and opacity of AI models, particularly those using machine learning (ML) and deep learning, can be daunting. This lack of transparency creates worries that organizations may struggle to effectively control or predict how AI systems will behave.

CHAPTER 7   FUTURE READY DATA SECURITY

In the earlier section, we discussed how we can leverage LLMs. As you read, I'm sure you considered the inherent threats they pose, starting with data collection. The threats posed by LLMs to security vendors and organizations are numerous. Let's briefly explore them.

Data Privacy and Security

LLMs require vast amounts of data for training, encompassing data collection and preprocessing of various types, including sensitive information. This collection of training datasets inherently becomes a honeypot for malicious actors seeking to steal data. Additionally, there is a risk of mishandling or exposing this data, particularly in the absence of proper security measures. Training should be conducted using software developed to secure data rather than sharing it with others, and all data must be safeguarded in the most secure manner possible.

Understanding Trained Models

LLMs can inadvertently reflect biases present in the data they are trained on, potentially leading to unfair or discriminatory outcomes in security assessments. LLMs, especially those based on deep learning, can be highly complex and opaque. This complexity may hinder understanding of how decisions are made, making it challenging to interpret and audit their behavior. Relying heavily on LLMs for security tasks could create a dependency that, if not managed carefully, might compromise the reliability of threat detection and response systems.

LLMs: A Threat in Themselves

LLMs face risks from adversarial attacks both in on-premise and cloud, where attackers exploit vulnerabilities to manipulate outputs, potentially undermining security measures. Implementing LLMs can also pose challenges in complying with data protection regulations, especially when handling sensitive personal information. To tackle these challenges, effective risk management strategies are crucial. This includes implementing strict data governance practices, employing bias detection and mitigation methods, ensuring transparency in AI decision-making, and continuously monitoring and adapting security practices to address evolving threats.

Safeguarding LLMs from Bad Actors

First and foremost, we should establish clear guidelines for the ethical use of LLMs, ensuring compliance with legal and regulatory requirements. Security products installed to ensure compliance within an organization should not undermine the compliance goals themselves by using LLMs in a non-compliant manner. This may involve addressing biases in training data and ensuring visibility and transparency throughout the entire process.

Secondly, educating and raising awareness among organizational representatives and all stakeholders about the benefits and threats posed by LLMs is crucial. Everyone involved should adhere strictly to the best security practices outlined and prioritize security at all costs.

Next, implement the best authentication and authorization mechanisms to protect LLMs from bad actors. Take utmost care to ensure that only authorized personnel and systems can interact with sensitive data and functionalities. Conducting regular security audits and vulnerability assessments of LLMs is a mandatory step to protect against compromise. All associated systems should be audited and monitored for potential security weaknesses or vulnerabilities.

Implementing strong data security measures throughout the lifecycle of LLMs—from data collection and preprocessing to model training and deployment—is essential. This encompasses encryption, access controls, and secure storage practices to prevent unauthorized access and data breaches. Additionally, it's crucial to incorporate adversarial training techniques during the model development phase to boost resilience against adversarial attacks. This means exposing the model to adversarial examples during training to enhance its robustness.

Therefore, by incorporating the above suggestions, security vendors and organizations can effectively harness the benefits of LLMs and mitigate the risks posed by bad actors who seek to exploit vulnerabilities or manipulate the model for malicious purposes.

Summary

In this final chapter, I discussed preparing our security product for future challenges. We explored in depth topics like data management and privacy, areas poised for significant growth. We also delved into intent-based security, a trend where organizations are increasingly expecting security vendors to automate processes and operate security products in autopilot mode. This shift reflects the evolving demands and expectations in the cybersecurity landscape. Lastly, we examined how to utilize LLMs in our security product and integrate them into the components we developed in previous chapters. Ethical and effective AI usage ensures that we can enjoy its benefits without encountering substantial drawbacks.

To wrap things up, remember: the challenges ahead might get as confusing as a goat on roller skates, but we're also getting smarter and more equipped to handle them. Keep learning, keep up with the latest tech, and stick to good security habits. That way, we'll make sure the digital world stays safe and sound for everyone. Thank you!

Index

A

AI, see Artificial intelligence (AI)
Analytics, 140
    feedback, 140, 141
    risk patterns/anomalies, 142
    spend management, 144
    SSPM software, 143, 144
    user risk assessment, 141–143
Analytics engine
    abnormalities, 249
        alarms, 252
        risk score calculation, 250, 251
        suspicious context, 249, 250
        vulnerabilities, 252
    aforementioned attributes, 243
    behavior analysis, 241
    cloud application posture management, 260, 261
    correlation/analysis, 244
        activity across channels, 244, 245
        data collection/comparison, 248
        peer analysis, 247, 248
        self analysis, 246, 247
    data audit trails
        following data, 253, 254
        monitoring data, 253
        transformation, 254, 255
        usage suspicion, 255, 256
    data collection, 242–244
    primary functions, 241
    violation monitoring, 256
        compliance, 259
        remediation process, 258
        risks/vulnerabilities, 257, 258
        security policies, 257
        trends, 259, 260
Artificial intelligence (AI)
    content detection, 344
    cybersecurity threats, 344
    LLMs (see Large language models (LLMs))
    organizations, 344
    potential threats
        adversarial attacks, 352
        cloud services/external vendors, 351
        privacy/security, 352
        trained models, 352

© Priyanka Neelakrishnan 2024
P. Neelakrishnan, *Autonomous Data Security*,
https://doi.org/10.1007/979-8-8688-0838-8

INDEX

B

Bring Your Own Device (BYOD), 71, 72, 129, 233, 242
    PRS heuristics, 297, 298
BYOD, *see* Bring Your Own Device (BYOD)

C

CASB, *see* Cloud Access Security Brokers (CASB)
Cloud Access Security Brokers (CASB), 68, 72, 76, 80, 129
Cloud Application Data Protection, 126
Cloud Security Posture Management (CSPM), 55, 56, 72
Content detection, 188
    classification/encryption, 192
    components layout, 193
    embedded content, 191
    encryption, 192
    endpoints/mobile devices, 195
    file content, 189, 190
    multi-tenant servers, 196
    policy set, 190
    remediation action, 192
    requirements, 198
    reviewing design, 197
    sharing content extraction, 194–195
    single-tenant environments, 193, 194

Content detection engine, 161
    asynchronous/synchronous processing, 163
    content matching message, 165, 166
    context rule possibilities, 166–168
    inputs/outputs, 162–165
    message-parsing solutions, 168–170
    security rules/policies, 162
    standardization/extraction, 170–172
    synchronous processing, 163
Content rule matching, 171
    Boolean expression, 182
    classification sensitivity labels/tags, 179, 180
    custom script, 182
    identity-based matching, 177–179
    keyword lists/pairs configuration, 172, 173
    machine learning-based matching, 181
    regular expressions, 172, 173
    structured content matching, 174–176
    suspicious intent, 180
    threat intelligence systems, 181
    unique identifiers matching, 173, 174
    unstructured data matching, 176, 177

INDEX

Continuous monitoring
    network traffic, 37
    storage systems, 37
    tracking, 36
CSPM, *see* Cloud Security Posture Management (CSPM)
Customer environments, 73
    hybrid environments, 75
    on-premise, 73, 74
    public cloud/private cloud, 74, 75
Cutting-edge technology, 330, 349

D

DAR, *see* Data-at-Rest (DAR)
Data-at-Rest (DAR), 59, 60, 101, 317, 321
Data-in-Motion (DIM), 58, 59, 101, 317, 321
Data management
    cloud computing, 331
    dark data, 331
    document identifiers, 332
    meaning, 331
    security product, 334, 335
    tracking URLs, 332, 333
Data privacy, 335–337, 348, 352
Data protection
    audit trails, 152
    components identification, 155, 159, 160
        auditing, 159
        block diagram, 154, 155, 160
        business continuity, 158
        external systems, 159
        generic perimeter protection, 154
        RBAC system, 159
        reporting engine, 157
        requirements, 153
        security policies, 155
        suspicious behavior, 157
        violation processor, 156
        zero trust, 158
    construction project, 149
    core requirements, 148
    integration, 151
    modular design, 149
    overarching goal, 150
    policies, 151
    primary goal, 149
    protect confidential data, 150
    use cases, 150–152
    violations/reporting, 151
    visibility/reporting model, 148
    zero trust, 151
Data security
    adversaries/tactics/attack, 5–18
    approach security, 2
    banking organization, 3
    business continuity, 29, 30
    challenges, 5
    comprehensive coverage, 76, 77
    confidential information
        content examination, 23
        content matching, 24
        contextual matching, 23

INDEX

Data security (*cont.*)
    data inspection, 22, 23
    remediation, 25
    scenario, 20
    sensitive *vs.* non-sensitive, 21
  configuration options, 82
  continuous (*see* Continuous monitoring)
  coverage points
    access points, 26
    cloud services, 28
    data centers, 28
    emails/messaging applications, 28
    endpoints, 28
    integration points, 25
    network perimeters, 27
    protection, 27
    remote access points, 29
  customer support, 85
  cybersecurity defense, 2
  definition, 3
  design (*see* Design process)
  detection gaps, 77
    cloud service, 78
    content extraction failure, 77
    content sizes, 79
    policy loading, 78
    security solution timeouts, 79
  extremes, 4
  feedback/learning, 35
    benefits, 32
    Excel spreadsheet, 32
    proactive security, 33, 34
    reactive security, 32
    supervised learning, 35
  inadequate integrations, 84
  internal and external data, 3, 4
  large-scale enterprises, 330
  matching technologies, 80
  monitoring, 83
  objectives, 4
  organizational intent/safeguarding sensitive data, 329
  organization infrastructure, 6
  reporting, 83
  requirements, 19, 20, 38
  scale/performance/resiliency, 81
  scaling, 37, 38
  security solution, 30, 31
  security vendors, 85, 329
  storage systems, 38
  unified policies, 79, 80
  upgrading software, 84
  usability challenges, 82
Deployment environment/channels, 127–129
Deployment/setup/maintenance, 136
  installation/upgrade administrators, 137
  channels, 139
  configuration, 136
  corporate/approved applications, 138, 139
  software, 137

INDEX

Design process
    cloud email violation, 188
    components, 161
    content detection, 188–198
    content detection
        engine, 161–170
    content rule matching, 171–183
    endpoint violation, 188
    feedback processor, 265–267
    matching algorithms, 183–185
    policy engine
        administrators, 199
        features, 199
        pre-defined models, 199, 200
        targeting/detection gaps,
          200, 201
    protection (*see* Data protection)
    remediation actions, 186, 187
    remediation execution
        engine, 205
        action types, 209, 210
        determiner's role, 207, 208
        executor's task, 208
        inputs/outputs, 205, 206
    reporting options, 210
        compliance, 214
        dashboard, 213
        distribution list, 211
        historical report, 211
        internal/external
          auditors, 214
        on-demand options, 212
        pre-configured criteria, 214
        scheduling options, 212
        specification, 211
        types, 213
        UI-centric reports, 213
        user experience, 213
    security violations, 186–188
    strategies, 147
    user/role processor, 214
        functions/RBAC, 216
        role definition, 215, 216
    violation processor, 201
        deduplication, 201
        remediation actions,
          203, 204
        retention period, 204, 205
        stages, 203
        subsequent phase, 202
DIM, *see* Data-in-
    Motion (DIM)

E, F

EDM, *see* Exact Data
    Matching (EDM)
EDR, *see* Endpoint Detection and
    Response (EDR)
Email security, 64–67, 71
Endpoint Detection and Response
    (EDR), 41, 50–51
Endpoint security, 70–73, 318
Exact Data Matching (EDM), 175
External infrastructure
    internal (*see* Internal
        infrastructure)
    malware, 14, 15

359

INDEX

External infrastructure (*cont.*)
    network, 15, 16
    physical attacks, 18
    social engineering, 17
    third-party components, 17
    types, 13, 14
    web application, 16

G

GAH, *see* Good American Hospital (GAH)
Good American Hospital (GAH), 88–90, 140

H

HA/DR, *see* High Availability and Disaster Recovery (HA/DR)
Healthcare organization, 88–90
High Availability and Disaster Recovery (HA/DR), 28, 44, 267

I, J, K

IAM, *see* Identity and access management (IAM)
ICAP, *see* Internet Content Adaptation Protocol (ICAP)
Identity and access management (IAM), 45, 55, 131, 133, 269
Intent-based security, 337
    advancements, 337
    cloud applications, 338

    configuration, 338–340
    continuous monitoring/feedback, 343
    ML-based policies, 342
    on-premise infrastructure, 339
    policy configuration, 341, 342
    requirement, 337
    threat-based/zero-day attack policies, 341
    violation remediation, 342–344
Internal infrastructure
    accidental data exposure, 9
    cyber espionage, 12
    data theft/exfiltration, 11
    destruction, 12
    financial attacks, 12, 13
    insider threats, 7, 8
    legitimate system, 6
    losing credentials, 10, 11
    malicious, 7, 11
    motivations, 13
    negligent user, 9
    shortcuts, 9
Internet Content Adaptation Protocol (ICAP), 69, 75
Internet Service Providers (ISPs), 65
ISPs, *see* Internet Service Providers (ISPs)

L

Large language models (LLMs), 97, 344
    detection process

INDEX

containerization tools, 349
content detection
   engine, 350
   gathering data, 347
   multi-tenant setting,
     348, 349
   performance, 351
   policy authoring, 350
   PRS/RRS integration, 350
   training/running, 348
features, 345
legal and regulatory
   requirements, 353, 354
legitimate activities/suspicious
   behavior, 346
proactive approach, 346
scrutinizing system logs, 345
threat detection, 346
traditional methods, 345
LLMs, *see* Large language
   models (LLMs)

M

Machine learning (ML), 181, 264,
   284, 351
MDM, *see* Mobile device
   management (MDM)
MFA, *see* Multi-factor
   authentication (MFA)
ML, *see* Machine learning (ML)
Mobile device management
   (MDM), 72
Mobile threat defense (MTD), 72

MTD, *see* Mobile threat
   defense (MTD)
Multi-factor authentication (MFA),
   269, 292, 295

N, O

Natural language processing
   (NLP), 344
Network channel security
   configuration, 68
   ICAP servers, 69
   low level/website traffic
     analysis, 68
   packet capture cards, 69
   shares/continuous
     monitoring, 69
   web/proxy server, 69
NLP, *see* Natural language
   processing (NLP)

P, Q

Personally identifiable information
   (PII), 111, 131
PII, *see* Personally identifiable
   information (PII)
Policy language
   AND/OR Boolean operator, 93
   context matching, 91–93
   creative, 96–98
   dependencies, 98
     response actions, 101, 102
     rules and guidelines, 98

INDEX

Policy language (*cont.*)
    static directives/inherent
        intelligence, 101
    structural elements, 99, 100
    targeting fields, 100, 101
  exceptions, 95, 96
  feedback, 107–110
  multiple rules, 93–95
  partial content
    matches, 103–106
  predefined rule types, 112–116
  rules setting, 90
  security violations, 116–123
  test mode policies, 110, 111
Policy Recommendation System
    (PRS), 334, 341
  autonomous policy
    creator, 271–273
  bottom layer, 304
  capabilities, 304
  design process,
    components, 304
  feedback processor, 271
  heuristics, 275
    BYOD devices, 297, 298
    categories, 300
    classification, 285–287
    compliance/regulation, 283
    continuous monitoring,
      302, 303
    coverage gaps, 277–279
    custom detection, 298, 299
    cybersecurity landscape, 284
    data trail discovery, 290, 291
    encryption, 286–288
    false positives, 279, 280
    high risk user, 289–291
    incorrect/outdated policies,
      280, 281
    loose policies, 282
    partial matches, 299–302
    policy deduplication,
      276, 277
    posture
      management, 292–294
    statistical trends, 294, 295
    zero-day threat
      prevention, 283, 284
  logical flow, 271
  recommendation system, 274
  responsibilities, 272
  RRS (*see* Remediation
    Recommendation
    System (RRS))
  test mode policies, 273, 274
PRS, *see* Policy Recommendation
    System (PRS)

R

RBAC, *see* Role-based access
    control (RBAC)
Reasoning module
  definition, 220
  executive email, 222
  feedback processor, 265–267
  partial matches, 238–240
  policies across channels

INDEX

BYOD channel, 233
cloud DAR channel, 229
contextual attributes, 230
DAR, 227, 228
email channel, 223–226
endpoint channel, 231, 232
intelligent system, 223
learning, 233, 234
network channel, 230, 231
network shares file, 227–229
share request, 228
successive user actions, 221, 222
violation remediators, 234
challenges/scenarios, 238
encryption/classification, 236
false positives, 234, 235
manual quarantine, 235
remediator lacks, 237
shares files, 236
threat, 235
user training, 236
workflow/integration, 237
Remediation Recommendation System (RRS), 335
auto-remediation rules, 305
components, 306
design process, 314
feedback processor, 306
heuristics, 306
auto-close, 307, 308
business workflows, 312, 313
false positives, 308, 309
manual remediation steps, 310
violation analysis, 310–312
tracking trends, 312
violation remediators, 305
Robust anonymization processes, 336
Role-based access control (RBAC), 45, 152, 159, 216, 295
RRS, *see* Remediation Recommendation System (RRS)

S

SaaS security posture management (SSPM), 143, 144, 260
Sarbanes-Oxley (SOX), 51, 156, 214, 272
Security background
access revocation, 48
alerting services, 52
characteristics (DIM and DAR), 59, 60
classification, 54
configurations, 44
access control/management, 45
channel-based, 47, 48
network infrastructure, 44, 45
Data In Motion *vs.* Data At Rest, 58, 59
data retention configurations, 57
deployment, 53

INDEX

Security background (*cont.*)
    digital/computer forensics, 57
    EDR configurations, 50
    encryption, 53
    incident severity, 57
    monitoring *vs.* prevention
        actions, 64
        differences, 61
        scenarios, 62
        threats, 62
    patching, 52
    policies/rules, 45
    posture management solutions, 55
    remediation actions, 47–50
    reporting, 51
    user personas, 42, 43
    user risk configuration, 56
Security information and event management (SIEM), 324
Security Orchestration, Automation, and Response (SOAR), 313
Security Service Posture Management (SSPM), 55
Security violations, 116
    enhancement options, 122, 123
    enterprise business, 131
    fields, 119–121
    IP, 131
    lifecycle, 117
    remediation, 117–119
    reporting, 130
    scale/performance, 132
    security vendor/enterprise administrator, 130–133
Self-learning assistant, 340
Settings Recommendation System (SRS), 340
    analytics/statistics engines, 315
    BYOD settings, 318
    cloud application settings, 321, 322
    configuring network channel, 320
    coverage points, 315, 316
    detection engine settings, 323
    email channels, 319
    endpoint channel, 317, 318
    general configurations, 316
    network channel, 319, 320
    network share settings, 316
    packet sniffer channels, 320
    policy engine settings, 323
    violation processor, 324, 325
        automated remediation settings, 324
        categorization, 324, 325
        integration, 324
        notification/reporting, 325
        performance optimization, 325
    web channels, 320
SIEM, *see* Security information and event management (SIEM)
Small and Medium Businesses (SMBs), 81, 124–126, 129

INDEX

SMBs, *see* Small and Medium Businesses (SMBs)
SOAR, *see* Security Orchestration, Automation, and Response (SOAR)
SOX, *see* Sarbanes-Oxley (SOX)
Spend management (SPM), 144
SPM, *see* Spend management (SPM)
SRS, *see* Settings Recommendation System (SRS)
SSPM, *see* SaaS security posture management (SSPM); Security Service Posture Management (SSPM)
Statistics engine
    data visualization, 263, 264
    modules, 262
    pre-processing techniques, 262
    unique features, 261

T

Target segments, 124–127

U

UEBA, *see* User and Entity Behavior Analytics (UEBA)
User and Entity Behavior Analytics (UEBA), 241, 334
Utilization (Personas)
    CISO/executives, 136
    compliance/audit manager, 135
    goals/objectives, 133
    IT Administrator, 134
    policy administrator, 134
    security analyst, 135
    violation manager, 135

V, W, X, Y

Virtual private networks (VPNs), 24, 29, 44, 70
VPNs, *see* Virtual private networks (VPNs)

Z

Zero trust security, 269